Classic New Zealand
Mountain Bike Rides

8th edition

Jonathan Kennett
Simon Kennett
Paul Kennett

Every effort was made to ensure that the information in this book was accurate at the time of publication. The authors accept no responsibility or liability for any accident or injury associated with its use. If you note any errors, please contact the authors and we'll post updates on www.kennett.co.nz

Maps in this book are intended as general guides only. For more detail, consult the recommended maps.

Published by
KENNETT BROTHERS LIMITED
info@kennett.co.nz   www.kennett.co.nz
Phone +64 4 499 6376   Fax +64 4 499 6533
PO Box 11 310, Wellington 6142

ISBN 978-0-9864641-3-3

Front cover	Photo by David Drake. Jess and Hazen Simson and Simon Kennett, Glendhu Bay Track.
Back cover	Photo by Zane Smith. Richard Goldworthy's home-made bike (featuring left-hand-side chain), Whites Bay – Mt Robertson Loop.
Editing	Angelique Tran Van, Bronwen Wall
Maps	Alex Revell
Design	Paul Kennett
Printer	Printlink, Petone New Zealand

Acknowledgements

We appreciate the assistance of staff from Department of Conservation, councils around the country and Bike NZ for all their help and information.

For their hospitality, encouragement, information and riding company we'd like to thank:

Invercargill–Lionel Benjamin.
Queentsown–Simon Smith.
Arrowtown–Liz and Grant Wood.
Wanaka–Tim Dennis, David Drake & Jennie Taylor.
Dunedin–Tim Armstrong, Pam Jackson, Derek Morrison, Hamish Seaton, Mike Wilson.
Westport–Phil Rossiter.
Christchurch–Lisa Carter, Chris Freer, Richard Goldsworthy, Scott Keir, Shailer Hart, Dave Mitchell, Zane Smith, Paul Topschij, Craig Tregurtha, Ditte van der Meulen.
Hanmer Springs–Mark Symonds.
Golden Bay–Andy Cole, Brent Hartshorne, Martin and Marie Langley.
Motueka–Guy Trainor.
Nelson–Murray Drake, Ginny Wood, Chris Mildon, Stew Thorpe, Paul McArthur, Dean Rainbow.
Wellington–Ashley Burgess, Richard Davies, Sarah Drake, Michelle Ducat, David Laing, Andrew McLellan, Jeff Lyall, Teresa Mcguire, Ron McGann, Patrick Morgan, Adam Perry, Clare Pascoe. John

Randal, Asher Regan, Rob Scott, Paul Smith, Bronwen Wall.
Kaitoke–Robert Lancaster.
Masterton–Karyn Burgess.
Fielding–Richard Lockett.
Wanganui–Doug@The Bike Shed.
Palmerston North–Phil Etheridge, Raewyn Knight.
National Park–Warren Furner.
Whakahoro–Dan Steele.
Turangi–John Carmen.
Taupo–Austin Hutcheon, Pete Masters, Thomas Schwarz.
Te Aroha–Geoff Buysman.
Napier–Paul McArdle, Meg Frater, Carl Larsen.
Tauranga–Ric Balfour, Bruce Galloway, Pete Roden, Karl Young.
Hamilton–Tui Allen.
Auckland–Ryan@Freeriden, Bill Fowler, Nick Lambert, Micheal May, Tim Welch, Callum Wilson.
Whangarei–Ruth and Jonathan Jarman, Brent Love, Kevin McKenzie, Steve Gwilliam.
Kaikohe–Lindell Ngata, Leif Pakai.

Thanks also to the private landowners who provide some of New Zealand's best riding areas and many helpful bike shops and information centres.

Research trips for this edition were kindly supported by:

Dedication

To the hundreds of mountain bikers around New Zealand who have volunteered their time and skills to build tracks and lobby for land access. Without their remarkable generosity, many of the rides listed in the following pages would not exist.

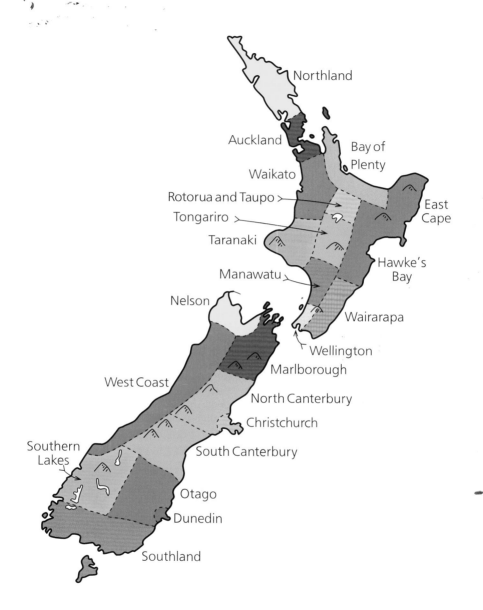

Northland

Auckland

Bay of
Plenty

Waikato

Rotorua and Taupo >

Tongariro >

East
Cape

Taranaki

Manawatu >

Hawke's
Bay

Nelson

Wairarapa

Wellington

West Coast

Marlborough

North Canterbury

Christchurch

South Canterbury

Southern
Lakes

Otago

Dunedin

Southland

Contents

Remember - OSM Bars !!
Chocolate and cranberry
are soooo good !!

Intro

You're holding the definitive guide to mountain biking in New Zealand. Over 300 rides are described, ranging from local mountain bike parks to wild multi-day adventures.

Over time, new tracks are built, old ones become overgrown and landowners change. Since the last edition, we've added 60 new tracks, removed 35 rides and significantly revised over half of the rest. It's a dynamic scene.

We produce a new edition of this book every three years, so if you know of any changes, please email info@kennett.co.nz or write to: Kennett Brothers, PO Box 11 310, Wellington 6142. If it's a change we haven't heard of, we'll send you a chocolate fish.

Terms we've used

To differentiate between vertical and horizontal, we've used **'m'** to refer to vertical height, and **'metres'** to refer to horizontal distance.

The heights shown on elevation charts are metres above sea level. Be wary of using elevation charts for route finding as small hills are not always shown.

The Department of Conservation are referred to most commonly as DOC.

Simon hard at work researching yet another great ride. Simon Kennett

Rating the rides

After rigorous and lengthy debate, we've rated every ride in the book based on our love of adventure, appreciation of scenery and appetite for flowing single track:

★ ★ ★ ★   A fantastic slice of mountain bike heaven.

★ ★ ★   A highly recommended ride, which we really enjoyed.

★ ★   Loads of fun with good mates on a fine day.

★   Enjoyed by locals but not worth a special trip.

👎   No way we'd go back for these duds.

Gradings

This mountain bike grading system is based on those used for kayaking and climbing. It is now used by DOC and NZCT and is similar to the International Mountain Bicycling Association (IMBA) grades. Remember, you and your bike risk being mangled by taking on tracks that are a grade or two higher than your ability. Choose carefully to ensure you have a great ride.

BEGINNER

Grade 1 Fairly flat, wide and smooth track or gravel road; suitable for all first-time riders.

EASY

Grade 2 Mostly flat with some gentle climbs on smooth tracks with easily avoidable obstacles, such as rocks, tree roots or pot holes.

INTERMEDIATE

Grade 3 Steeper grades on a loose surface; trickier obstacles may be present but are avoidable; may be some exposure at the outside edge of the track.

ADVANCED

Grade 4 A mixture of steep climbs, loose track surfaces and obstacles that are tricky to avoid or jump over; generally exposed at the outside edge of the track. Most riders will find some sections easier to walk.

EXPERT

Grade 5 Prolonged steep climbs; generally exposed at the outside edge of the track, with technically challenging obstacles and sharp corners. The majority of riders will need to walk some sections.

EXTREME

Grade 6 Downhill or free-ride specific tracks; extremely steep sections with large drop-offs and other unavoidable obstacles; may include huge man-made structures and jumps.

Note: Tracks are usually a grade or two harder in the wet.

Stuff to take

Don't ride alone; always take a buddy and a tool kit. Let someone know where you're going and when you'll be back. If there's a chance you'll be caught out overnight, take a small survival kit (including an emergency blanket, torch and extra food).

First aid

It's almost inevitable. Sooner or later you or one of your buddies is going to wipe out big time. Blood, stress, shock, broken bones, deep gashes ... maybe worse. Don't panic! Do a first aid course now and be ready to impress with your flash first aid kit.

Food and drink

Drink early and often. Once you start to feel thirsty, your energy levels are already dropping. The best drinks for your body are water, diluted fruit juice and sports drinks.

On any ride over 2 hours long, take something to eat. Some of our favourite 'inner tube fillings' are muesli bars, scroggin and bananas.

Maps

Don't go into any seriously wild country without a good map, such as a 1:50,000 scale map. We've listed any map you might need at the start of each ride's write-up.

Be aware that a completely new 1:50,000 topomap series came out in 2009. The NZTopo50 series replaces the old NZMS 260 series and is more compatible with GPSs. All grid references given in this book relate to the new maps.

A GPS or compass may also be useful – and for some rides essential. GPS's don't work well under thick forest canopy, especially pine. When using a compass don't stand over a steel bike frame.

Tool kit

You might have been lucky for a few weeks, or months even, but your time will come. Be prepared for a flat tyre and some loose bolts, at the very least. A small multi-tool is bound to save you a long walk home, sooner or later.

Cell phone

If you are lost or injured you can *sometimes* use your cell phone to contact Search and Rescue (phone 111 and ask for Police). Although reception is unreliable in most of the back country (especially the valleys), it's still worth taking one if you can. Make sure it's fully charged.

Jeff Carter, Rotorua autumn

Attitude

To help keep tracks open to mountain bikers, try to ride dual-use tracks as diplomatically as possible. Avoid startling other track users, call out a friendly 'hello' well before reaching walkers and accept that really popular dual-use tracks won't be worth biking at busy times such as national holidays.

Weather reports

We often check these sites before heading into the hills – they have the most up-to-date weather reports:

- www.metservice.co.nz/forecasts/
- www.metvuw.co.nz/forecast/

All other things being equal, expect the temperature to drop a degree for every 100 m height you gain. If there's any risk of getting caught out on the tops, pack an extra layer.

Stuff to leave behind

Rock Snot

Bicycles can spread didymo! Cleaning your bike not only helps it last longer, it also stops invasive species such as didymo and African clubmoss spreading from one area to another.

Ripping it up

The impact of a mountain biker is usually on a par with that of a walker, unless the biker is skidding, in which case, the erosion is several times greater. It takes just a little skill to be able to roll rather than skid those tyres. Go easy on the back brake and enjoy the tracks for years to come.

Trains, planes and buses

If you're on a tight budget, want to do a through trip or simply don't like cars, public transport might be your best option.

Tranz Scenic (train)	0800 872 867
Interislander (ferry)	0800 802 802
Bluebridge (ferry)	0800 844 844
Air New Zealand	0800 737 000
Auckland commuter trains	(09) 366 6400
Wellington commuter trains	0800 801 700
Christchurch buses (many now have bike racks)	(03) 366 8855

Smaller operators are mentioned in the relevant ride notes.

Fees for unbagged bikes

Some ferries and trains, and most buses, charge $10–15 for an unbagged bike. Wellington commuter trains no longer charge for bikes, but space can be limited; some peak-hour trains have no room for bikes. Auckland trains charge $1 per bike; don't expect peak-time commuter trains to have space either.

The Interislander ferries charge $15 for a bike. Bluebridge Cook Strait Ferries charges $10 for a bike, but they waive the fee for members of the New Zealand cycling advocacy group RideStrong (see www.ridestrong.org.nz). You'll be required to walk your bike on and off these ferries.

Air New Zealand does not charge for bikes but does charge for your second bag or item ($15 for a bag up to 25 kg). They expect you to pack your bike well, or at least wrap the chain and cogs in newspaper, remove the pedals and turn the handlebars.

Qantas charges $20 per bike and sell bike boxes for $25. If your bike weighs more than 15 kg, there may also be an excess luggage charge.

Budget airlines will charge an arm and a leg!

The cost of travel

Like any human activity, the sport of mountain biking is impacted by the rising cost of fuel. To help you estimate your travel expenses and carbon emissions, we've given you the actual driving distance from the nearest main town for every ride.

The AA estimates that an average-sized, fully loaded car costs around $100 per 100 km to run (taking into account fuel, tyres, maintenance, etc).

Landcare Research estimates that an average-sized car will emit whopping 1 tonne of CO_2 for every 4,000 km driven – larger cars emit much more.

You can save money and reduce emissions by packing your bikes inside your car and sharing your trip with others. Maybe check out the public transport options. And the ultimate solution? Cycle to and from the ride!

With a bag full of food and a good bike, the possibilities are endless.   Caleb Smith

Northland

1 **Tutu Trail**
2 **Kaitaia Walkway**
3 **Twin Coast Cycle Trail**
4 **Waitangi Forest**
5 **Glenbervie Forest**
6 **Parihaka MTB Trails**
7 **Whanui Loop**
★ Plus seven other rides

NORTHLAND HIGHLIGHTS

Whangarei remains the hub for Northland's mountain biking, with Glenbervie Forest continuing to offer the best purpose-built trails in the region. But further north, beautiful beaches and tropical weather provide the setting for four cruisy coastal rides and the country's most northern New Zealand Cycle Trail.

1 Tutu Trail ★★☆☆

Ahipara, 14 km southwest of Kaitaia

INTERMEDIATE

One of the most interesting and scenic rides of Northland. Make sure you get the tides right and go prepared for desert like conditions.

Grade 3+
Time 4–6 hours
Distance 27 km return

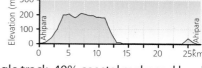

Track conditions 5% sealed road, 25% gravel road, 20% 4WD track and single track, 40% coastal rocks and hard sand, 10% semi-ridable sand

Maps NZTopo50 AV25 Tauroa Peninsula is useful for working out where to ride in the gumfields.

Route description

You must return along the coast during low tide; before departing, ring Information Far North, (09) 408 0879, for tide times.

From Ahipara beach, ride southwest past the changing sheds and up the hill. Veer left at the first Y-intersection (1 km from the changing sheds) and, after another kilometre, right at the second Y-intersection. After about 30 minutes, you'll reach a plateau. Follow the metal Gumfields Road until you see a group of corrugated iron buildings on the left side of the road; one of them is a museum featuring relics from the gum-digging days. At the museum, turn hard right onto a sandy clay track. This is the Tutu Trail.

Not far down the Tutu Trail, you may notice a small set of steps cut into a bank on your left. They lead up to the gumfields; no place for cycling, but they offer a fascinating glimpse of heritage digging sites. Continue past these steps down the main trail. After about 3 km, there is a minor turn-off on the

Perfect colour coordination on the Tutu Trail.

right leading up to a lookout spot and then a few hundred metres later a minor turn-off on the left, which is the Erewhon Trail. This used to be the main route to the coast but is now overgrown.

Continue following the main track out to the top of the sand dunes another kilometre away. If you really love your bike, turn back here (or carry your bike down to the coast). If you're not too fussy, glide down the sand dunes to the coast. Make sure you follow the main set of quad bike tracks at all times; wandering off the main track will exacerbate erosion, and you might get lost.

At the coast, turn right and ride on firm sand, where you can find it, back towards Ahipara. As you get close to Ahipara, you'll encounter flat patches of rock, and the sea will force you to ride close to the cliffs. This section is only passable during low tide.

Notes If the tide conditions are not right for this ride, limit yourself to checking out the gumfields and the view from the top of the dunes before riding back the same way. Drinking water is scarce – take an extra bottle. Clean your bike thoroughly after the ride (salt and sand are murder on metal components). Please remember that sand dunes are a fragile environment and avoid riding over any vegetation.

2 Kaitaia Walkway

INTERMEDIATE

7.5 km south of Kaitaia

This is a fun, but short, single-track ride through native forest.

Grade 3   **Time** 1–2 hours   **Distance** 12 km return

Track conditions 30% narrow gravel road, 70% single track

How to get there Head southeast from Kaitaia on Highway 1. After 3 km, turn right onto Larmer Road and head to a quarry 3.5 km away. If you're in a car, we recommend liberating yourselves at the quarry.

Route description

Follow the narrow gravel road that drops down to the right from the quarry and ride 2 km to the start of the Kaitaia Walkway (signposted). A former bullock track, the walkway passes through native bush at an easy gradient. After about 30 minutes, you'll pass a short detour to a kauri grove (unridable but worth the 10-minute walk). Another few minutes takes you to another side track, this time to a lookout point 30 metres away. From there, turn round and follow your tyre tracks back to the quarry.

Notes The track that goes on from the lookout to Diggers Valley is partly overgrown and mostly unridable.

3 Twin Coast Cycle Trail ★★ ☆ ☆

BEGINNER

Central Northland

It doesn't get cruisier than this: a smooth, wide trail wending its way along what was once New Zealand's northernmost railway line offers the best of the far north heartland.

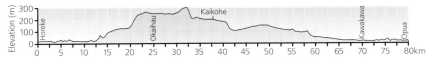

Grade 1 **Time** 1–2 days **Distance** 80 km when finished

Progress 13.5 km built; 66.5 km under construction

Track conditions 80% rail trail, 20% cycle path

How to get there Head north from Whangarei to start your ride at Kaikohe or Kawakawa. In future, when the full trail has been completed, you'll also be able to start from Horeka (near Rawene) or Opua (near Paihia).

Route description

By January 2012, the first 13.5-km section will have been built from Kaikohe to Okaihau. It is scenic and easy, includes a tunnel for a refreshing change and passes the tranquil Lake Omapere – an ideal trip for families and those looking for a cushy jaunt.

Plans are afoot to open the 34-km section from Kaikohe to Kawakawa and the 25-km section from Okaihau to Horeke.

Locals are building the trail and are rightly proud of it. They are also planting native trees along the route and generally looking after the environment. The whole area is also steeped in fascinating Maori and Pakeha history, so it can be more than just a bike ride, if you want it to be.

Jonathan Kennett

A long-abandoned rail tunnel near Kaikohe.

Notes This is one of the Government's New Zealand Cycle Trail projects. For more info, get yourself a copy of our book *Classic New Zealand Cycle Trails* due out in 2012.

4 Waitangi Forest ★ ★ ☆ ☆

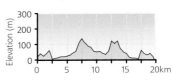

Waitangi, Paihia

You wouldn't travel to the Bay of Islands for its mountain biking, but if you happened to be there with a bike, this is the place to go.

Grade 2
Time 1–3 hours
Distance 20 km

Track conditions   10% sealed road, 60% gravel road, 30% 4WD track

Maps DOC has a good pamphlet on the forest that includes a useful map.

Landowners Gifted to the nation by Lord and Lady Bledisloe; managed by Rayonier Forestry and the Waitangi National Trust.

Route description

From Waitangi (near Paihia), ride north up past the golf course and down to the Wairoa Bay picnic area (a great spot for lunch and a swim after your ride). Just past the recreation area, turn left and cruise up Te Wairoa Road for 3 km. Turn left again at Rosella Road and, just before the top, turn right and climb up Lookout Road to check out Scoria Cone (Te Puke).

From the cone, freewheel back down Lookout Road and turn right, out to the main gravel road (Te Puke Road). If you're feeling tired here, head left to take a short cut to Mt Bledisloe. Otherwise, turn right and ride around to

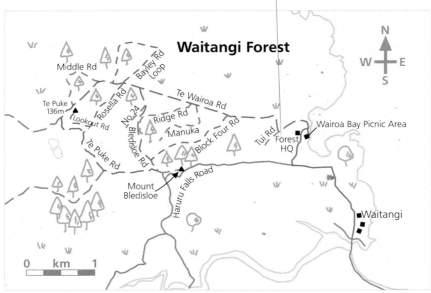

Te Wairoa Road via Middle Road Loop and maybe Bayley Road Loop as well. When you reach Bledisloe Road, follow it up to the forest entrance near the top of the hill and down the other side a hundred metres or so to follow an obvious 150-metre-long track to Mt Bledisloe for some great views.

After taking in the views, backtrack along Bledisloe Road for a few hundred metres and take the first track on your right after passing the mapboard at the forest entrance. This is called Block Four Road and is a fun downhill that leads you back to Te Wairoa Road less than 2 km from the recreation area. Now follow your front wheel back home.

Notes No smoking or dogs allowed in the forest as it is home to endangered kiwi. Watch out for logging trucks. Ridge Road also offers a good downhill. Te Wairoa Road continues across Waitangi Forest and leads to Kerikeri Inlet, but at times, that part of it may be closed for logging.

5 Glenbervie Forest ★ ★ ★

10 km northeast of Whangarei

The single tracks in Glenbervie Forest have received a lot of TLC in the last few years, and several excellent new ones have been added. It is now the most popular riding area in Northland.

Grades 3–5
Time 2–10 hours
Distance 10+ km

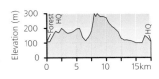

Track conditions Single tracks connected by forestry road

Maps You can buy a trail map from Whangarei bike shops for $4. Check out NZTopo50 AW30 Whangaruru for longer exploration trips.

Landowners Rayonier Forestry. No permit required, but please drop some coins in the donation box and respect all forestry operations.

How to get there Head north through Tikipunga and out of town on Ngunguru Road for 3 km before turning left down Maruata Road at the 'Glenbervie Forest' sign. Two kilometres down this road, you'll reach a signposted car park area on your left.

Route description
Hop over the stile beside the car park and follow the fun Eveready Track into the forest. Within a few minutes, it takes you to the MTB noticeboard beside the forest HQ, 400 metres away as the crow flies. Have a look at the map for any new tracks or logging information. Local mountain bikers have built a number of cool tracks, but they take a bit of hunting out. Best to go riding

with the mountain bike club if you can. Check out their website at: www.bikenorthland.co.nz If you can't ride with the club, try the fun 1-hour loop described below.

Single Tracks Loop

From the noticeboard, ride up Mains Road and take the second left onto Marsden Road. Ride past the Tin Bum turn-off (overgrown) and take the next left down Flipper.

At the bottom of Flipper, turn right and ride up Burma Road for 10 minutes until you see a little bridge on your right: that's the start of Far-2-ezy. Blast your way across to Mangakino Road, turn left and ride to Nursery Flat Road.

Turn right at Nursery Flat Road to get back to Mains Road, then hang another right to get to Quarry Road. This leads to B'ware the Troll, which is a ripper of a downhill. It leads to Waitangi Road. Turn left, then take the next three right-hand turns to get to the top of Bluff Trail (signposted). This is also a cool downhill. We loved it so much that we rode up for another run, but the second time down Bluff Trail, try turning left onto Shoelace. This gives you the option of riding Frump back to the MTB noticeboard. From there, take The Antidote back to the car park.

Next time try out Lovers Lane, Ward One, Bone Garden and Nancy.

Notes The forest is constantly being logged, so watch out for speeding trucks.

6 Parihaka MTB Trails ★ ★ ☆ ☆
Whangarei city

In 2007, this forest was logged, destroying several mountain bike tracks in the process. The Council is now leaving the area to regenerate, and local mountain bikers are beavering away at a series of new tracks.

Grade 2–5
Time 1–3 hours
Distance 15 km

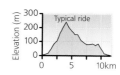

Track conditions A mixture of 4WD and single track

How to get there Ride or drive north on Mill Road then out of town on Whareora Road for 3 km. Turn onto Abbey Caves Road and, 200 metres up the road on your right, you'll see a car parking area.

Route description

At the car park, study the mapboard to plan your route up to Memorial Drive and back. One possibility is to start off with White Tail and The McKenzie.

There is a lookout at the Parihaka Memorial that provides great views of the city. This is the highest point for miles around.

From the top, there are a number of grade-5 trails to try on the way back down, or you can play it safe and take the forestry roads.

Notes Beware! In the wet, the single tracks are slippery as snot. If you'd love a bit more single track in this area, contact the mountain bike club via www.bikenorthland.co.nz and help them dig it.

7 Whanui Loop ★ ★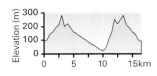

15 km east of Whangarei

This is good old-fashioned fun on a bike. The single-track downhill is awesome, but you have to earn it.

Grade 3
Time 2 hours
Distance 17 km

Track conditions 70% gravel road, 30% sweet single track

Maps NZTopo50 AX30 Whangarei and AX31 Bream Head show the details.

Landowners For access permission, contact Hancock Forest Management Ltd, (09) 470 1300.

How to get there Head east from Mairtown, northern Whangarei, on Whareora Road (which becomes Pataua North Road), for 12.4 km and park at the 'Whanui Forest' sign on your right.

Route description
Hop over the gate and ride up Tuatua Road, climbing up through a farm and into a forestry area, then through a quarry. Stay on Tuatua Road until you reach a gate 5 km from the start. Turn hard right and head down into the bush on a superb, benched single track.

If you come across a slip near the top, just look for a track to the right. Cross a couple of streams, jump a Taranaki gate and head out to a farm. Swing over the fence and turn right on the track marked 'Mussel Road'. After a few minutes, cross a ford and grunt up the big hill.

Near the top, you reach a Y-intersection. Both forks take you back to Tuatua Road, but pick the left one to get back to where you started.

Notes Logging vehicles use the gravel road section.

Seven Other Rides

Ninety Mile Beach ★ ☆ ☆ ☆
Riding the big beach is like crossing the Sahara; desolate, stunning and windswept. It helps to follow the prevailing northwesterly wind.

Grade 1   **Time** 4–6 hours (no headwind)   **Distance** 93 km

From Te Paki, 24 km south of Cape Reinga, cycle down Kauaeparaoa Stream (also called Te Paki Stream) to the northern end of Ninety Mile Beach. From there, it is 86 flat kilometres south to Ahipara, which lies 14 km southwest of Kaitaia.

During low tide, the beach is as hard as concrete; easy but boring, so best to ride it with an entertaining bunch of friends. Try cycling with your eyes closed. Even better is no hands with your eyes closed. You can check tide times at Waitiki Landing or Information Far North in Kaitaia, phone (09) 408 0879.

Waitiki Landing and Ahipara are the first and last places to buy food, so stock up. Food isn't sold or allowed to be eaten at Cape Reinga because of the spiritual importance of the site. Bikes should be thoroughly cleaned of salt and sand straight after the ride.

Takahue Saddle ★ ☆ ☆ ☆
This is an easy ride along an old public road that is no longer drivable.

Grade 2   **Time** 2–3 hours
Distance 38-km loop

Head southeast from Kaitaia on Highway 1 for 11 km and turn right at the 'Takahue 8 km' sign. From Takahue, take Takahue Saddle Road southeast for 10 km through to Broadwood. It goes like this: about 2.5 km from Takahue, where Warner Road begins following the river, veer right up the side valley. About 350 metres later, you'll cross a small stream and climb up to the saddle at 380 m.

At Takahue Saddle, go straight ahead for 10 minutes before scrambling around a slip to a gate.

Jonathan Kennett

One hundred metres from the gate, you will pop onto a gravel road, which leads to Broadwood. At the very end, take a short cut across a swing bridge on your right to get to the Broadwood general store.

To return to Takahue, turn right when you hit the sealed road, ride 13 km, before turning right again onto Waiotehue Road and pedalling another 15 km back to the start.

Puketi Kauri Forest   ★ ☆ ☆ ☆
A few 4WD tracks provide access to some huge kauri trees. Great scenery but boring riding.

Grade 3-   **Time** 2 hours   **Distance** 20 km return

From Kerikeri, drive 4 km northwest to Waipapa. Then follow Highway 10 north for 1 km before turning left and following the signposts to 'Puketi Recreation Area' 13 km away.

At the recreation area car park, check out the mapboard and head up Pirau Road. This soon becomes a good 4WD track that climbs up and down, but generally up, into imposing kauri forest.

After almost 10 km, keep your eyes peeled for a signposted turn-off called Takapau Track. This marks the top of the ridge and the end of the line for mountain bikes. You can continue on foot to take in more of the kauri forest though.

When you're ready, turn around and enjoy the rolling downhill back to the car park.

The Manginangina Kauri Walk, not far from the car park, takes 15 minutes and offers excellent interpretation boards – definitely worth getting off your bike and stretching your legs. We walked it at night, which was awe inspiring!

Waoku Coach Road   ★ ☆ ☆ ☆
An interesting place to visit for its scenery and history, but also a ride that can leave you wallowing in mud.

Grade 3   **Time** 2 hours   **Distance** 40 km return

Start from Tutamoe, 52 km northwest of Dargaville. From Tutamoe School, ride north on Waoku Road. After 4 km, you'll pass a picnic area beside a large 'Walkways' sign. From here, the gravel road gradually turns into a muddy, but ridable, 4WD track. Within an hour, you will reach a gate bearing a 'Private Road...walking only' sign, which you should ignore – this is definitely a public road!

Continue up through the native bush and over the occasional stone culvert (built in the 1890s) to a signposted intersection. Turn left off the main track and ride past Honeymoon Hut and the old Honeymoon Commune site. Cross a clearing on a 4WD track before entering the bush, where the track becomes a diabolical bogfest. Turn around here and head back the way you came.

Whananaki Walkway, Sandy Bay   ★ ☆ ☆ ☆

This rough old walkway provides an interesting trip to the longest footbridge in the Southern Hemisphere.

Grade 3+   **Time** 1–2 hours   **Distance** 8 km one way

Head northeast out of Whangarei to the southern end of Sandy Bay, 24 km away. There is a car park with toilets by a popular surfing beach.

Whananaki Walkway footbridge at low tide.   Bronwen Wall

From the car park, ride 100 metres inland and turn right onto McAuslins Road. Climb up a short hill to the start of the walkway. There is a gate with an old 'No Cycles' sign. Ignore it – the walkway is on legal road. Follow orange marker poles around several spurs to Te Ara O Tunua Road, only 400 metres from the Whananaki Inlet Bridge. There are a couple of markers leading up above, or down below the walkway in places. Ignore them.

The bridge is quite narrow, so hopefully you have narrow or high bars. There is a dairy 100 metres from the far end of the bridge. Return the way you came.

Western Hills   ★ ★ ★ ★

This council-owned area of native bush and exotic forest on the edge of Whangarei has a few short technical tracks, which are fun when dry.

Grade 3+   **Time** 1–2 hours   **Distance** Various lengths

Head out of Whangarei on Western Hills Drive, then turn left up Whau Valley Road. Go to the dam and just as the reservoir comes into view, veer left, across some grass, to a gate where a narrow track begins.

After 20 minutes climbing, you'll reach another gate on a ridge top, by a pylon. Cross the gate and turn right. Follow the main track for 5 minutes as it veers right twice more and eventually reaches a well-defended trig, the highest point in these hills.

After checking out the view, backtrack 50 metres and turn right. Soon you'll come to a right-hand bend with two 4WD tracks heading off to the left; take the first left. Follow this track as it undulates and comes to a sudden stop. On your right, there is a single track, which forks almost immediately; head left onto Frank Holman Track.

In fairly quick succession, you'll have to veer right, then left, then left again. At the bottom, cross the paddock and hop over a stile onto Russell Road. Go right and then turn right again onto the main road to get back to town.

Waimahanga Track   ★ ★ ★ ★

This is an excellent track for complete beginners, and it's only 5 km from Whangarei.

Grade 1   **Time** 30 minutes   **Distance** 3 km return

The track is marked on the council pamphlet "Walking Tracks in Whangarei" available at the local information centre.

From Whangarei, follow the airport signs along Riverside Drive towards Onerahi for 5 km. Then take Old Onerahi Road on your right and after another 100 m turn right again onto Waimahanga Road and take this road to its end.

From the end of the road, follow the signposted track around to George Point Footbridge and on to Cockburn Street. The track follows an old railway line through the mangroves between Sherwood Rise and Onerahi. Return the same way.

Notes This area can be busy at times; please take it easy.

Waimahanga Track.

Jonathan Kennett

Auckland

1 **Great Barrier Island**
2 **Woodhill MTB Park**
3 **Riverhead Forest**
4 **Totara Park MTB Track**
5 **Whitford Forest**
6 **Hunua Ranges**
7 **Puni MTB Park**
★ Plus five other rides

AUCKLAND HIGHLIGHTS

Woodhill Forest is the most popular riding area in Auckland, offering over 100 km of wicked single track. In dry weather, however, the purpose-built tracks at Riverhead and Hunua give it a run for its money. Mangere Coastal Walkway is great for beginners, and Great Barrier Island makes for a great fat-tyred holiday.

1 Great Barrier Island ★ ★ ☆ ☆

INTERMEDIATE

80 km northeast of Auckland (as the sea gull flies)

There are 180 km of roads and 4WD tracks on Great Barrier Island. The 80-km anti-clockwise loop described here covers the best of them.

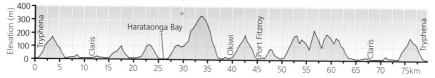

Grade 3   **Time** 2 days   **Distance** 80 km

Track conditions 50% sealed road, 25% gravel road, 25% 4WD track

Maps Refer to NewTopo Aotea, Great Barrier Island.

How to get there Check out travel options at www.thebarrier.co.nz or go straight to Fullers Ferrys. They are well set up for bikes and only take 2–2.5 hours, as opposed to 5–6 hours on the car ferry.

Route description

From Tryphena, ride over a short, sharp hill to Medlands Beach, which has a camping ground. Head northwest to Claris, a few kilometres away, where there are some shops, including a surprisingly large Thai restaurant. After stocking up, head north past more campsites at Awana Bay and Haratonga Bay (a 3-km side trip along a 4WD track, but it's the best campsite on the island).

Out of Haratonga Bay, there's a big climb (330 m) over to Okiwi where there's a cafe that serves awesome mussel fritters. At dawn or dusk, watch out for pateke (the critically endangered New Zealand brown teal) around here. There's a 200-m climb over to Port Fitzroy (shop and bar) and another minor climb over to Kaiarara Bay. From here, the seal stops and traffic is banned. Follow the scenic 'Forest Road' to Kaiarara Hut, set in sub-tropical forest.

After the hut, the road becomes a 4WD track, which is slippery in places when wet. There are also several stream crossings. After 12 km (and at least 3 hours), you'll come out at a saddle above Whangaparapara. Turn left and coast down to Claris. From there, follow the roads you cycled in on, back to Tryphena to catch the ferry to Auckland.

Notes Spend at least two days on the island to take advantage of the great beaches, bush walks and Kaitoke hot pools. There are accommodation options at Whangaparapara, Tryphena, Medlands, Claris, Kaitoke and Okiwi as well as the DOC Kaiarara Hut.

There are general stores at Port Fitzroy, Claris, Whangaparapara and Tryphena and a bike shop at Tryphena that hires out bikes (Paradise Cycles, phone (09) 429 0700). Water from streams that cross farmland needs to be treated.

In October each year, there is a great event called the Wharf to Wharf marathon, open to bikers, runners and walkers. It is a hilly 42 km that traverses the island from Port Fitzroy to Tryphena Harbour.

2 Woodhill MTB Park ★ ★ ★ ☆

40 km northwest of Auckland city centre

This is the most popular riding area near Auckland city. There are more tracks than you could possibly ride in a day, and everyone is catered for, from beginners to complete adrenalin junkies. Because it's a sandy area, the tracks get even better after rain.

Grades 1–6
Time 1 or 2 days
Distance Up to 120 km

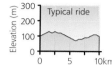

Track conditions 5% forestry road, 95% single track

Landowners Managed by Bike Parks Ltd. A permit is required with a range of fees. A one-day pass in 2011 cost $7 per adult (over 15), $5 for a 'youth' and $2 for children under 5. The pass comes with a free park map. An adult's 6-day pass is $35 and a year costs $109. Check out www.bikepark.co.nz

Tim Hunter and Mark Harrowfield on The Wall, Woodhill.   Thomas Lloyd

How to get there Drive west from Auckland on Highway 16 for 37 km. Turn left at the 'Woodhill Forest' road sign and drive a further 2 km to a large car park (it's well signposted). The main entry gate is open from 7 am to 7 pm daily (except Wednesdays when it stays open till 10 pm).

Route description

At the huge car park, you will find a staffed information centre, toilets, a cafe, bike wash stands, and a bike shop with bikes for hire.

The map you are given when you register has all the tracks marked on it. There are 68 tracks in total to explore, including six signposted favourite courses to follow, ranging from 6 km to 25 km in length.

It's interesting that, even on a day when the car park is totally packed, the far ends of the mountain bike park feel almost empty! Our strategy was to cruise around asking locals what their favourite tracks were and then go and ride them. This worked a treat and helped us discover some real classics like Big Mumma, Cookie, SPCA and Slippery's Delight. Then there are some new advanced tracks like Charlies Angel, Evil Offspring and Treasure Island, enough to satisfy any mountain biking enthusiast.

Although the easy tracks are by far the most popular, it is the difficult wooden structures that make Woodhill unique. We really enjoyed some of these, but a word of caution: ride to your ability. The jumps and structures here have led to a world of hurt. If in doubt, take the bypass.

Notes Because Woodhill Forest is sandy, it's one of Auckland's best wet-weather riding areas. However, the wooden obstacles are slippery after rain.

There's a dirt jump playground near the car park plus some short easy stuff for very young kids. Don't forget to clean the sand out of your drive train after your ride.

3 Riverhead Forest ★ ★ ☆ ☆

10 km west of Albany

In the middle of summer, when Woodhill becomes sandy, Riverhead is the place to go. There are over 30 single tracks to explore and dozens of forestry roads.

Grades 1–6   **Time** 1–4 hours   **Distance** Up to 50 km

Track conditions 45% gravel road, 25% 4WD track, 30% single track

Bruce Boardman, Riverhead.   Daniel Murphy

Landowners Rayonier Forests Ltd. No permit required.

Other users Logging trucks, motorbikes and war-game soldiers. The forest is closed during motor sports events.

How to get there The track network is complicated and still evolving, so you'll need a map: www.freeriden.co.nz/WCRC2010map.php You should also drop in to FreeRide'n' at 318 Main Road, Huapai (it's only 3 km south of the forest) and talk to Ryan. He'll show you the best access points and tracks.

Route description

Riverhead Forest is a large pine forest criss-crossed by gravel roads and tracks. Over the past few years, logging operations have closed some of the old favourites, but new tracks are being built by the West Coast Riders Club. The forest is large enough to get lost in for a few hours, so get into the exploring spirit of things, or hook up with some locals or the Auckland Mountain Bike Club to get the best intro to this forest.

The terrain consists of rolling hills up to 200 m high. Most riders cycle up forestry roads to a high point and then blast back down on single tracks.

For a first time ride, start from the Waitemata Motorcycle Club building on Barlow Road, and head up to Patterson Road. From there you can choose from three tracks that head back down to the club buildings. The Number 13 track (signposted) is a good aperitif.

Notes It's not a good idea to park too close to access gates. If there's a forest fire, your car may be shoved out of the way by a fire truck in a hurry.

There's a Dual Slalom Track on Ararimu Valley Road, 500 metres down on the right.

After heavy rain, Riverhead is a bogfest! Head for Woodhill instead.

4 Totara Park MTB Track

INTERMEDIATE

2 km east of Manukau city

This is one of the few riding opportunities in South Auckland. It's in a farm park, so although the track is very well built, it gets hammered by the cattle and its condition varies.

Grade 3 **Time** 1 hour **Distance** Up to 7 km

Track conditions 100% single track

How to get there Drive or ride east of Manukau city on Redoubt Road. Totara Park is well signposted on your right, 1.5 km from the motorway overbridge.

Route description

Manukau City Council have built 7 km of track in this farm park. From the car park, the track drops to a 'hub' and then climbs to the far side of the park. Then the fun really begins. The track flows across the hill and down into the main gully. Then you have to climb back up to the car park.

There's a skills area planned for some time in the future.

Notes You can also ride on the bridle track, but it's got zero flow.

5 Whitford Forest

40 km southeast of Auckland city

A series of purpose-built trails weave through this privately owned forest. The tracks have been designed and refined over many years, making Whitford Forest a popular destination for local mountain bikers.

Grades 3–4
Time 2–4 hours
Distance 1–20 km

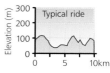

Track conditions 100% purpose-built single track

Landowners Rayonier Forests Ltd, entry by permit only.

How to get there First up, head to the Howick information centre to buy a forest permit, or you can get a year's access by joining the Pohutukawa Coast Bike Club (pohutukawabike@gmail.com) for $25, which includes a forest permit. Then drive to Whitford and turn northeast on the Whitford-Maraetai Road, driving a further 6 km. Park at the top of the hill.

Route description

Most people head for the single tracks near the entrance before exploring further afield. Hop over the gate, ride for 20 metres and turn left down Keanu Track (a 300-metre-long bus stop). At the bottom, follow the road to your left for a few hundred metres, turn left again at the next fork and stop just down the road to check out the mapboard.

There are several grades 3–4 tracks around this small area. The jumps and drop-offs are a hoot, but they demand respect – especially after rain. Start with Joshua's Track and work your way up to Pete's Track.

Notes Beware of the archery club near Breadhead Track. If you're not fit enough to climb the steep forest roads, you will be after a few rides here.

An alternative entrance is 1 km up Waikopua Road.

Since 2010, the Pohutukawa Coast Bike Club has been busy building 15 XC and DH tracks in nearby Maraetai Forest. Join the club to find out more.

Michael May and Blair Stansfield, Whitford.   Paul Kennett

6 Hunua Ranges ★ ★ ★

28 km southeast of Papakura

The Hunua Ranges Regional Park has the best collection of free-to-ride tracks in the Auckland area.

Grades 1–6
Time 1–5 hours
Distance Up to 42 km
Track conditions Gravel roads and single track

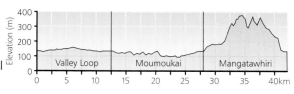

How to get there From Hunua township, follow Hunua Road southeast for about 7 km before turning left onto Moumoukai Road and driving 6.6 km over the hill to the Mangatawhiri Dam car park . Note that logging trucks use this narrow gravel road. There is a mapboard, emergency phone and toilets at the car park.

Valley Loop Track/Family Trail

Grade 1+   **Time** 1–2 hours   **Distance** 13-km loop with lots of detours possible

From the car park, ride back down the road, veer left at the first intersection and slip round a large steel gate. Ride along the gravel road, signposted 'Mangatangi Hill Road', for 800 metres and veer left at the first main intersection. Pop across the ford to start the gravel road loop marked on the map. There is a tiny bit of single track near the end of the loop that needs to be walked (turn left when you hit the gravel road); otherwise this track is a piece of cake.

River Track and Moumoukai Farm Track

Grade 3+   **Time** 1.5–2.5 hours   **Distance** 17-km loop

Most riders head straight for these tight and twisting mountain bike tracks. From the car park, follow the directions for the Valley Loop Track for about 2 km, then turn right at the 'River Track' signpost. After a short stretch of old gravel road, you'll pop into a tight 2.3-km single track. Near the end, there's a stream crossing that can get knee deep after rain. When you pop back out

Cranking it up on the Valley Loop Track.

onto a gravel road, head left back up the valley for a couple of hundred metres and look for a sign pointing to the Moumoukai Farm Track.

This single track twists through forest, fields and fords. Countless roots and ruts combine to ensure the trials and tribulations of everyday life are quickly forgotten. When you reach a 4WD track, turn left, then after 50 metres, right onto more single track. After a while, you'll reach a T-intersection where you need to turn hard left and climb beside a fence (don't go down to the 4WD track to the right). Then, after another 10–15 minutes, you'll merge with a grassy 4WD track (don't turn hard left – look for the track marker hidden in the grass ahead).

A few hundred twists later, you'll hit a gravel road. Turn right, then left onto another diverging single track after a few hundred metres. At the very bottom, follow the Valley Loop Track back to the car park. Sweet!

Mangatawhiri Challenge Track

Grade 4+   **Time** 1.5–3 hours   **Distance** 15-km loop

From the car park, ride north up the main gravel road, climbing high above the reservoir. After about 5 km, at the top of a large hill, turn left onto a 4WD track, which soon becomes a single track and traverses the main ridge. Great views and gnarly little hills. At each of the next four intersections, turn left. Don't miss the cool 1.5-km section of single track halfway down the main gravel road back to the car park (it's signposted).

This track has many steep, slick sections of moss-covered clay – not recommended when wet. Even in the dry, expect some walking.

Notes Track building is continuing, so keep an eye on the mapboard at the car park or check www.aucklandmtb.co.nz for updates. Please keep well left on all park roads.

7 Puni MTB Park ★ ★

4.5 km southwest of Pukekohe

A small pine forest absolutely packed with fun single track.

Grade 2+   **Time** 30 minutes   **Distance** 6-km loop

How to get there Drive southwest out of Pukekohe on West Street, Puni Road and Waiuku Road. After 4 km, turn left onto Attewell Road. Less than a kilometre away on your right is the Puni Rugby Club. Park there.

Route description

Ride up past the left side of the rugby club to the grassy slope and then veer right onto a 4WD track to climb to the top of the forest. After 1 minute, you will reach the start of the single track (signposted) and be ready to zigzag your way back and forth through the pine forest. At the bottom, the track exits the forest and climbs up to a BMX track quite close to the rugby club. Make sure you avoid the 'bear trap' jump near the end.

Notes This is about the smallest mountain bike park in the country. The track builders have done well to get so much out of it. For more info, check out www.franklinmtb.org.nz

Five Other Rides

Royal Albany Bicycle Reserve   ★ ☆ ☆ ☆

Grade 4   **Time** 1–2 hours   **Distance** 14 km

For North Shore riders, this twisty single track next to Massey University provides a welcome diversion from Woodhill and Riverhead.

The farm gate entrance is across the road from number 3 Bush Road in Albany (or you can start from the university car park). Head up the 4WD access road for 500 metres until just before the cell phone tower. Jump over the fence on your right, and you'll pick up the start of the Fairlane trail. Download the latest map from www.aucklandmtb.co.nz/trails/ and explore. The fenced block is owned by Massey University and the bush around it is public reserve.

Sanders Reserve   ★ ☆ ☆ ☆

Grade 3+   **Time** 1 hour   **Distance** 5 km

The new tracks at Sanders Reserve feel like they were designed by a blindfolded giant who chucked a bucket-load of fettucini on the ground, then laid some gravel over the top. They are super tight and twisty, with zero flow.

If you're a track bagger and want to ride these tracks anyway, good on you! From Albany, head southwest on The Avenue, which turns into Paremoremo Road. After several kilometres, turn left at Merewhira Road, then left again at Sanders Road. Park by the mapboard entrance.

The track network is quite confusing. Just head in and see if you can find something that tickles your fancy. This is a beaut' spot for a picnic!

Mangere Coastal Walkway   ★ ★ ☆ ☆

Grade 1   **Time** Up to 2 hours   **Distance** Up to 14 km return

From Auckland city, head south through Onehunga, over Mangere Bridge on Highway 20, and turn off to Mangere Domain. Drive 1 km west of Mangere Domain down Ambury Road to the Ambury Farm Park information centre.

Free from Auckland city bustle on the Mangere Coastal Walkway.   Jonathan Kennett

From the car park by the information centre, follow blue posts across the farmland to the Mangere Coastal Walkway, which is a wide smooth gravelled path. The walkway skirts south around the coast to the Mangere Lagoon. You can ride all the way round the lagoon (on your left) or go straight ahead for a short cut. The lagoon track is a lovely ride.

Beyond the lagoon, the track continues past the waste-water treatment plant – not so nice. There are a few turns to make, but they are all signposted, and apart from a few steps, the track is still easy. You can continue all the way to the Oruarangi Creek picnic area (3 km from the lagoon). Most people turn back here, but the track does continue for another 1 km if you cross the bridge. The track ends at a quieter part of the coast.

Tapapakanga Regional Park   ★ ☆ ☆ ☆

Grade 3   **Time** 1 hour   **Distance** 7-km loop

To be perfectly frank, this little trip ranks at the bottom end of the fun scale and only just made it into the book. But it's worth doing if you're in the park.

From Clevedon, 15 km from Papakura, drive northeast to Kawakawa Bay and then south on Kawakawa-Orere Road. Turn right again onto Orere-Matingarahi Road and then veer left onto Deery Road, 28 twisty kilometres from Clevedon. After a few hundred metres, turn left again at the large carved poles (poupou) and drive down to the car park by the beach.

There are usually map pamphlets at the car park. The 7-km-long mountain bike route is marked by yellow posts. It follows a mixture of gravel road, 4WD track and pasture up to a trig station and back via a different route. Anticlockwise is the best direction, but either way involves short steep hills.

Waharau Regional Park ★ ★ ☆ ☆

These old tracks provide a good range of opportunities. As long as you don't mind a little 'foot cycling', you'll be rewarded with awesome views and lengthy downhills. There are three loops to choose from (see below).

From Clevedon, 15 km east of Papakura, drive east to Kawakawa Bay and then south towards Kaiaua. About 40 km from Clevedon (and beside the Firth of Thames), turn right at the Waharau Regional Park signpost and drive up to the second car park.

The Auckland Council's "Southern Parks" pamphlet, available at the car park, includes a map of the tracks.

Upper Link Track

Grade 3   **Time** 1 hour   **Distance** 4.5 km

From the mapboard, head left (not straight ahead) over a fence, then follow the yellow markers up a steep track to the spur on your right. Some walking may be required. After 2 km, turn left and follow a steep single track down to another fork, where you should turn left again to head back to the car park.

Waharau Ridge Track Loop

Grade 4-   **Time** 1.5–2.5 hours   **Distance** 11 km

Ride the first 2 km of the Upper Link Track and then continue climbing up to the ridge, following the red markers. Three kilometres from the car park, there is a fantastic lookout platform beside the track. This is only 600 metres from the ridge. There's a fair bit of walking in the second half of this climb, especially when wet. Once on the main ridge, it's a 100% ridable vehicle track – turn left and enjoy. Keep an eye out for the left-hander off the ridge that will loop you back down to the start – it's pretty obvious if you're not moving too fast.

Whakatiwai Ridge Route

Grade 4   **Time** 2–3 hours   **Distance** 18 km

From the mapboard, follow the Waharau Ridge Track Loop for 6 km, then carry straight on along the ridge. The old logging track gets rougher further along but is mostly ridable. Turn left at the 'Whakatiwai and Coast Rd 2 hrs' signpost for a long downhill, which spits you out at a non-signposted spot on the main coast road. Turn left to return to the car park 4.5 km away.

Waikato

1 **Te Aroha MTB Trails**
2 **Pukete MTB Park**
3 **Te Miro MTB Park**
4 **Waikato River Trail**
5 **Pureora Timber Trail**
★ Plus four other rides

WAIKATO HIGHLIGHTS

Biking opportunities have improved dramatically over the last few years in the Waikato. Two new trails, the Waikato River Trail and the Pureora Timber Trail, provide excellent multi-day rides. Te Aroha, with its nearby hot pools, is still a popular destination, and Te Miro MTB Park has some great tracks, built by mountain bike enthusiasts for mountain bike enthusiasts.

1 Te Aroha MTB Trails ★★★☆

EASY   INTERMEDIATE

Te Aroha, 40 km northeast of Hamilton

Some fine riding for fit riders with varying levels of experience, these fun trails start at the entrance to the Te Aroha Domain, right next to the hot springs.

Grades 2–3+   **Time** 1–2.5 hours   **Distance** Up to 11 km

Track conditions 99% single track, 1% road

Maps You can grab a free trail map from the information centre and the Outdoor Adventure bike shop, but it's not essential for the ride.

Route description

From the hot springs, head out of the domain, right up Boundary Street and follow your handlebar stem to the town water tank.

From the water tank, the track is signposted all the way round and has a few optional 'hard' loops, which add a couple of challenging kilometres to the main track. Watch out for other users when coasting back down the last section of dual-use track.

The blue route markers are reflective, so this also makes a good night ride. A lot of effort has gone into making the

Simon Kennett

tracks enjoyable all year round, but they're still a grade harder when wet. New tracks have been built since 2010.

Notes The bike shop located at 204 Whitaker Street (phone (07) 884 4545) has bikes for hire. There's some interesting history on display at the museum in the domain.

2 Pukete MTB Park

EASY

Hamilton city

The Hamilton Mountain Bike Club has packed a bunch of nice grade-2 tracks into this small area on the outskirts of town.

Grade 2
Time 20–40 minutes
Distance 2–6 km

How to get there Head north from the centre of Hamilton on Highway 1 for 7–8 km; turn right onto Kapuni Road and right again after 100 metres onto Maui Street. After 200 metres, look for a 'Pukete Farm Park, Hamilton Mountain Bike Club' sign on the left.

Route description
Ride through the paddock and around to the left until you see a gate and more mountain bike related signs. Follow the arrows and enjoy the flow. Give yourself

Paul peruses Pukete MTB Park.

Paul Kennett

30 minutes to blast around or longer if you head out on the grassy tracks beyond the official park.

Notes A lot of tree planting is changing this area from a wasteland to a green bush park. Hopefully, as the trees grow, the industrial noises and smells will diminish.

3 Te Miro MTB Park

16 km south of Morrinsville

INTERMEDIATE   EXPERT

Te Miro is an active logging forest, so expect things to change without warning. However, there are some great tracks to enjoy. Best ridden when dry to avoid the slippery clay.

Grades 3–5
Time 1–3 hours
Distance 5–20 km
Track conditions 10% forestry road, 20% 4WD, 70% single track

Maps Pick up a map from Rex at Kaimai Cycles or the information centre in Morrinsville or www.kaimaicycles.co.nz/temiro.html

How to get there From Morrinsville, drive southeast on Studholme Street. This becomes the Morrinsville-Walton Road and 1 km from town, at a railway line, veers right. About 10 km from town, veer right onto Chepmell Road and then, after another 700 metres, turn left onto Waterworks Road. This is a narrow windy road in places. After about 7 km, stop at the parking area overlooking the reservoir. The road is sealed up to here – if you hit gravel, you've gone too far.

Route description

From the car park, there's a short track among pampas on your left. This takes you to the start of the PD Track only 100 metres away. The PD boys have built a long, mostly downhill track into the forest; it's good fun.

From the bottom of the PD Track, cross an old bridge and head left on a gravel road for 150 metres, then cut across an old skid site onto an old 4WD track. After 10 minutes, you will have climbed to the top of Gobblers Knob, one of the best tracks at Te Miro. It's 4 km long and mostly downhill. Follow the Joiner Link and Kaimeleon to return to the car park. This is a neat introductory loop, but there's lots more to explore.

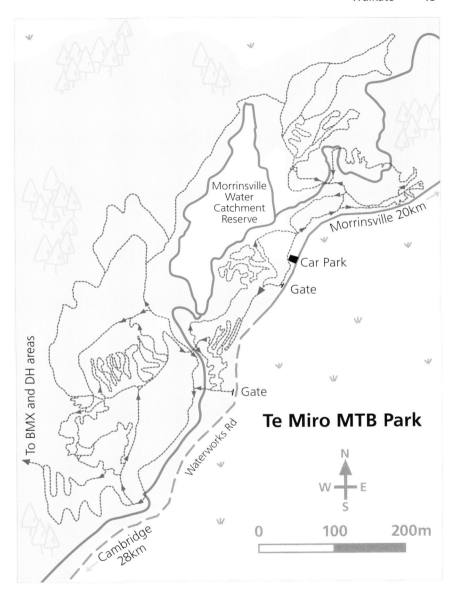

Morrinsville
Water
Catchment
Reserve

Morrinsville 20km

Car Park

Gate

To BMX and DH areas

Gate

Waterworks Rd

Te Miro MTB Park

N
W E
S

0   100   200m

Cambridge
28km

4 Waikato River Trail ★ ★ ★ ★

Between Cambridge and Taupo

Also known as the 'Hidden Trail' this is one of the little-known gems of the Waikato River. In 2011 it became the second of the New Zealand Cycle Trails to be officially opened. It is a fully gravelled, all-weather track, ready to ride any time of year.

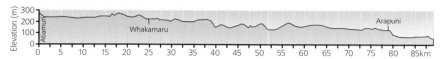

Grades 2 and 3   **Time** 1–2 days   **Distance** 90+ km

Track conditions 98% gravelled single track, 2% road and footpath

Maps Check out www.nzcycletrails.com for a map.

Route description

There are three main sections of this trail that can be ridden separately or continuously.

Karapiro Trail: Arapuni to Pokaiwhenua Bridge car park

At the northern end, there is a fun 11-km section, which most people ride there and back. Allow approximately 1 hour each way. The Rhubarb Cafe in the small village of Arapuni is an ideal place to start/finish, and they have maps of the trail.

From the Rhubarb Cafe, ride south down the main road for 200 metres and then turn right at the 'Waikato River Trails' signpost. There is an impressive swing bridge across the Waikato River only 100 metres away. It is worth checking out at the start or end of your ride. You have to drop down to it on a little side track.

The main trail passes by a picnic table 20 metres above the swing bridge, and heads north, running parallel to the Waikato River. It is well gravelled and easy to follow. After 5 minutes you'll pop out onto a road, turn left, and after a few seconds you will see the trail again on the other side. There are lots of great views, a couple of picnic tables, and a few short climbs that some cyclists will have to walk. The highlight of this section is a 500-metre long board walk through the Huihuitaha wetlands.

Turn back from either the Little Waipa Reserve, which has toilets, or a few kilometres further on at the Pokaiwhenua Bridge car park, which is just a car park in the middle of nowhere.

500-metre long boardwalk, Waikato River Trail

Arapuni to Whakamaru

This 60-km section was the last stretch of the trail to be built and the toughest. There are a few big hills, and a lot of country that is hardly ever seen. At the time of writing we had only walked and ridden short bits of it, so we can't give you a complete account. Suffice to say that it will be fully signposted, and ready to ride by the end of 2011. When we explored it, there were a few short walking sections.

Whakamaru to Atiamuri

There is 25 km of grade 3 trail open and ready to ride at the southern end of the Waikato River Trail. Intermediate level mountain bikers should allow 2 to 3 hours for this section.

You can ride the trail in either direction. At the Whakamaru village end, park near the dairy/cafe beside Highway 32, and ride across the Whakamaru Dam. It's only 600 metres away, and there is a footpath to ride on. At the far end of the dam, turn right onto the Waikato River Trail. It is well signposted and easy to follow all the way to the Atiamuri end.

If you want to start at the Atiamuri end, it is a little less obvious. If travelling from Taupo, drive north on Highway 1 for 40 km until you reach a long bridge across the Waikato River. Less than 100 metres after crossing the bridge, turn left onto Ongaroto Road at the 'Waikato River Trails' sign. Drive down this road for 200 metres before parking on the left, at the start of the trail. From here the trail is easy to follow all the way to Whakamaru village.

Notes Parts of this track were initially built for walkers, and a few short bits are unridable.

5 Pureora Timber Trail   ★ ★ ★ ☆

70 km southeast of Te Kuiti

By mid 2012 DOC will have finished building one of the most exciting grade 2 trails in the country. This is one of the New Zealand Cycle Trail projects, and it winds its way through Pureora Forest at an easy gradient, from Pureora village to Ongarue (near Taumarunui). Much of it is on an old tramline, and it includes a spiral and some very long swing bridges.

Grade 2+   **Time** 1–2 days   **Distance** 77 km

Track conditions 25% new and old logging roads, 40% old bush tramline, 35% new single track

How to get there Pureora is in the middle of nowhere. That's part of its charm. From Te Kuiti, head southeast on Highway 30 for just over 60 km. Just short of

Kay Meekings crossing the Mangatukutuku Stream swing bridge.

Rachel Kelleher

Barryville, turn right onto Barryville Road and drive 2.5 km to the DOC Forest Field Centre.

Route description

The ride starts 100 metres from the visitor centre. Sweeping through an impressive chunk of the Pureora Forest Park, this trail takes you through four ecological areas, passing 800-year-old trees, a bush tramway and historic timber-milling sites along the way.

Although the full trail takes two days to cycle, there are several options for shorter rides, with trackside shelters, toilets, and interpretation panels positioned at regular intervals along the route. For a 25-km loop trip, check out the Maraeroa Cycle Trail, the last ride mentioned in this chapter.

The trail features some of New Zealand's highest and longest suspension bridges (the biggest is 140 metres long and 45 m high!), and the amazing Ongarue Spiral bush tramway is being restored to become a significant feature of the adventure.

From the visitor centre, head to the signposted trail head, 100 metres away. Follow the signs around the southwest side of Pureora (1165 m). From there the trail squiggles its way through the forest, generally southwest, crossing several major rivers, and passing a number of historic sites. There is a camping site at Piropiro Flats about half way.

The trail ends at Ongarue, a small village 24 km north of Taumarunui. Less than 1 km before Ongarue, there is a back country road trail, signposted to Taumarunui, where you will find shops, accommodation, and public transport.

Notes Parts of the trail will be opened before the end of 2011, and the full trail will be ready to ride by April 2012. At the time of writing, there were no shops at Pureora or Ongarue; the nearest facilities to Pureora are at Benneydale or Mangakino, and the nearest facilities to Ongarue are at Taumarunui.

Four Other Rides

Wires Road   ★ ★

Rough 4WD tracks provide plenty of exploration potential on the Coromandel Range.

Grade 3+   **Time** 2–3 hours   **Distance** 20–30 km

Check out NZTopo50 BC35 Paeroa. DOC has a pamphlet on this area, titled "Maratoto and the Wentworth Valley".

About 9 km north of Paeroa, turn right onto Maratoto Road. After 7 km, turn left onto Wires Road and park at the ford 500 metres down the road.

From here, the gravel road soon becomes a rough 4WD track and climbs onto the Coromandel Range. There are a few tracks to explore up here before heading back down the same way.

This is a popular off-road vehicle area, but it is sometimes closed due to bad weather; best ridden when bone dry.

Notes The Wentworth Track is not open to bikes.

Karangahake Gorge Historic Walkway   ★ ★ ★

Here is a fascinating trip for history buffs along an old railway line. There are two impressive bridges and a 1-km-long tunnel. Don't forget your lights.

Grade 2   **Time** 1–2 hours   **Distance** 8 km each way

Start from the Karangahake car park, right beside Highway 2, only 6 km southeast of Paeroa (120 km southeast of Auckland).

From near the end of the car park, cross the bridge and follow the track up valley for almost a kilometre before taking another bridge across the river and Highway 2. You then enter a long tunnel, which takes you to another bridge across the highway and river again! From there, the track takes you through the gorge to the Waikino Station Cafe, 6 km from Waihi.

After a cuppa and a browse through the information centre, head back the way you came.

Notes This is part of the 77-km Hauraki Rail Trail Cycleway, one of the New Zealand Cycle Trail projects that is currently being constructed between Thames, Paeroa and Waihi. It should be finished by the end of 2012.

Pirongia Forest ★ ★ ★ ★

Here is a mountain bike park in the making. Not much to ride in 2011, but the potential is huge and the local club is keener than a ferret in heat.

Grade 3+   **Time** 1.5 hours   **Distance** approximately 18 km

Pirongia village is 32 km south of Hamilton on Highway 39. From the public toilets, head south on Highway 39 for 600 metres and turn west onto Baffin Street, over the Waipa River, then right onto O'Shea Road, then take the next right on to Sainsbury Road. It's 8 km uphill to the forest gate entrance.

In June 2011, there were just a couple of single tracks in this 200-hectare forest. Have a look at www.waipamtb.org.nz for the latest track and events information.

Kids flocked to the opening of the Pirongia Forest tracks, May 2011.

Tui Allen

Maraeroa Cycle Trail   ★ ★ ☆ ☆

Mountain biking with a difference! This easy trail provides a great loop trip with the added bonus of a new eco-cultural centre to visit en route.

Pureora, 70 km southeast of Te Kuiti

Grade 2   **Time** 2–3 hours   **Distance** 25-km loop

The ride starts at Pa Harakeke eco-cultural centre, approx 3 km west of Pureora Forest village. Ride through Pa Harakeke, cross KK Road and follow the cycleway signs to Pureora village. A hundred metres east of the visitor centre, the ride joins the start of the Pureora Timber Trail and winds through the magnificent Pikiariki ecological area. After a further 6 km, turn right onto Cabbage Tree Road and follow the cycleway signs through private forestry roads all the way back to Pa Harakeke.

The private section of this trail may occasionally be closed to riders due to logging operations. Check the Pa Harakeke website for details at www.paharakeke.co.nz Bikes are available for hire. They also do coffee, and have a model fortified pa site.

Bay of Plenty

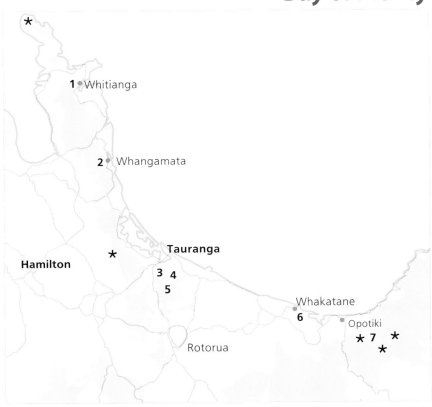

1 **Whitianga MTB Park**
2 **Whangamata Forest**
3 **Oropi Grove Freeride Park**
4 **Summerhill Recreation Farm**
5 **TECT All Terrain Park**
6 **Rawhiti MTB Park**
7 **Pakihi Track**
★ Plus five other rides

BAY OF PLENTY HIGHLIGHTS

There's a huge diversity of mountain biking options in the Bay of Plenty, ranging from freeriding at Oropi to classic cross-country through the remote and recently restored Pakihi Track. The most popular trails are at Rawhiti MTB Park near Whakatane and Summerhill Recreation Farm just out of Tauranga.

1 Whitianga MTB Park ★ ★ ☆ ☆

3.5 km from Whitianga

This small park is packed with a dozen single tracks and contains enough variety to suit most riders. There is also a skills area and a BMX track.

Grades 3–5   **Time** 1–2 hours   **Distance** Up to 10 km

Track conditions 100% single track

Maps Pick up a trail guide for $4 from The Bike Man at 16 Coghill Street in Whitianga, or the Whitianga Information Centre.

How to get there Head out of town on Joan Gaskill Drive, turn left onto Highway 25, then right onto Moewai Road. Park at the small, signposted car park.

Route description

From the parking area, cross the road and enter the park at the signposted gate. There are several signs there, just in front of all the wooden structures. Follow the track across to the forested hill. There are about 6 km of track to explore, starting with Tank Entry.

Notes See www.whitiangabikeclub.co.nz for more details, including gradings for all the tracks. There is a bike wash near the car park. If you enjoyed your ride, leave some coins in the donation box.

2 Whangamata Forest ★ ★ ☆ ☆

Whangamata

This pine forest has a mixture of forestry and single tracks. Like most pine forest mountain bike parks, navigation is hard the first time and gets easier the more you explore. There's a kids' skills area next to the old forest HQ car park, 250 metres up from the main gate.

Grades 3–4
Time 1–4 hours
Distance Up to 50 km

Track conditions An even mix of forestry roads and single tracks

Landowners You need a permit to ride in this commercial pine forest ($10 for one month's access). Drop in to the Whangamata Information Centre, Port Road (phone 07 865 8340) or Whangamata Cycles on Port Road to get one.

Maps You will get a map with your permit – and you'll definitely need it.

How to get there From downtown Whangamata, ride 4.4 km northwest along Highway 25 to a white gate with a small 'Mountainbike Track Way In' sign. It's on your left, 500 metres after passing Allan Drive on your right.

Route description

Here's a starter loop: Ride up (1) Fritz, then down (6) Cruiser and (7) HQ.

For a bigger loop, cycle via tracks (7) HQ, (4) Dons and (2) Newby to Otuwheti Road. There is a lookout about 50 metres west of the top of Newby. Then sweat your way up Middle Ridge. Drop down Manuka Road and head back along Otuwheti Road.

3 Oropi Grove Freeride Park ★ ★ ☆ ☆

5 km southwest of Tauranga

This park features jumps and stunts ideal for expert freeriders rather than cross-country riders.

Grades 2–6   **Time** 1–2 hours   **Distance** Up to 15 km

Track conditions 5% gravel road, 95% single track

Maps Oropi Grove MTB Park maps are available at Tauranga bike shops.

How to get there From Highway 29 on the southern edge of Tauranga, follow Oropi Road south for 3 km to the well-signposted car park.

Route description

Check out the mapboard at the car park to plan your trip, then head into the forest on the single track to the left, behind the mapboard (that's 'Entry Track').

For your first ride, you should at least aim to get across to Joyce Road (the far side of the park) and back. This area is not huge, so you can't get lost for long.

Notes There's a toilet and wash-down pad adjacent to the car park. These tracks are best ridden when dry. The Council nearly shut down this park because they were worried about all the hardcore North Shore style structures. Some have been removed, and track building is now led by old-school legend Clive Vail.

4 Summerhill Recreation Farm ★ ★ ★ ☆

11 km southeast of Tauranga

This working farm has 20 km of hand-built single tracks for walkers, mountain bikers and equestrians. It's the location for many local mountain bike races. Expansive views, specimen forests, Mongolian gers and great single track combine to make Summerhill a truly unique experience.

Grades 2–4   **Time** 1–3 hours   **Distance** Up to 20 km

Track conditions 10% 4WD track, 90% single track

Maps Recreation Farm map available at information kiosk.

Mark Leuschke and Karl Young on SRAM Track, Summerhill.

Brian Rogers, *The Weekend Sun*

How to get there From Welcome Bay on the outskirts of Tauranga, head east on Welcome Bay Road for several kilometres. Turn right on Reid Road and, after another 3 km, you'll reach the car parking area on your left with toilets, showers and an information kiosk.

Route description

At the information kiosk, register, give your donation, check out the noticeboard and pick up a map. Ride through the kiosk and veer left to follow the track of your choice. The tracks are well signposted and cover areas of pasture and forest (exotic and native) on single track and 4WD track. Most are grade 3–4 tracks, but there is also an easy track through the avocado grove.

Notes Leave all farm gates as you find them. For more info, email info@summerhillfarm.co.nz or phone (07) 542 1838. Entry is by gold coin donation.

5 TECT All Terrain Park ★ ★ ☆ ☆

Halfway between Tauranga and Rotorua

This recreation park now has several short mountain bike tracks, and the potential for a lot more in future.

Grades 1–4   **Time** 1–3 hours   **Distance** Up to 17 km

Track conditions 100% single track

How to get there From Tauranga's Barkes Corner on Highway 29, head 27 km south along Pyes Pa Road (Highway 36). Or it's 28 km north of Rotorua; head northeast around Lake Rotorua, through Ngongotaha and stay on Highway 36. Once you reach the park, you'll find the mountain bike track area 1.6 km from the park entrance. It's well signposted.

Route description

In June 2011, there were several tracks ready to ride, including:

Kids a 300-m grade 1 track ideal for children going out on their first mountain bike ride.

Uno a 2-km grade 2 track for anyone wanting a basic cruise.

Lookout a 6-km grade 3 track mostly on gravel roads.

Buffalo Girl a 9-km grade 4 track with 6 km of single track, the rest gravel road.

Notes For the latest information, see www.mtbtauranga.co.nz and/or www.tectallterrainpark.co.nz

Riders enjoying the new tracks at TECT Park.   TECT Park

6 Rawhiti MTB Park ★★★☆

11 km southeast of Whakatane

INTERMEDIATE   ADVANCED

The tracks here have been well designed and built and are definitely worth a visit.

Grades 3–4

Time 1–3 hours

Distance Up to 15 km

Track conditions 100% single track

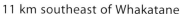

Maps This is an active logging area, so you need a permit and a map, which you can get for $5 from the Whakatane Information Centre, the Ohope Beach holiday park or the Whakatane Cycle Centre.

How to get there Head 6.6 km east of Ohope on Wainui Road to Burma Road. There is a small parking area 1.1 km up Burma Road in front of the main forest gate.

Route description

From the car park, swing your bike over the access gate and ride up the main forestry road. Head up the hill and onto the Ground Effect Grinder. You will then have two choices of downhill: Mal's Mayhem is a purpose-built track with some awesome berms on the way down (at the bottom, turn left and hook onto the Bobcat Exit Track). Alternatively, for a more old-school ride, take Works Whoops. Either way you'll have a blast.

There are more tracks being built, and more forest being logged, so expect major changes. The Whakatane Mountain Bike Club does a great job, so the new tracks will be guaranteed fun.

Burma Road Riders who aren't into steep hills or narrow tracks could well enjoy riding Burma Road. It heads from the car park across a bridge on the right and through farmland to a gravel road a few kilometres away, making an ideal easy ride for those wanting to keep fit.

Notes This is a production forest. If logging is happening, consult with the foreman before entering the park. If you're into racing, don't miss the Ohope Ordeal in late March.

The ups and downs of Mal's Mayhem, Rawhiti MTB Park

Paul Kennett

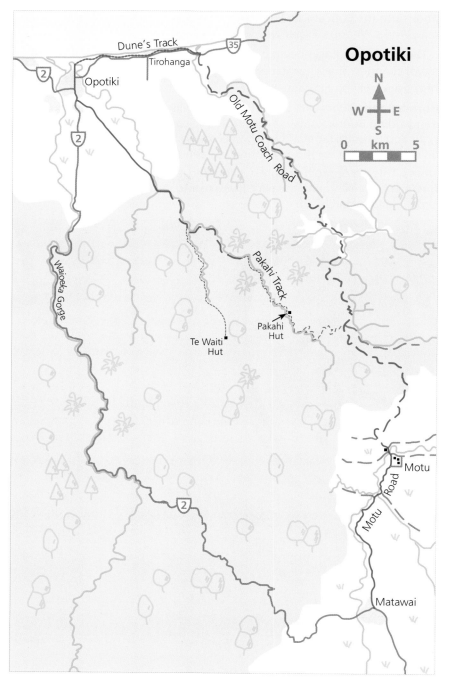

7 Pakihi Track ★★★☆

INTERMEDIATE

Bay of Plenty

This historic stock route through the Urutawa Conservation Area has been resurrected as one of three New Zealand Cycle Trail projects in the Bay of Plenty.

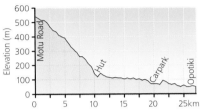

Grade 3

Time 3–4 hours

Distance 27–33 km

Track conditions 100% single track

Maps NZTopo BE41 Opotiki and BF41 Oponae are recommended.

How to get there From Opotiki, drive south on Highway 2 to Matawai, then turn north to get to Motu. The road narrows and becomes rougher as it climbs into the hills. About 10 km past Motu, you will reach the top of the ridge. From there, it's considerably faster and more fun to bike to the start of the Pakihi Track, 6 km away.

Route description

The Pakihi Track used to be a grade-5 epic, and then it was all but destroyed by a massive storm in 2008. In 2011, it was upgraded and reopened as a grade 3 trail that almost anyone can ride. Also, a bridge has been built across the Pakihi River. All in all, this is a much faster trip now.

From the signpost beside Motu Road, dive off into the bush. A benched single track descends to Pakihi Hut 10 km away. Almost 1 km past the hut, you cross the river on a new bridge and continue down valley on a completely upgraded single track. You will reach the road end next to a second swing bridge about 9 km down valley from the hut.

Most people ride from here back to Opotiki. It is 15 km of gravel and sealed road, mostly gently downhill.

Notes You can make an 80-km loop by riding from Opotiki to the Pakihi Track via the Dunes Track and the Old Motu Coach Road. See Other Rides below.

Five Other Rides

Stony Bay ★☆☆☆☆

Grade 4   **Time** 1–2 hours   **Distance** 7 km

It's hard to be grumpy in such a beautiful part of the world, unless you're trying to 'ride' a really poxy track.

Drive 50 km north from Coromandel township to Stony Bay. The last 7 km is 'Unmaintained Road' and makes for better riding than the track we're about to describe.

From Stony Bay, a steep, semi-ridable 4WD track hauls its way over a huge hill to Fletcher Bay. Be warned – this track is slippery when wet and is often covered in cow pats.

It's well signposted for mountain biking, with the aim of keeping cyclists off the sweet walking track, which is illegal to ride (except during the annual Colville Connection event).

Thompsons Track   ★ ☆ ☆ ☆

To be honest, in wet conditions this is the bog ride from hell; but, in dry conditions, some people love it for its remote scenery and sense of achievement at having crossed the Kaimai Range.

Grade 3   **Time** 2–3 hours   **Distance** 20 km one way

Maps NZTopo50 BD35 Matamata and BD36 Lower Kaimai

To be honest, in wet conditions this is the bog ride from hell; but, in dry conditions, some people love it for its remote scenery and sense of achievement at having crossed the Kaimai Range.

About 30 km west of Tauranga, turn off Highway 2 down Thompsons Track Road. We recommend parking at the highway and riding up to the road end 5.5 km away. It's a good gravel road ride.

Cycle a rough 4WD track over the Kaimai Range to Shaftesbury or just to the top (480 m) and back. It takes 1–2 hours to the top from the tarseal and about 40 minutes down the other side, which is very rocky. There are a few bike gobbling bogs on the eastern side. Thompsons Track is also used by 4WD vehicles, which have wrecked parts of it.

At the top, it's worth taking a hard left turn and checking out the views from the trig 200 metres away.

Te Waiti Hut   ★ ★ ☆ ☆

This is a scenic single-track ride through native bush.

Grade 3+   **Time** 2–3 hours   **Distance** 21 km return

Maps NZTopo50 BE41 Opotiki

Head south from Opotiki on St Johns Street. Just past the edge of town, turn left onto Otara Road and drive/ride for another 14 km to a single-lane bridge. Don't cross the bridge. Instead carry straight ahead and cross a ford. About

10 minutes on from the ford, the narrow road drops down to Bushaven Lodge, and the track is signposted to the right.

There are some scary drops off the side of this track, so take care. After almost an hour, you'll descend to Te Waiti Stream. The hut is only 500 metres further on in a large clearing, but be aware that this stream becomes uncrossable after heavy rain.

Most locals turn around and head back from the hut. If you're keen, you can bash up valley a few more kilometres to Stag Flat, but it's hardly worth it.

Old Motu Coach Road   ★ ★ ☆ ☆

Motu Road is one of the roughest, most scenic public roads in the North Island. It's part of the New Zealand Cycle Trail project and connects with the Pakihi Track and the Opotiki Dunes Track.

Grade 2   **Time** 4–8 hours   **Distance** Up to 77 km one way

Maps See our Opotiki map earlier in this chapter.

Matawai (550 m), the starting point on this ride, lies halfway between Gisborne and Opotiki on Highway 2. It has the last dairy, hotel and restaurant for 70 km. Stock up well.

From Matawai, ride north to Motu, 14 km away. From there, a narrow road climbs into the hills and forest. There are awesome views for kilometres during the ride along the ridge and then plenty of downhill en route to the coast.

Once you reach the coast, you can turn left and follow the highway to Opotiki, or take the Dunes Track to Opotiki.

Dunes Track (Grade 2, 15 km): an easy gravelled path that was constructed as part of the New Zealand Cycle Trail in 2011. It starts 2 km east of Tirohanga on the coast and heads west to the War Memorial Park at the north end of St Johns Street, Opotiki.

Notes To simplify transport arrangements, some people do an 80-km loop trip by riding from Opotiki along the Dunes Track, then up Motu Road and down the Pakihi Track back to Opotiki. This is one long day or two easy days.

Otipi Road   ★ ★ ☆ ☆

This scenic back-country ride follows a road that was built in 1952 when the Motu River was proposed as a hydro dam site.

Grade 3   **Time** 4–5 hours   **Distance** 60 km return

Maps NZTopo50 BE42 Houpoto

From Opotiki, drive east for 10 km before turning right onto Motu Road. After another 23 km, you will reach Toatoa at the 'Takaputahi Rd' sign. Park here.

Murray Drake coasting down Otipi Road.

Jonathan Kennett

From Toatoa, ride east on Takaputahi Road for 10 km. This is a rough but scenic road. Just after breaking out of a particularly narrow gorge, you'll reach a large bridge with a DOC parking area by the start of the Otipi Road.

Cross the ford and follow the old road up into the forest. The views from the top are worth the climb, and although some people carry on down to the Motu River, many prefer to turn around at this point. This is a there-and-back ride.

Notes In 2011, there was one large slip 3 km from the river, which you had to carry your bike across.

Rotorua and Taupo

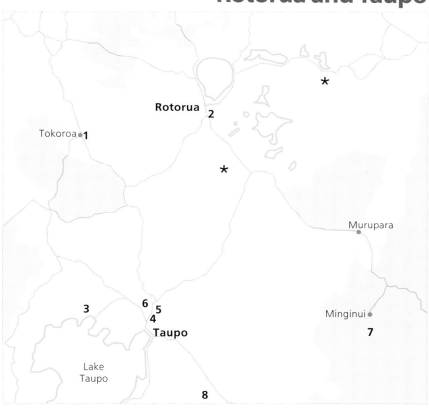

1 **Cougar Park**
2 **Whakarewarewa**
3 **Lake Taupo Track**
4 **Rotary Ride to Huka Falls**
5 **Aratiatia Dam Loop**
6 **Wairakei MTB Tracks**
7 **Whirinaki Forest**
8 **Te Iringa**
★ Plus two other rides

ROTORUA AND TAUPO HIGHLIGHTS

Many of the rides in this chapter are exceptional. First mention has to go to Rotorua's Whakarewarewa – one of the biggest and best track networks in the country. That's why Rotorua has more bike shops per capita than anywhere else in New Zealand. But Taupo, with its excellent Lake Track and well established tracks around Huka Falls, is also jostling for top spot. Meanwhile, out in Whirinaki Forest, DOC has built one of the longest native forest single tracks in the country. It's all good.

1 Cougar Park ★ ★ ☆ ☆

Tokoroa

For a quiet alternative to Rotorua, Cougar Park is a good choice. It's well signposted, so you can just rock up and ride.

Grades 2–5
Time 1–4 hours
Distance Up to 35 km

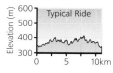

Track conditions 95% single track 5% 4WD track

Maps Pick up a park map from the Tokoroa information centre, South Waikato Cycles or the Tokoroa MTB Club www.tokoroamtb.co.nz

How to get there From town, head southeast on Highway 1 for 500 metres, turn left onto Mossop Road and left again after another 500 metres. The Cougar Park car park is at the end of the road, overlooking the cricket ground.

Route description

Head around the right-hand side of the field, through the well signposted entrance, over the bridge and warm up on the gentle Entrance Track.

A great 12-km starter loop is to pedal up 3 Blind Mice, 'down' Pig Jumps and Triple Down, then across to Go Go Gadget and out the tail end of The Nationals, then to Maber Mile and Log Drops.

Notes The Tokoroa MTB Club has a 25-year lease on this area and will be building new tracks as time allows.

Samara Sheppard enjoys the sure-fire traction on the Volcanic Plateau.   Nick Lambert

2 Whakarewarewa ★ ★ ★ ★

3 km southeast of Rotorua

Described as the 'Disneyland of mountain biking', Whakarewarewa contains some of the best purpose-built mountain bike trails in New Zealand.

Grades 1–6
Time 1 hour to 2 days
Distance Up to 100 km

Track conditions 70–80% single track, 20–30% forestry roads

How to get there Head out of Rotorua towards Taupo for 3 km. One kilometre past the '100 km/h' sign, turn left at the 'Cycle Trails' sign and ride 200 metres down Waipa Mill Road to the car park on the left. Alternatively, follow the cycle track from town to the Long Mile Road visitor centre entrance.

Route description

Pick up a $6.50 trail map from the forest visitor centre on Long Mile Road, the MTB car park or any bike shop in town.

The trail map shows all the forestry roads and mountain bike trails. Every trail is signposted at the start and finish and graded from 1 to 6 on the signposts and the trail map. The sheer number of possibilities can be bewildering, so here are some suggestions for starting off.

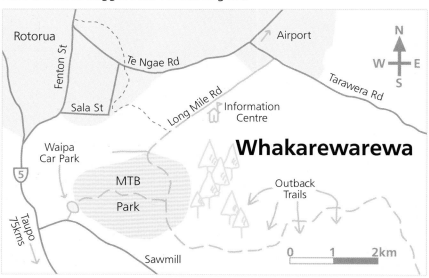

Wade Garmson and Flyn fly through Whakarewarewa.

Derek Morrison, Adventure Media Group

For the easiest possible ride, stick to the forestry roads. You can just cruise along, side by side and head out for 20 minutes or 2 hours. There's a nice picnic area to aim for at Lake Tikitapu (Blue Lake). No stress – just a good bit of exercise.

Next up are the fun grade-2 single tracks close to the Waipa Mill Road car park. Head out on the Tahi Trail, blast around The Dipper and fly home on the second part of the Tahi Trail. If you enjoyed that, head back and try the grade-3 Challenge Trail that links onto the grade-4 Rock Drop.

For experienced riders, the real drawcards at Whakarewarewa are the newer, and longer, 'outback trails'. The trail map shows four great outback loops, ranging from 2 to 4 hours, on mostly grade 3 and 4 tracks. They are all worth doing. If for some silly reason you only have one day to ride in Rotorua, we recommend the following 30-km loop.

From the car park, cut straight to the chase by riding the gravel roads to the bottom of the A-Trail, a single-track treat that flows onto the similarly scenic Tickler. This ends at a rest area with a mapboard and water fountain. From there, follow Direct Road and Frontal Lobotomy up to Billy T, one of the best intermediate downhills in the forest, surpassed by only one – the single-track perfection of Split Enz. From the bottom of Billy T, ride Moerangi Road and Loop Road across to the start of Split Enz. There is a good rest spot halfway down, which has great views over Whakarewarewa. The downhill leads straight onto Pondy and Chinese Takeaways. Finish off with Be Rude Not 2 and Mad If You Don't.

There's lots more to explore, including some advanced DH trails. While most areas are covered in exotic production forest, the epic Tuhoto Ariki delves deep into lush native bush.

Notes Walkers are not allowed on the mountain bike trails and vice versa, so it's best not to wander off the marked MTB routes. Most difficult sections of trails are marked with 'XXX' signs.

There is a mapboard and wash-down stand at the car park. Thanks to the Rotorua Mountain Bike Club, there's also a toilet a couple of hundred metres into the forest from the car park. New mapboards have been put at several key intersections around the forest.

Southstar Adventures provide a shuttle service. It costs $10 per trip to shuttle riders to the main downhill tracks (or $40 for a six-trip pass). Check out www.southstaradventures.com

For the latest trail info, check out http://riderotorua.com/trails.php

3 Lake Taupo Track ★★★★

Also known as W2K and Kawakawa Bay

15 km west of Taupo

As part of the New Zealand Cycle Trail project, a 100-km track is being built around part of Lake Taupo. It starts with two well-established and much-loved tracks: the beautiful Whakaipo Bay to Kinloch (W2K) track and the recently upgraded Kawakawa Bay track.

Grade 3
Time 4 hours
Distance Up to 33 km, another 67 km being constructed

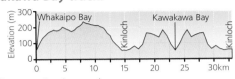

Track conditions 2% sealed road, 98% single track

Maps See www.nzcycletrails.com for a map of this ride.

Squeezing through the rocks, Lake Taupo Track.

Simon Kennett

Sarah Drake and John Randal take in the view of Lake Taupo.

Simon Kennett

How to get there Ride or drive north out of Taupo on Highway 1 and within 1 km turn left at the large 'Acacia Bay' sign. After 8 km, you'll reach the small Acacia Bay suburb and should turn right up Mapara Road. After a further 6 km, at the bottom of a downhill, watch out for a small turn-off on your left that is signposted 'Whakaipo Bay Recreation Reserve'.

Route description
The W2K track starts from the western end of this small bay and is well signposted. Hop over a large stile and check out the signboard. Once you pick up the first marker post, you can't get lost. This is an ideal intermediate track through native bush with occasional views out over the lake.

At the top of the climb, you have the option of heading round the Headland Loop – just over 9 km of brilliantly contoured single track that hooks back into the W2K track 1 km further along. The Headland Loop is a bit more challenging, but it's one of those rare gems that feels more downhill than up. If you have some spare time and energy, go for it!

From the highpoint on the W2K track it's a brilliant 6-km downhill to Kinloch. When you finally reach the edge of town, follow the marker posts across the street and enter the last bit of track down to the bay. A boardwalk leads you towards the lake. Head right at the lake and then follow the marker posts slightly away from the lake to get around the back of the marina. The track ends near the toilets and shops in the centre of town.

Your choices are now; (a) retrace your tracks for a double dose of sweet single track, or (b) carry on and ride the somewhat more technical track to Kawakawa Bay (18 km return in late 2011).

To ride to Kawakawa Bay, from the shop at Kinloch, head west along the lake front on a minor track for a few hundred metres. It leads you over a small bridge and onto the main signposted track.

The track was upgraded in 2010 and is now of similar quality to W2K. Ride through sweet native-bush single track to one particularly awesome vista at the top of the last climb. It takes about 1–2 hours to get to Kawakawa Bay, where there's a secluded beach and toilet. It was still a dead-end track in October 2011, but that was OK. It actually rides better on the way out. Enjoy!

Notes Construction to extend this track by another 67 km began in late 2011 and should be completed in 2013. The track will end at the Waihaha River bridge on Highway 32 (Western Bay Road), 57 km from Taupo.

4 Rotary Ride to Huka Falls ★ ★ ★ ☆

Taupo

There are several great mountain bike tracks to ride on either side of the Waikato River between Taupo and Huka Falls. The most popular is the Rotary Ride to Huka Falls. From Huka Falls, riders can cross the bridge and spin back down stream to Taupo on the Redwoods Track.

Alternatively, you can continue down valley to Aratiatia Dam (see Aratiatia Dam Loop overleaf). There is also a good single track linking Huka Falls to the Wairakei MTB tracks.

Grade 2+   **Time** 1–2 hours   **Distance** 10 km to Huka Falls and back
Track conditions 80% single track, 20% sealed road
Maps Pick up the 'Bike Taupo' map for $3 from the Taupo Information Centre, one of the local bike shops or the Helistar Hub Cafe (beside Highway 1, near Huka Falls – with a big helicopter outside).
How to get there Starting with the Rotary Ride, head northeast of downtown Taupo on Spa Road for a few minutes and turn left onto County Ave (there is a cycle path beside the road). From the car park at the end, you can just make out a Rotary Ride logo post straight ahead.

Route description
From the car park, the Rotary Ride is 4 km of varied single track to Huka Falls. When you reach Huka Falls, be aware that there is a new bypass track in place, so you can either view the falls from above and then carry straight on to Aratiatia Dam (see below), or turn left and drop down to the falls for a closer look.

From Huka Falls, you can return to Taupo on the Redwoods Track. Cross the falls bridge and turn left to enter a single track at the end of the car park. The track leads you back to Huka Falls Road. Just across the road, you'll find the start of Kev's Track. At the top of the hill, turn left onto the 2.5-km-long Redwoods Track, which pops out onto Huka Falls Road again about 2 km from town. Turn right, climb back to Highway 1, then hang a left to blitz back to the nearest cafe along the concrete cycle path running beside the highway.

The other popular choice from Huka Falls is to cross the bridge and head right on a single track to climb to the Helistar Hub Cafe. From there, you can ride through a tunnel track to the Wairakei Forest Tracks shown on the other side of the "Bike Taupo" map and described below. After exhausting yourself there, return to Taupo via the cycle path described above.

Notes There are toilets at Huka Falls. Be warned that the Huka Falls car park is locked at 5:30 pm each day. For the most up-to-date information on these tracks, check out www.biketaupo.org.nz

Taupo Cycle Challenge

Even while racing, Eddie Kattenburg has time for a smile on Taupo's awesome tracks.

5 Aratiatia Dam Loop ★ ★ ★ ★

INTERMEDIATE

Taupo

From Huka Falls you can ride down one side of the Waikato River to Aratiatia Dam and back along the other side of the river.

Grade 3 **Time** 2–3 hours **Distance** 20 km return

Track conditions 90% single track, 10% sealed road

Maps Pick up the "Bike Taupo" map for $3 from the Taupo Information Centre, one of the local bike shops or the Helistar Hub Cafe (beside Highway 1, near Huka Falls).

How to get there Start by either driving to Huka Falls, or riding there via the Rotary Ride (see above).

Route description

After checking out Huka Falls, backtrack 100 metres to take the Aratiatia Dam track. It starts with a short, sharp uphill and then eases as it follows the true right side of the river on a good quality track all the way down to Aratiatia Dam. Time things just right, and you'll be there to watch the impressive water flow when the dam gates open for 30 minutes.

During **summer,** the gates open at 10 am, 12 noon, 2 pm and 4 pm

During **winter,** the gates open at 10 am, 12 noon, and 2 pm.

Cross the Aratiatia Dam, turn left past the Aratiatia power station, past a green locked gate and onto a dirt road. Head straight past the power station, under the new Taupo bypass flyover road to the top of the hill, then turn left onto new meandering single track, and cross the Wairakei Stream Bridge.

Straight after the bridge, turn left to go behind the Wairakei Resort and then past a beautiful green thermal stream to the signposted grass intersection. Head uphill and onto Karetoto Road. Then cross the road at the Volcanic Centre.

There are two options from here down to Huka Falls. Go straight past the Hub Cafe and down to the falls for an easy option. For the more technical option, turn left down Ferguson's Track, and then right and follow the track beside the river to Huka Falls.

Notes Please, no racing on these tracks as they are popular with many bikers, walkers and runners. There are toilets at Huka Falls and the Aratiatia Dam. For the most up-to-date information on these tracks, check out www.biketaupo.org.nz

6 Wairakei MTB Tracks ★ ★ ★

Also known as Craters of the Moon

5 km north of Taupo

This area is popular with Taupo riders as it's close to town and provides lots of curly loop tracks to test your skills on. It's good for any rider and any length of time. These sweet purpose-built single tracks weave through mature pine forest at one of New Zealand's oldest MTB areas.

Grades 1–6 **Time** 1–4 hours **Distance** 5–25+ km

Track conditions 90% single track, 10% 4WD track and gravel road

Maps Pick up a map from the Taupo Information Centre, the Helistar Hub Cafe or one of the local bike shops.

Land owners Wairakei Tourist Park – no permits required.

Other users Walkers, equestrians, forestry vehicles. Steer clear of the designated horse riding tracks.

How to get there You can drive or ride to these tracks from Taupo township. If driving, head north on Highway 1 for 5.5 km and turn left into Karapiti Road. After another couple of hundred metres, turn left onto Powerline Road, where there's a car park and mapboard. If riding, use the "Bike Taupo" map to take the Rotary Ride, or the Redwoods Track (described in Waikato River MTB Tracks above) to the Helistar Hub Cafe beside Highway 1.

The feng shui of Wairakei.

Raewyn Knight

Route description

Assuming you rode to the Hub Cafe, look for the start of the Tunnel Track a stone's throw away. It leads underneath the highway and across to the main track system.

The first track is Inward Goods, which leads to the Tourist Trap, an excellent starter. This will pop you out at the main mountain bikers' car park.

From the car park, ride through the tunnel and generally uphill on Lake Hire Link, Tank Stand and then Ground Effect Grinder. Phew! Now you have earned a rest and, more importantly, a long downhill. Fly down Mr and Mrs, followed by Better than P and the last section of Young Pines. Then pedal up Incline and roll the Coaster back to the car park.

Notes   This is a commercial pine forest with many stands of mature trees. Logging started in 2010 and will continue for some time – please observe track closure signs. The neighbouring Craters of the Moon is a geothermally active area open to walkers only.

7 Whirinaki Forest   ★ ★ ★ ☆

95 km southeast of Rotorua

DOC has built two fantastic mountain bike tracks in the incredible Whirinaki Forest: one is easy and the other epic. Head to Whirinaki, 2 hours drive southeast of Rotorua and take your pick.

Whirinaki Forest Mountain Bike Track   ★ ★ ★ ☆

Grade 2   **Time** 1.5–4 hours   **Distance** Up to 16 km

Track conditions 100% single track

Maps Pick up the DOC pamphlet for this ride from the visitor centre in Murupara, phone (07) 366 1080.

How to get there Whirinaki Forest lies adjacent to Minginui, 90 km from Rotorua via Murupara (on Highway 38). As you approach Minginui, veer right to stay on Minginui Road, right again onto Old Te Whaiti Road, cross the river and turn left onto Fort Road (there's a car park/picnic area at the end).

Route description

There are short and long loop options, with information panels along the way. The loops are best ridden in an anticlockwise direction. From the car park, follow the MTB signs, climbing gently into the forest. After several minutes, turn right to begin the first loop. This becomes 104 Track, which comes out at Okurapoto Road. Turn left to complete the short loop or right for the longer ride back via the Tangitu Track.

Moerangi Track ★ ★ ★

Grade 4   **Time** 1–2 days   **Distance** 35 km

Track conditions 100% single track

Maps NZTopo50 BG38 Wairapukao and BG39 Ruatahuna

How to get there The best option for transport is to park your car at the Jail House farmstay and have them drive you to and from the road ends, which are 37 km apart. That way your car will be safe. Check out their details at www.jailhousefarmstay.co.nz

Alternatively, drive or ride to the end of Ohaku Road (grid reference 315 123). This is about 30 km from Minginui village, which is about 7 km from the end of the track.

Route description

This is one of the longest continuous native forest rides in the country and passes three traditional tramping huts along the way. Awesome! The ride involves around 1000 m of climbing.

From the end of Ohaku Road, ride up the valley to Whangatawhia (Skips) Hut. This takes 1–2 hours.

Over the following 2–3 hours, the track leads you over a 700-m high saddle and down to Rogers Hut (Te Wairoa).

Blasting down Moerangi.

From there, head up beside Moerangi Stream to Moerangi Hut (1–2 hours). The hut is 500 metres off the main track. Turn left, just before a big swing bridge.

After visiting the hut, and signing the hut book, go back to the main track, cross the swing bridge and continue climbing to a 900-m high point beside Moerangi. From there, it is mostly downhill to River Road. This final stage takes 2–3 hours.

Notes You can ride this track in either direction, but if you start from Ohaku Road then you have less climbing and finish with a long downhill – wahoo! Take it easy on the track, however, and be prepared to meet trampers around any corner.

8 Te Iringa

43 km southeast of Taupo

This arduous bike 'n' hike mission is a true classic for lovers of the outdoors with good fitness and bike handling skills.

Grade 5   **Time** 1–2 days   **Distance** 38 km return

Track conditions 100% sweet technical single track

Maps Take NZTopo50 BH37 Rangitaiki.

How to get there Turn right off Highway 5 (Napier-Taupo Road) 27 km southeast of Taupo and drive down Taharua Road. After 9.5 km, turn right on to Clements Mill Road. Stop at the car park 6.5 km down this road.

Route description

The semi-ridable track climbs 330 m from the car park to a clearing where the old Te Iringa Hut used to be, then skirts around Mt Te Iringa (1241 m) before dropping down to a swing bridge just downstream from the junction of Tikitiki Stream and Kaipo River.

Cross the swing bridge and take the main track down Kaipo Valley toward Oamaru Hut (which has 12 bunks) by the confluence of the Kaipo and Oamaru rivers.

This is a big day, packed with technical riding, so we recommend staying at the hut overnight and soaking up the wilderness rather than racing through. From here, you have to head back the same way as all the other tracks are closed to bikes and this one is just open on trial.

Notes The track through Poronui Station along the poled route to Taharua Road crosses private land and is not open to mountain bikers.

Jungle riding in Te Iringa.

Two Other Rides

Lake Rotoma Forest   ★ ★ ☆ ☆

This ride is an honest mix of heaven and hell. There's some magnificent native forest, but the track tends to get overgrown from time to time.

Grade 3   **Time** 1–2 hours   **Distance** 13-km loop

The track entrance is difficult to spot. Park at the picnic area at Lake Rotoma (40 km east of Rotorua), and ride east on Highway 30 for 2.4 km to an obscure opening in the bush on your right, just over the hill.

Ride into the forest. Within 15 minutes, you will reach a fork in the track – this is the start/end of the loop. Continue along the main track for a good 20 minutes. During a short downhill stretch along a waist-deep rut, you'll reach a fork. Go right and ride down to a clearing by Waikanapiti Stream.

Next comes a steep 30-minute climb. At the top, you'll enter a clearing with some pines ahead. Turn right and head back into native forest for a curly downhill. When you rejoin the main track, turn left and pedal back to the highway.

Pathway of Fire   ★ ★ ☆ ☆

The first half of this New Zealand Cycle Trail is mostly off road and visits several unique geothermal areas that include explosive geysers, bubbling mud and soothing hot pools. It's a great holiday trip.

Grade 2   **Time** 3–5 hours   **Distance** 30 km

The Pathway of Fire starts at Te Puia, right in Rotorua and heads out past Whakarewarewa on a cycle path beside the highway. After dropping into the picnic area beside Green Lake, it continues southeast, past Lake Okaro, and around Mt Rainbow to the Waiotapu Thermal Wonderland. Construction is due for completion in mid 2012. This is the first day of a two-day trail. The second day is mostly on road and heads down to Lake Ohakuri.

Notes For more information on this and the other New Zealand Cycle Trail projects, check out our book *Classic New Zealand Cycle Trails* (published 2012).

Tongariro

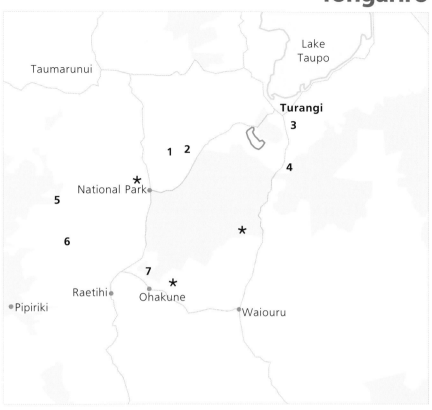

1 **42 Traverse**
2 **Tongariro Forest Loop**
3 **Tongariro Walkway**
4 **Tree Trunk Gorge**
5 **Kaiwhakauka Track**
6 **Bridge to Nowhere**
7 **Ohakune Old Coach Road**
★ Plus three other rides

TONGARIRO HIGHLIGHTS

For experienced mountain bikers, the best Tongariro trails are the crème de la crème of adventure back-country riding in the North Island, with the Bridge to Nowhere, the Kaiwhakauka Track and the 42 Traverse leading the charge.

1 42 Traverse ★★★☆

INTERMEDIATE

Tongariro Forest, 18 km northeast of National Park

This is one of the most popular adventure rides in the North Island. It involves brilliant biking on old logging tracks through a remote location teeming with native bush, and with an overall descent of 570 metres, it's hard to beat.

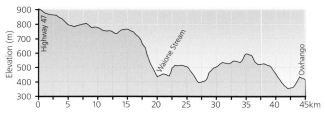

Grade 3   **Time** 3–6 hours   **Distance** 45 km

Track conditions 35% gravel road, 65% 4WD track

Maps For safety, NZTopo50 BH34 Raurimu is essential, but it has some old tracks marked on it that don't exist anymore. For this reason, we recommend you take a compass or GPS.

Landowners Department of Conservation

How to get there From National Park township, head northeast on Highway 47. After 18 km, you'll reach Kapoors Road on your left (signposted with a DOC route description board). This is the usual drop-off point for the ride as it's predominantly downhill riding from here.

Route description

DOC has signposted this track with camouflage green roadside markers 10 metres before and after most major intersections. However, don't count solely on the markers for navigation – some have disappeared, and when you're spinning along quite fast, they can be hard to spot.

As you head up Kapoors Road, keep going straight ahead around the 3-km mark (do not veer right onto an enticing turn-off that was well-gravelled in

Listen for the call at Coo-ee Lookout, 42 Traverse.   Jonathan Kennett

2011). Seven kilometres along Kapoors Road, you'll reach a large cleared area with a few motorbike jumps and another big DOC sign. Head right along a 4WD track that follows the main ridge north, past high point 831. After 1.5 km, there is a smaller clearing on your left (Kiwi Clearing), with great views back to Mt Ruapehu, on a fine day.

The next few kilometres are undulating, and there are a few major turn-offs to ignore, until you get to an intersection at grid reference 146 752. Miss this right turn and you will soon be seriously lost (trust us, we've been there). Last time we were there, it had a 'Kiwi Zone' sign standing proud. After turning right, cruise past high point 793.

Now here's a hot tip. Just over 1 km down from 793, you might notice a little track heading off on your right. This leads to a fantastic lookout over Echo Canyon. The lookout is only 100 metres off the main track, at grid reference 163 770, and offers the best spot for a break and a view of the whole ride.

From the Echo Canyon lookout, the downhill is a universally popular rip snorter all the way to Waione Stream. If it's wet, just be wary of the odd slippery patch of clay.

When you reach Waione Stream, follow the main track right and down valley for a few hundred metres. The track then hangs another sharp right and climbs steeply away from the stream for a couple of minutes then swings left and sidles down valley again. Before long, you'll dive down steeply to meet the main ford across the Waione.

This is the halfway mark, but it's not all downhill from here; there are still a few good uphills to tackle.

The first significant turn-off on the right is the Pony Club Track, and from here, you can look down into the head of the Whanganui River. Awesome! But don't take any of the enticing-looking turn-offs. Just stick to the main track, called Dominion Road, and you will ride through lovely native bush and past Te Kaha and Waterfall Bridge before blasting down to the Whakapapa River Bridge. This is where most people arrange to be picked up, although it's only a 10-minute ride up to Owhango if you're keen to finish the ride in style. There is a picnic area, toilets and a swimming hole near the bridge and, up at Owhango, a pleasant pub and plenty of accommodation.

Notes This is an isolated area that has seen many bikers become totally lost. Take extra clothes, food and a first-aid kit and make sure someone responsible knows what you're up to.

National Park Backpackers offers a shuttle service ($30 per person) – phone (07) 892 2870 or email nat.park.backpackers@xtra.co.nz

Budget accommodation is available at Owhango and National Park, and there is a free camping area at the Owhango end of the track (1 km east of Whakapapa River).

The Overlander train can take you and your bike to National Park.

After big storms, it's worth checking with the Whakapapa visitors centre (phone (07) 892 3729) that all the tracks are open; the Waione Stream ford is occasionally impassable due to flooding.

2 Tongariro Forest Loop ★ ★ ☆ ☆

Also known as John McDonald Loop

20 km northeast of National Park

This is a fantastic trip for fit and skilled jungle riders with lots of outdoors experience. Choose a dry day and take grippy shoes, safety glasses, a long-sleeved top and full-fingered gloves. Expect a toitoi thrashing, a freezing tramp down a mountain stream and difficult navigation. In return for these tribulations, you will be rewarded with stunning scenery and an honest adventure.

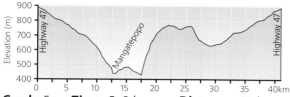

Grade 5+   **Time** 5–8 hours   **Distance** 41 km

Track conditions 35% gravel road, 30% 4WD track, 20% single track, 15% unridable

Maps NZTopo50 BH34 Raurimu is essential, although not all the roads are marked on them accurately. A GPS is also a good idea.

How to get there Start at the picnic area where John McDonald Road meets Highway 47, 4 km south of the Outdoor Pursuits Centre (OPC) turn-off.

Route description

This ride used to be called John McDonald Loop, but that road was logged in mid-2008. To avoid the devastation we started from Taurewa, just 2 km south of the OPC road. All the old buildings at Taurewa are now part of the OPC as well.

Making the most of the Mangatepopo Stream.   Sarah Drake

At Taurewa, park your car out of the way and carry your bike across a carpeted footbridge at grid reference 230 717. Nip around the side of the Lions lodge and ride down the obvious old forestry road (Pukehinau Road). You will pass John McDonald Road on your left, then the Taurewa Intake track on your right. Then, after one more kilometre, at grid reference 194 740, you'll reach Danahars Road (signposted).

Turn right down Danahars Road. The main track narrows to single track and delivers you to a flat area directly above the Mangatepopo Stream. At the northwest corner of the small clearing, a tiny track drops steeply down to the stream. There are ropes to help, but carrying a bike makes the descent difficult all the same. Expect to take about 15 minutes to reach the bottom.

When you hit the stream, walk and wade down valley for about 45 minutes to connect with the old OPC-Owhango track where it fords the Mangatepopo Stream. You might see the OPC end of the track on your right first, but you'll have to continue walking down the stream for another 200 metres to find an über-steep quad-bike track on the left bank. Grovel your way up this for 5 minutes, and you'll reap the reward of being able to return to your saddle.

At the next major intersection, turn right and tackle a steep downhill leading to a bridge (of sorts); and 300 metres later, veer left. Watch out for two more dodgy bridges in short succession. Continue on the main track and, after about 20 minutes, you'll sidle around the east side of a large knoll and meet up with the 42 Traverse track just above Waione Stream.

Head southwest above Waione Stream on the 42 Traverse – it's a 40-minute climb, all ridable (honest!), to the Echo Canyon lookout at grid reference 163 770. After a well-deserved rest, the riding flattens out as you continue along the 42 Traverse, then descend to the Pukehinau Track turn-off, on your left, at grid reference 152 743.

Now, blast down this forestry road for 1 km, then keep a sharp look out for a small track branching off on your left. This seems to be the sole domain of quad bikes these days, and in 2011 was dangerously rutted from top to bottom. Eventually it leads out to a large picnic area with toilets and back to Pukehinau Road where you started. Enjoy, if you dare!

Notes Don't even think about attempting this ride during or soon after heavy rain. Take the same gear as mentioned in the 42 Traverse write-up above.

3 Tongariro Walkway ★★★
Turangi

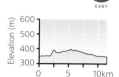

This scenic loop is suitable for all riders. However, it's heavily used by walkers and anglers – ride carefully, give way to other users and avoid it during holiday seasons.

Grade 2   **Time** 1–2 hours   **Distance** Up to 12 km
Track conditions 25% sealed road, 75% single track

Route description

From the Turangi information centre, head east across the main highway and make your way down to the Tongariro River on Arohori Street. Ride through the park at the end of the street and you'll find the Tongariro Walkway beside the river.

Turn right and follow the walkway up river for at least 5 minutes. New sections of track have been added – turn right at the 'Waikari Loop' sign if you feel like adding a few more minutes to your ride. Before long, you should turn right again to follow a short road out to the highway.

Ride south on Highway 1, and 4 km from Turangi, turn left at the 'Red Hut Pool' sign. Drop down to the river and cross the large swing bridge 100 metres away.

After crossing the bridge, follow the main track down river to Turangi. Don't be tempted to turn left down any of the anglers' tracks: they soon peter out at the river. The track rolls up and down through a mixture of scrubby forest and farmland on its way down to another swing bridge at Major Jones Pool, just next to town (you passed it on the way up).

From the bridge you have two options:

Option one: Re-cross the Tongariro River here and head back into Turangi via any one of the several obvious access roads. This is the easiest option.

Option two: Don't cross the bridge, but instead head straight down on the Tongariro Lookout Track. The track climbs high above the river, then drops down a swag of switchbacks to a big bridge on Highway 1. Cross the bridge and pick up the last section of riverside track, which leads back to the park you rode through an hour or two ago.

Notes A newish section of track has been built on the east of the river to avoid a steep section with steps.

4 Tree Trunk Gorge ★ ★ ★ ☆

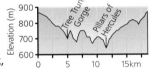
INTERMEDIATE

22 km south of Turangi

This popular ride follows beautiful native forest single track and is within cooee of a couple of the most impressive gorges in the central North Island.

Grade 3

Time 2–4 hours

Distance 19 km

Track conditions 45% sealed road, 25% 4WD track, 30% single track

Maps NZTopo50 BH35 Turangi is worth taking.

How to get there From Turangi, head south on Highway 1 for 22 km before turning left onto Tree Trunk Gorge Road (signposted). Park just out of sight of the main road.

Route description

From the highway, coast 5 km down to the Tongariro River Bridge and check out the gorge. Cross the bridge and carry on for 500 metres before turning left onto a track signposted 'Kaimanawa Rd 1 hr'. This is the start of the Tree Trunk Gorge track.

For almost 6 km, this track weaves through native forest, dealing out a steep little climb, a couple of picturesque river fords and two wooden bridges en route. At the first stream crossing, look upstream to find the ford (which is impassable when in flood). On the other side, continue following the orange markers. You'll be well ready for a rest by the time you reach the picnic/camping area beside a gravel road.

Carefully crossing a flooded stream en route to the Pillars of Hercules.   Simon Kennett

Cycle out of the picnic area on the gravel road. After 50 metres, turn left onto another single track. At the end of that satisfying little trundle, hang a left to cross the Pillars of Hercules Bridge.

After crossing the bridge, follow the main 4WD track gradually uphill, past several turn-offs, for 4.5 km, out to Highway 1. Turn left at the highway to return to Tree Trunk Gorge Road (less than 2 km away).

Notes Be careful not to spook any walkers.

5 Kaiwhakauka Track ★ ★ ★ ☆

INTERMEDIATE

Whakahoro, 35 km west of National Park

This old tramping track has been upgraded as part of the New Zealand Cycle Trail project, and now provides a stunning alternative route to the Bridge to Nowhere ride.

Grade 3   **Time** 2 hours   **Distance** 20 km

Track conditions 25% 4WD, 75% single track

Maps The best map to take is Whanganui Parkmap 273-05.

How to get there The Kaiwhakauka Track starts from Whakahoro and finishes near the Mangapurua Trig (on the way to the Bridge to Nowhere). You can use New Zealand Cycle Trail routes to cycle to Whakahoro from either National Park or Taumarunui. From National Park it's 45 km and from Taumarunui it's 65 km. Both routes are mostly downhill and well signposted.

You can also drive 44 km down Oio Road, which starts off Highway 4, only 2 km south of Owhango.

Route description

There are a few ways to cycle this track, and planning your trip is half the fun. We guess most people will want to do either a through trip to the Bridge to Nowhere or a there-and-back from Whakahoro. Here are the directions for both options.

To do a **there-and-back** trip, ride from Whakahoro, down the Whanganui Valley for 1 km on a farm track that will soon veer left up the Kaiwhakauka Valley to the Whanganui National Park boundary, where the Mangapurua Track starts – fit bikers will reach the Mangapurua Track within a couple of hours. Ride along to the trig for a view, and if you are feeling really keen, drop down to the Bridge to Nowhere and back. It takes about 2 hours to get from the trig down to the bridge.

To do a **through trip**, start by riding from either National Park, Owhango or Taumarunui (close to the Pureora Timber Trail) to Whakahoro. Then ride the Kaiwhakauka Track and continue on to the Bridge to Nowhere and down to the Mangaparua Landing, from where you can canoe or jet boat to Pipiriki.

From Pipiriki you can get a shuttle up to Raetihi, or ride down the River Road to Whanganui. See the Bridge to Nowhere write-up for more details.

Notes Check out www.blueducklodge.co.nz for accommodation, food and transport options at Whakahoro. Whakahoro is a surprisingly cool place – you may want to hang out there for a while.

Paul, Jonathan and Simon in search of sweet single track.

Adam Perry

6 Bridge to Nowhere ★ ★ ★ ★

ADVANCED

Whanganui National Park

If you only have the chance to do one adventure ride this year … you need to get out more! There are loads of great rides to do; this is one of the North Island's best. There are several ways to tackle this beauty. Below, we describe the most popular.

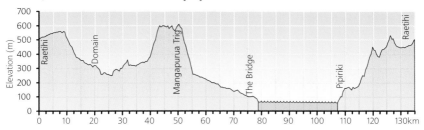

Grade 4   **Time** 2–3 days   **Distance** 135-km loop

Track conditions 30% sealed road, 24% gravel road, 8% 4WD track, 15% single track, 23% river

Sneaking around Battleship Bluff.   Jonathan Kennett

Maps The best map to take is Whanganui Parkmap 273-05.

How to get there The best place to start and finish this ride is Raetihi, 11 km west of Ohakune.

Route description

Day One This is a biggish day, so you really want to be away by 9 am. First of all, there is a 40-km back-country road ride to the start of the track. The first half to Ruatiti Domain is mostly downhill – fast fun on a sealed road. Then the road narrows and breaks into gravel: from Raetihi, give yourself 2–3 hours to reach the signposted start of Mangapurua Track.

The history of this road is mind-boggling. After the First World War, returned servicemen were given a portion of the Mangapurua Valley to farm. The government assisted by building the impossible road to the Bridge to Nowhere. It didn't last long, and neither did most of the settlers.

All going well, it'll take you about 3–4 hours to ride the next 38 km along the Mangapurua Track to the Bridge to Nowhere. From the start of the 4WD track, head left through a gate and cruise up a well-graded 4-km climb. When you reach a second gate, near the top of the hill, take a look back; the views are stunning on a clear day. This is the one big climb of the day. After an hour, you'll reach a letterbox and see a 'National Park' sign ahead.

About 2 km after entering the national park, you will reach a Y-intersection and must go left (to the right is the Kaiwhakauka Track, down to Whakahoro). Continue rolling along the ridge, and you'll soon pass a steep walking track (signposted) on your left that goes up to the Mangapurua Trig.

The track is all downhill from here, and will take fit riders about an hour and a half to get to the Bridge to Nowhere; it's a real hoot. Make sure you veer right at the 'Stafford' sign. Half an hour after that sign, you will reach a large clearing in the valley that is a good place for a rest and regroup.

The track follows the valley gently downhill all the way to the bridge; so gently, it's almost flat. There are many narrow swing bridges, a few bluffs and several large clearings en route.

The bridge itself, quite aptly, appears out of nowhere. It was opened in 1936 and had become overgrown by 1948. DOC has restored it, and it now looks weirdly fresh and new.

There is a lookout track 100 metres on from the bridge and then toilets a few hundred metres further on again. The steep ride down to Mangapurua Landing and the Whanganui River takes about 15 minutes. There is a shelter 200 metres before the landing (not a bad place to camp if need be).

From the landing, we caught a jetboat down to the Bridge to Nowhere Lodge and stayed the night before canoeing down to Pipiriki. This allows you to do the whole trip without camping gear and with the bonus of a big dinner and breakfast at the lodge.

The good, the bad and the ugly [in no particular order].   Jonathan Kennett

Day Two The paddle down the river takes about 5 hours from the lodge if you allow plenty of time for photos. Much of the river is like a long narrow lake with hardly any flow at all, but there are several grade two rapids to negotiate.

The most obvious alternatives are: save time by getting a jetboat all the way down the river or save money by cycling back out the way you came.

From Pipiriki, cycle 28 km up to Raetihi (2–3 hours). It's a quiet winding road, with great bush scenery in the first half and mountain views in the second. We stayed the night at the Raetihi Holiday Park (good value) but there are other fancier options.

Notes To organise transport and accommodation, contact Bridge to Nowhere: email info@bridgetonowhere.co.nz, phone toll free 0800 480 308, or check out their website, www.bridgetonowhere.co.nz for ideas on all the different options available. In 2011, the jetboat, lodging and meals, and canoeing option cost about $285 per person. Transport only from Mangapurua Landing down the river, and up to Raetihi costs about $115 per person.

7 Ohakune Old Coach Road ★ ★ ★ ★

EASY

Ohakune

Historically and scenically, this is one of the best easy rides in the North Island.

Grade 2   **Time** 1.5–2.5 hours   **Distance** 14 km one way

Track conditions 35% gravel road, 15% 4WD track, 50% single track

How to get there From the Ohakune railway station it is impossible to miss the start of the trail.

Route description

Ride northwest under the huge New Zealand Cycle Trail sign, and across a new cycle trail bridge. From there, the trail runs beside Old Station Road and Marshalls Road for about ten minutes before crossing a small bridge on your right and heading up into the hills. The track surface is rocky in places – remnants of the century-old cobbled coach road. There are several fascinating interpretation panels along the way, many massive rimu to admire and, just off the main trail, two huge viaducts. The last stretch to Horopito follows farm roads. Give yourself two hours to complete this 14-km trail to Horopito, and one hour to whiz back down it (assuming you don't stop to look around).

Notes This trail is the first section of one of the government's New Zealand Cycle Trail projects, the Mountains to the Sea. The next stage is the Bridge to Nowhere (see above) followed by the Whanganui River Road. For more info, get yourself a copy of *Classic New Zealand Cycle Trails*, due out 2012.

Stunning native forest on
Ohakune Old Coach Road.

Three Other Rides

Fishers Track   ★ ☆ ☆ ☆

Here's a scenic trip for fit cyclists in search of smooth riding.

Grade 2   **Time** 3–5 hours   **Distance** 50-km loop

From National Park township railway station, Fishers Road heads over a hill and down a long way to a war memorial in the middle of nowhere. The ride is mostly gravel roads these days, but there is still 5 km of dirt track that is fun and scenic.

Once you reach the memorial, turn right and follow the 'Raurimu' signposts up to Raurimu, then turn right again at Highway 4 and continue climbing back up to National Park.

Tukino Mountain Road   ★ ☆ ☆ ☆

This ride involves just over 600 m of climbing/descending and offers great views of Mt Ruapehu.

Grade 2   **Time** 2–4 hours   **Distance** Up to 28 km return

From Turangi, head south on Highway 1 for 32 km. Turn right onto the Tukino ski field access road and park a few hundred metres in from the highway.

Jonathan barrelling down Tukino Mountain Road.   Bronwen Wall

Follow the main 4WD track towards Mt Ruapehu. Just over halfway up, you'll pass DOC signs pointing out where the round-the-mountain walking track heads off. Carry on past these signs up a steep section to the Telecom transceiver and then around the hill to tackle the last stretch up to the ski field.

From the ski field, head back the same way, watching out for the sandy/snowy patches.

Rangataua Forest   ★ ☆ ☆ ☆

A pleasant ride, in dry conditions, through native bush on quiet old forestry roads and quad bike tracks.

Grade 3+   **Time** 1–2 hours   **Distance** 10–20 km

Maps The pamphlet "Ruapehu Great Bike Rides" includes a rough map of the area (available from the Ohakune information centre). NZTopo50 BJ34 Mt Ruapehu is out of date, but not entirely useless.

Mangaehuehu Stream.   Andrew McLellan

From Ohakune railway station, ride around to Railway Row, on the other side of the tracks. A hundred metres beyond the last house in this street, cross an overbridge to get to Dreadnought Road.

Ride east down Dreadnought Road to Rangataua village 5 km away. At the far end of the village, veer left onto a gravel road running beside the railway line, to Mangaehuehu Stream.

Head left under the railway bridge, and then cross the stream to follow a 4WD track east beside the railway line for 5 km. Then turn left and climb up Rangataua Road, which starts just west of Karioi railway station (if you want to keep your feet dry you can ride from Rangataua to Karioi via Highway 49).

Climb up this old gravel road for about 10 km. It is well graded and passes some fantastic forest. After several kilometres, the track veers right and the surface becomes a mixture of grass, bare earth and stones, eventually petering out in dense forest. Before it does that, veer right onto North Track, which soon becomes single track (just past a clearing on your left). Sniff your way down this track, back to the main gravel road. You've just done a big loop around spot height 714. Now, hang a left and, 600 metres later, turn right down Middle Track, which takes you back down to the main trunk line. Turn right to follow the 4WD track next to the railway back to Ohakune.

The last settlers abandoned their farms in 1942 after 25 years battling the vegetation, Kaiwhakauka Track.

Hawke's Bay and East Cape

1 **Whataupoko MTB Park**
2 **Old Mahanga Road**
3 **Eskdale MTB Park**
4 **Yeoman Track**
5 **Pukeora MTB Park**
★ Plus four other rides

HIGHLIGHTS OF HAWKE'S BAY AND EAST CAPE

Pickings are slim around East Cape, which is disappointing for such a beautiful part of the country. Further south though, in Hawke's Bay, the mountain bike scene is humming with 99% of the action happening in Eskdale MTB Park.

1 Whataupoko MTB Park ★ ★ ☆ ☆

INTERMEDIATE

Fox Street, Gisborne

This small reserve on the edge of town is riddled with purpose-built single track.

Grade 3
Time 1–2 hours
Distance 1–10 km
Track conditions 10% 4WD track, 90% single track
Maps Check out www.gdc.govt.nz/walkways-and-trails/

Murray Drake swings back down towards Gisborne.

Jonathan Kennett

How to get there The park is well signposted near the eastern end of Fox Street. There is not much parking at the road end, but it is only a 5-minute ride from town.

Route description

First timers will definitely need to download the map or memorise the mapboard at the entrance because the park offers the typical maze of single tracks.

Ride to the top of the park by heading up the grass bank and taking the Village Trail to the left, followed by Norm's Track and finally the Ground Effect Trail (all signposted). That should take 15–30 minutes.

Take in the views of the city and coastline before descending the Ground Effect Trail again and swinging onto Annette's Trail. A couple of minutes later, you will see a track heading into the forest on your left. This is the best track in the park. It's unnamed, but we call it 'Maximus Single Track' because it's so long.

At the bottom, you'll probably want to ride back up just to do that one again, only faster.

Notes This is also a popular walking and running area.

2 Old Mahanga Road

40 km south of Gisborne

This pleasant old road offers expansive views of the Pacific Ocean and a peaceful escape from the rat race.

Grade 2 **Time** 2–4 hours   **Distance** 26 km one way

Track conditions 70% gravel road, 30% 4WD track

Maps Take a good road map and NZTopo50 BH43 Wharerata.

Landowners This is mostly on a legal road, but it is important to ask for permission from Te Au Station owners Malcolm and June Rough, phone (06) 837 5751, as farming operations pose health and safety risks from time to time.

The Roughs offer modern accommodation with flawless sea views and meals by arrangement (www.quarters.co.nz).

The road also passes through Crown forest. To check on logging activities, phone Juken Nissho Ltd on (06) 869 1180.

Sweating it out on the Old Mahanga Road.

Route description

From the lookout at the summit of the Wharerata Range (40 km south of Gisborne on Highway 2), ride north for 700 metres to Paritu Road and head east on a major gravel road. For much of the way, the route follows the border between farmland on your left and forest on your right. As you head south, the track becomes rougher.

Along the way, you'll see the Railway Road and Top Circuit Road turn-offs – ignore them. Shortly after the Top Circuit Road intersection, you'll pass a house on the left. At the next fork, go left onto the dirt road that leads up the hill. After about an hour's riding, you'll reach a point (just after gaining your first good views inland) where the route is blocked by a fence with no gate. Jump over the fence, take the left fork towards the pine trees and continue along the farm track.

The track hugs the hillside overlooking the Pacific Ocean, with views of Mahia Peninsula. Please leave all gates as you find them. At the Te Au Station stockyards, watch out for dogs. From here, it's back onto gravel roads. From Kopuawhara Railway Station, it's a further 14 km west to Nuhaka back on Highway 2.

3 Eskdale MTB Park ★ ★ ★

EASY   EXTREME

19 km northwest of Napier

This is the premier spot to ride on the east of the North Island. It's also the reason why the Hawke's Bay MTB Club is the largest in the country, with over 1850 members. There are more than 60 named tracks, averaging 1 km in length, and all are signposted.

Grade 2–6
Time 1–10 hours
Distance over 60 km of tracks

Track conditions 70% single track, stitched together with new and old forestry roads

Landowners Pan Pac Forests. You must have a permit to access this privately-owned production forest. Either join the Hawke's Bay MTB Club or buy a three-week permit, which comes with a map, for $7 from any Napier bike shop, the Bayview 4 Square or the Napier Information Centre. One permit covers Eskdale and Pukeora MTB parks. You can also get a permit, and/or join the club at www.hawkesbaymtb.co.nz

How to get there Head north from Napier on Highway 2, then left on Highway 5 to get to Eskdale. Turn right onto Waipunga Road 18.5 km from

Napier, at the 'Eskdale Mountain Bike Park' sign. There is a signposted car parking area 500 metres up the road.

From your car, swing your bike over the gate and ride up Burden Road for 300 metres until you reach the forest. The Hawke's Bay MTB Club has posted a large mapboard here.

Route description

For an easy 7-km ride, start with Barley, Pace and Lower Magog before heading back on Merv's and Burden Road and finishing off with Blink.

For an average difficulty ride, try the following 1-hour loop. Blast along Barley, link up to Twoman, heading for Upper Magog, through and down to Luge and then left into Lower Magog, right down the Drop, left around into Boulder, through all of Boulder onto Burden Road. (Check it all out on the mapboard.) Cross Burden Road to connect with Merv's, turn right along Merv's, and left onto Burden Road again, right into Pace (just before the cattle stop), out of Pace, bunny hop the cattle stop and right into Barley to finish this seamless 10 km of single track.

For a harder 2- to 3-hour ride, head out to Ridgeline via Twoman. Then pedal up to the 120-m high trig via Fenceline and Ledge, taking in the views over Napier. From there, fly down the popular Dam Canyon, across Zip and return via Dingo Valley, Blackberry Nip, Lower Pond, Forrest Gump and Eskdrive down to Burden Road. Whew! Finish off by doing part of Lower Magog, Boulder, Pace and Barley.

After those three options, you will have only scratched the surface of Eskdale. Return another day to explore further.

Notes There is another car parking area at the east end of the forest. It's off Highway 2 and Tait Road. Only a couple of hundred metres from this car park is the cool Trials Arena, where you can easily spend an hour or two playing. If you go exploring, keep well clear of the Pan Pac mill, and the Gun Club.

Carl Larson and Jonathan head for the top of Eskdale MTB Park.

Jonathan Kennett

4 Yeoman Track ★★☆☆

Ruahine Range, 50 km northwest of Waipukurau

This ride has a fine mix of logging roads and vintage single track through exotic and native forest.

Grade 2+
Time 2–3 hours
Distance 17-km loop

Track conditions 65% gravel road, 5% 4WD track, 30% single track

Maps NZTopo50 BK37 Tikokino shows the route but is not essential.

How to get there Turn down Wakarara Road (3 km north of Ongaonga on Highway 50). Follow it to the road end at the Makaroro River ford – half an hour's drive away.

Route description
From the road end, head straight across the ford and up the overgrown 4WD track for a few hundred metres before taking the first right-hand turn. Carry

on along this gravel road through exotic forest for several kilometres. About 10 minutes after passing the Leatherwood Road turn-off, you'll cross a creek and pedal up a small climb to a major intersection. Turn left onto Ellis Road – this is mostly downhill to Ellis Hut, 5 minutes away. Veer left 150 metres past the hut, onto a grassy track leading into native bush. There is a sign pointing to Yeoman Track.

Yeoman Track is an overgrown logging road and generally has a reasonable gradient, but there are one or two steep, slippery sections. When you rejoin the main gravel road, head down hill for almost 2 km and you'll reach the Makaroro River again.

Riverbed option: After you exit Yeoman Track, take the gravel road past Craig's Hut to the Makaroro River. If the river is low, you can ride down it back to the road-end ford.

Notes This ride includes 6 km of walking track, which is popular on summer weekends. If you meet walkers, greet them well in advance and pass slowly.

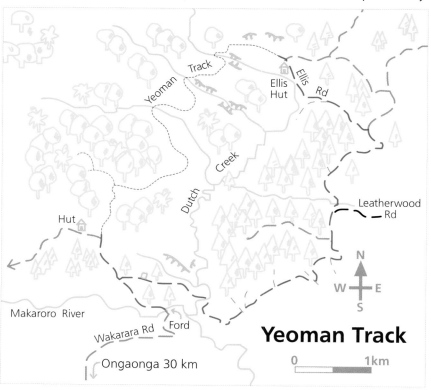

The Yeoman Track beckons.

Simon Kennett

5 Pukeora MTB Park   ★ ★ ☆ ☆

INTERMEDIATE ADVANCED

6 km west of Waipukurau

This mountain bike park through pine forest was opened in 2008 and is a smaller version of Eskdale.

Grade 3–4   **Time** 2 hours   **Distance** Up to 12 km

Track conditions 100% single track

Landowners You need to buy a permit, which comes with a map, to ride in this private forest (a three-week permit costs $7). You can get both from the club website www.hawkesbaymtb.co.nz or Hatuma Cafe on your way out of Waipukurau.

How to get there From Waipukurau, drive west on Highway 2 for 6 km. Stop at the car park on the corner of the highway and Pukeora Scenic Road.

Route description

From the car park, head east to cross a bridge and climb a gentle single track beside Pukeora Scenic Road. After 10 minutes, you'll start the 'Main Loop Trail', which is best taken in a clockwise direction. There are some fun berms and dippers that will keep you on your toes. We spent quite a while just swinging back and forth through the biggest dipper.

After completing the main loop, and exploring the extra few tracks, we recommend riding out on the track you started on. It flows better than the entry/exit trail that goes through the Paint Ball Area.

Notes The climbs are never more than 50 vertical metres. This park is another creation of the Hawke's Bay MTB Club.

Four Other Rides

Cave Road, Gisborne   ★ ☆ ☆ ☆

Grade 2+   **Time** 1 hour   **Distance** 18-km loop from Gisborne

If you've done all the other local rides and are eager for more, try this satisfying little loop. Head north from Gisborne on Riverside Road for 7.5 km. Turn left on the gravel Cave Road. Follow this road for 2 km to the end, veering left at the Stewart farm gate/cattle stop. Carry on up the farm track, through two or three gates and past a house on your right. You are now on an unformed legal road. Follow the fluoro orange arrows sprayed on fences and gates. Pop over the hill and ride down the dirt track to Matokitoki Valley Road, which leads back to town. Please leave all gates as you find them.

Heading in to start the Main Loop at Pukeora MTB Park.

Simon Kennett

Hawke's Bay Trails   ★ ★ ★ ☆

Grade 1   **Time** 1–8 hours   **Distance** 160 km

Over the last few years, millions of dollars worth of off-road cycle trails have been constructed in Hawke's Bay. Most of them are dead flat and run around the coast or up the side of major rivers on stopbanks. You'd hardly call it mountain biking, but for a cruisy day's cycling in the sun, they really can't be beaten. Pick up a trail map from the Napier i-Site and ride from there.

These trails are another one of the New Zealand Cycle Trail projects, and we describe them fully in *Classic New Zealand Cycle Trails*, due out 2012.

Cape Kidnappers   ★ ★ ☆ ☆

Grade 2   **Time** 2–4 hours   **Distance** 12 km return

During low tide, you can cycle from Clifton along the beach past a small gannet colony towards Cape Kidnappers. But first, contact the Napier i-Site for tide times, on phone (06) 834 1911.

From the road end at Clifton, ride through the motor camp and onto the beach. After half an hour, you'll pass a minor gannet colony (be careful not to scare them). Five minutes later, you'll reach a track leading away from the beach to a DOC shelter. This is a walking only track, so you'll have to leave your bike to go to the main gannet colony 20 minutes away.

Notes Because of the tide, you can't spend more than 4 hours on this trip. Any longer, and you will get wet! The gannets are only present from November to March.

Te Mata Peak   ★ ☆ ☆ ☆

Grade 4-   **Time** 1–2 hours   **Distance** 12-km loop

Biking on the established tracks in this area was banned years ago, so the local PD workers have built a special-purpose mountain bike track. Their supervisor designed it after watching a Red Bull event full of jumps on TV. The result? The country's humpiest track. At speed, it would be suicidal. We took it slowly and kind of enjoyed it.

Head south out of Havelock North on Te Mata Peak Road. For good views, ride to the top (399 m). The start of the mountain bike track is well signposted 200 metres from the top of Te Mata Peak. Three-quarters of the way down, navigation becomes tricky. After crossing a fence and entering the pine forest, head left, down to the redwoods. Then aim for the farm track on the other side of the main valley. It will lead you down valley to a road on the edge of Havelock North. Follow your front wheel back into town.

Taranaki

1 **New Plymouth Walkways**
2 **Mangamahoe Forest**
3 **Moki-Rerekapa**
4 **Bridge to Somewhere**
★ Plus three other rides

TARANAKI HIGHLIGHTS

With the Tasman Sea at one shoulder and the mountain at the other, Taranaki mountain bikers are stuck between a rock and a wet place. Still, there are a couple of rides well worth getting kitted up for.

1 New Plymouth Walkways   ★ ★ ☆ ☆
New Plymouth city

This is an interesting urban ride with a few different options for variety. Pick up a free map from the New Plymouth information centre, down by the waterfront.

Grade 2
Time 1–2 hours
Distance 12 km one way

Track conditions 25% sealed road, 75% single track (including many concreted sections and a few flights of steps)

Route description
From downtown New Plymouth, head to the Coastal Walkway and turn right. Follow the walkway until you reach Te Henui Stream.

Now follow the Te Henui Walkway up stream for 4–5 km, until it ends at houses. Then follow your nose west through the suburbs on Junction Street, Tarahua Road, left onto Carrington Street, then right onto Huatoki Street until you hit Huatoki Stream, which has another walkway starting on your right.

Follow the Huatoki Stream track back to town as far as Vivian Street. The last 100 metres of walkway has a 'No Biking' symbol, so cruise the streets back to the coast.

Notes These tracks are very popular with walkers and runners – take it easy and slow down when overtaking. You may want to use a New Plymouth street map to navigate the bits between the walkways.

If you're looking for a slightly longer ride, take the Coastal Walkway right out to the magnificent Waiwhakaiho River Bridge and beyond to Bell Block.

2 Mangamahoe Forest

10 km south of New Plymouth

This has been the premier mountain biking destination in New Plymouth for several years now. There are several purpose-built single tracks and plans for many more.

Grades 2–5+   **Time** 1–3 hours   **Distance** up to 20 km

Track conditions 30% old gravel road, 15% 4WD track, 55% single track

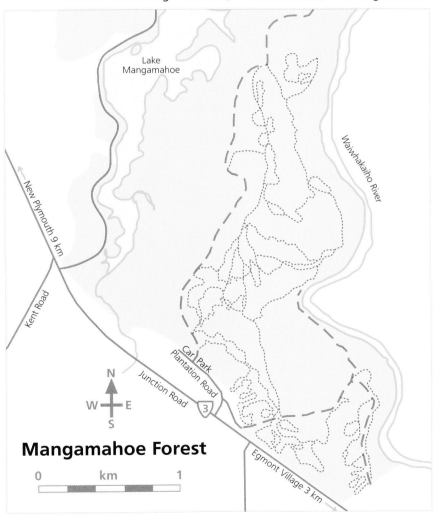

Lake Mangamahoe

Waiwhakaiho River

New Plymouth 9 km

Kent Road

Car Park

Plantation Road

Junction Road

3

Egmont Village 3 km

N
W — E
S

Mangamahoe Forest

0   km   1

Maps There's a mapboard at the car park entrance and a trail map available from the New Plymouth MTB Club at http://npmtb.co.nz/?q=node/13

Landowners New Plymouth City Council so no permission is needed for casual use.

How to get there Head south 10 km out of New Plymouth on State Highway 3 until you see the Lake Mangamahoe turn-off, then carry on 800 metres to the next left turn-off (Plantation Road). Turn left and, 200 metres later, stop at the obvious row of angle parks by a gate. The gravel road beyond the gate denotes the western border for mountain bikers – everything between it and the Waiwhakaiho River is open to cycling.

Route description

Start by riding up the obvious gravel road for 100 metres, then turning right onto the Kiwi Trail. After a few minutes you can branch off and do a quick loop of the Kea Trail, before carrying on to finish Kiwi Trail. This brings you back to the gravel road near the car park. That's a great intro-duction.

Now ride down the main gravel road for about 3 km to get a feel for the area. You will reach an area that was logged and replanted in 2008, but before the new trees went in, the locals built a few kilometres of track.

After exploring these tracks, head back to the car park and start exploring the tracks that go east towards the river. Closer to

Mark Kent

Simon rolling through Mangamahoe Forest.

the car park are some downhill tracks with a few extreme jumps to watch out for. The steeper tracks have been built on slick clay and are best avoided when wet.

Fast-growing vegetation and logging will change the picture over time.

Notes Mangamahoe Forest is riddled with an invasive weed called African Club Moss. The spores are viable for up to two years. Please clean your bike before riding elsewhere.

3 Moki-Rerekapa   ★ ★ ★

85 km northeast of Stratford

After a week of fine weather, this is one of the best adventure rides in New Zealand and certainly the best in Taranaki.

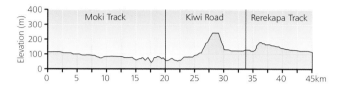

Grade 4   **Time** 5–10 hours   **Distance** 45-km loop

Track conditions 5% sealed road, 20% gravel road, 50% 4WD track, 20% semi-ridable single track, 5% unridable

Maps Refer to NZTopo50 BH31 Whangamomona.

How to get there Head 21 km north of Whangamomona on Highway 43, through the 'Hobbit Hole' tunnel to Moki Road on your left. Head down Moki Road, then Mangapapa Road for 8 km to park at the small DOC camping area.

Route description

From the camping area, nip back to Moki Road and follow it west. It soon becomes a farm track. After passing a farm shed, keep your eyes peeled for a fork, at which you veer right. You will follow the Waitara River down valley.

After about 40 minutes of farm track, you'll come across an old tin hut and the start of the single track. If the vegetation has been cut back recently, there's about 2 hours of uninterrupted, tight and technical riding.

The last of five swing bridges marks the return to farmland at the far end. Turn right to stay with the river. After 30 minutes, you'll reach a concrete bridge, and the farm track becomes an old gravel road. Turn right soon after you hit the gravel of Kiwi Road. It's 12 km of gravel road with a bit of a climb till you reach the start of the Rerekapa Track – signposted on the right.

Be sure to follow the orange triangle markers, which cross to the left side of the valley after less than a kilometre. The track then sidles up the side of the hills. After the very slippery stile, the track narrows and the surface improves a little but continues uphill. Once you reach the Boys' Brigade Hut at the top, riding becomes a bit easier.

Soon you'll reach more farm track, which leads down valley until you hit Mangapapa Road again (turn right) 5 minutes north of the DOC camping area.

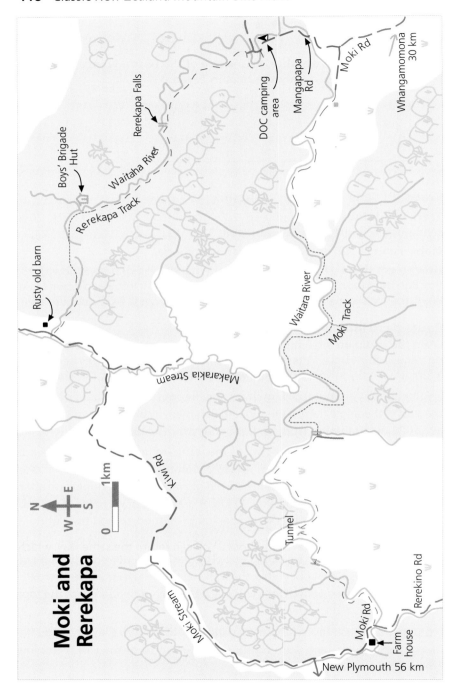

Moki and Rerekapa

Notes At both ends of the Moki and Rerekapa tracks are sections of somewhat unpleasant farm track on a papa mud base. In summer, the mud sets to a lumpy concrete and is easy to ride across. In winter, it's hopeless. If it's wet, go elsewhere.

The Forgotten World Highway (Highway 43) is a mighty fine road ride with some gravel. In 2011, a cycle route down the Forgotten World Highway and across various country roads to New Plymouth was signposted as part of the New Zealand Cycle Trail project.

4 Bridge to Somewhere ★ ★ ☆ ☆

65 km northeast of Stratford

This ride takes you to a bridge that's identical to the Bridge to Nowhere, (see the Tongariro chapter) except it's still open to traffic.

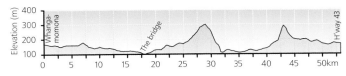

Grade 3　**Time** 1 day　**Distance** 54 km, 85-km loop

Track conditions 35% sealed road, 35% gravel road, 30% 4WD track

Maps If doing the full loop, take NZTopo50 BH31 Whangamomona and BJ31 Strathmore.

How to get there From Stratford, drive 65 km inland on Highway 43 to Whangamomona.

Route description

From the pub, ride down Whangamomona Road. After 2 km the gravel road becomes a grassy 4WD track. The route follows the old road to the Bridge to Somewhere, about 20 km away. There are many bogs and a couple of washed out bridges, but the Council gave the road a good spruce up in early 2011. Still, it's best ridden in dry weather.

The ride to the bridge takes 2–4 hours. You can return the same way, which is what most people do or tackle the full loop as described below.

From the Bridge to Somewhere, backtrack 100 metres and ride 25 km southwest on Upper Mangaehu Road to Makahu. Then turn north onto Brewer Road, which leads back to Highway 43 at Strathmore. Complete the loop by turning right and riding 31 km back to Whangamomona on one of New Zealand's most scenic highways.

Notes The Whangamomona camping ground costs about $5 per night.

Travelling light and fast to the Bridge to Somewhere.

Three Other Rides

Colson Forest, New Plymouth landfill

Grade 4   **Time** 15–30 minutes   **Distance** A couple of kilometres
Maps There's a trail map at http://npmtb.co.nz/?q=node/12

Imagine grovelling through scrappy pine forest, with an undergrowth of wind-blown rubbish from an old landfill – welcome to Colson Forest. Locals have been building short tracks and jumps here for years. Access is off Colson Road, on the east side of town.

Meremere Road, Hawera   ★

Grade 2   **Time** 1.5–3 hours   **Distance** 20–34 km

If you're desperate for a ride in South Taranaki, Meremere is as good as it gets. From Hawera, head inland 12 km to Ohangai School (a good place to park). Meremere Road is 100 metres east of the school. Ride inland for 9 km, and you'll reach the edge of the forest. The road ends 8 km further in. Return the same way. NZTopo50 BK30 Patua doesn't cover the whole ride but will get you started. Expect plenty of mud if it's rained heavily recently.

Pukeiti Trails

In late 2011, after this book went to print, locals began building new trails in the forest around Pukeiti Gardens (Carrington Road, 23 km southwest of New Plymouth). Check out www.npmtb.co.nz for more details.

Manawatu

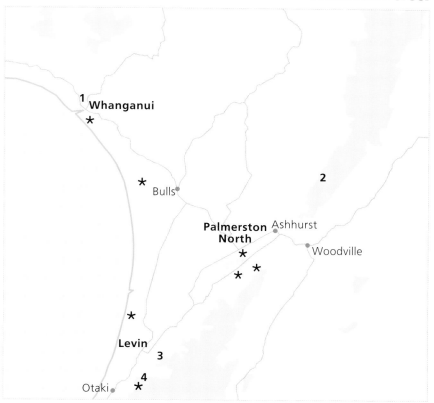

1 **Hylton Park**
2 **Takapari Road**
3 **Kohitere Forest**
4 **Mt Thompson**
★ Plus seven other rides

MANAWATU HIGHLIGHTS

Manawatu is a region dominated by farmland and inaccessible mountains. Hylton Park and Kohitere Forest provide a few purpose-built tracks, while Takapari Road and Mt Thompson give riders a chance to sample some rarified mountain air.

1 Hylton Park ★ ★ ☆ ☆

Whanganui

It takes 10 minutes to climb to the top of this humble little forest, and there are several great tracks to ride back down on. Feel the flow.

Grades 3–4
Time 1–2 hours
Distance Up to 10 km

Track conditions 10% gravel road, 15% 4WD track, 75% single track

How to get there From downtown Whanganui, head to Somme Parade on the western bank of the Whanganui River and ride upstream 5 km to Brunswick Road. From the corner dairy, it's only 600 metres to the old fertiliser works on your left and the gravel road entrance to Hylton Park on your right.

Route description

The Whanganui MTB Club has built several kilometres of fun single tracks in the park. Hop over the gate and blitz up the gravel road to a flat area with jumps. There are single tracks sprouting off both sides of this road, as well as the sides of the jumps area.

We followed red arrows up to the top of the park and explored tracks back down. Once just wasn't enough, so we repeated the exercise on different tracks. They were all well designed with good flow and options for repeating specific sections.

Give yourself at least an hour to explore this maze of grade 3–4 tracks. The area isn't large enough to get lost in for more than a few minutes.

Notes If you're not used to getting big air, watch out for the double jumps.

Weaving through Hylton Park forest.   Simon Kennett

2 Takapari Road ★★☆☆

INTERMEDIATE

50 km northeast of Palmerston North

A simple and scenic back-country ride up onto the spine of the Ruahine Range and back.

Grade 3

Time 3–7 hours

Distance 32 km return

Track condition 30% gravel road, 70% 4WD track

Maps The 'road' is shown on the Kiwimap Road Atlas.

How to get there 34 km northeast of Ashhurst, turn right onto Takapari Road, just past Pohangina Scenic Reserve (east of the Pohangina River).

Route description

Head up the road to a locked gate and throw your bike over. The road then deteriorates (i.e. improves) to a 4WD track as it climbs to Delaware Ridge at 800 m elevation. It then winds steeply onto the Ruahine Range. Take warm clothes as you will cool off quickly on the exposed tops.

Once you reach the main Ruahine ridge, turn south and ride on to Travers Hut or beyond. Head back the way you came.

Notes According to an old log book at Travers Hut, this ride was once conquered on a Raleigh 20 and two ancient 28″ Triumph bicycles.

3 Kohitere Forest ★ ★ ★ ☆

INTERMEDIATE   ADVANCED

Levin

This is Levin's main riding area, and locals have been building tracks here for years.

Grades 3–4+
Time 1–4 hours
Distance 5–20 km

Track conditions Some gravel road and lots of purpose-built single track on a clay base that denies traction when wet.

Landowners Rayonier NZ Ltd – check the signboard at the forest entrance for access restrictions, or ask at Southend Cycles, 117 Oxford Street, Levin, phone (06) 368 5459.

How to get there From the Levin clock tower, head east on Queen Street East for 3.9 km to Denton Road on your left. Head north for 300 metres to a gate and signboard.

Route description
Generally, people start up Trig Road, but there is an alternative nearing completion.

Simon Kennett

Kurts Track is a grade 4 climb starting near the bottom of Trig Road and topping out on Greys Bush Road (near the top of The Edge).

The Edge: This popular, grade-3+ descent is narrow, rutted and steep in places; definitely on the edge.

Russell Track: A very cool, twisty, grade-3 track; our favourite track in the forest. This is most easily accessed via the grade 4 Stump Track (which is signed as grade 3, but has suffered the ravages of a thousand skids since construction).

Gardiner Road Track: A long, grade-3 downhill that starts on a logging road then cuts through rank grass beside a deer fence.

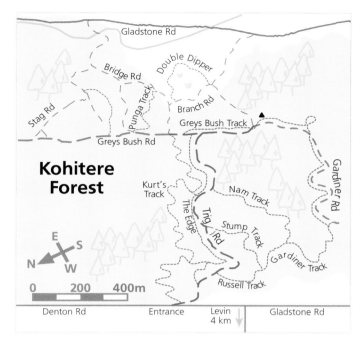

Nam Track: This less used grade-4 track is steep and rutted. Put your seat down and treat that front brake with respect.

Notes Te Araroa (the length of New Zealand trail) uses Trig Road, making it particularly popular with walkers.

4 Mt Thompson ★ ★ ☆ ☆

ADVANCED

11 km northeast of Otaki

A grunty granny-gear climb, followed by a chunky rock-garden type descent scares most people away from conquering the 711-m Mt Thompson, but on a fine day, most advanced riders will love it.

Grade 4+   **Time** 3–4 hours   **Distance** 26-km full loop

Track conditions 46% sealed road, 17% forestry road, 36% 4WD track, 1% single track

Maps NZTopo50 BN33 Levin gives a pretty good idea of the route, but be warned that Rayonier NZ Ltd have done some roading work to log the forest, so the map's a bit out of date.

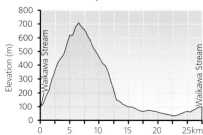

How to get there Access is via the Waikawa Stream recreation area, 3.5 km up North Manakau Road (10 km northeast of Otaki).

Route description

If your bike has a good granny gear and full suspension, the ride over Mt Thompson to Waitohu Stream is primo. With map in hand, cross the concrete ford and climb south. After 1 km, veer left up Judds Road. When you reach the main ridge, turn right and continue south. Soon after high point 595 you will enter lush native bush and turn right a couple of times – one of those turn-offs is a short, unridable push up to an old track. When you get to an intersection with an old 'Mt Thompson' sign, turn right again for the final slog to the top.

After taking in the view, backtrack 200 metres to the signed intersection and turn right to continue south for 500 metres. Turn right, yet again, and descend 600 vertical metres of uncompromising, super-slippery, uber-rocky, 4WD goodness.

Watch out for the barbed wire 'Taranaki gate' near the bottom. Once at Waitohu Valley Road, you've got a 12-km road ride back to the picnic area.

Seven Other Rides

Harakeke Forest, Whanganui   ★ ★ ☆ ☆

Local mountain bikers are building several new tracks in the rolling forest southeast of Whanganui.

Grade 2+   **Time** 1–2 hours   **Distance** 6 km and growing

Head east out of Whanganui on Highway 3 for 6 km, then turn right onto Pauri Road. After 2 km, at a Y-intersection, veer left and park after 500 metres. The track entrance is on your left.

These new tracks are being built in a forest that won't be logged for 20 years, so the job is being done with long-term commitment. There are a few loops, and the track network will grow with time. Join the Whanganui Mountain Bike Club, and/or drop into The Bike Shed, on Ridgway Street, Whanganui, for more information.

Riverside Bridle Track   ★ ★ ☆ ☆

This is an easy riverside track just south of Palmerston North. In 2011, it followed the Manawatu River for 12 km, and there are plans to extend it up to Ashhurst.

Grade 1+   **Time** 1–2 hours   **Distance** 12 km one way

Head northeast out of Palmerston North on Highway 3 for 1 km before turning right onto Te Matai Road. After 500 metres, veer right and head down Riverside

Sasha and Megan rock on down Mt Thompson.

Simon Kennett

Drive for another 500 metres. You will reach the start of the Bridle Track on your right.

The Bridle Track meanders its way down valley beside the Manawatu River, passing a couple of golf courses and ducking under Fitzherbert Bridge. This is the halfway mark.

From the bridge, cruise through Fitzherbert Park and then take back streets to Maxwells Line, at the southern edge of Palmerston North. There is a new MTB skills park near the riverside end of Maxwells Line, suitable for average to expert riders.

This track is popular with walkers and runners and is really only suitable for a leisurely ride.

North Range Road ★ ☆ ☆ ☆

On a fine day, this is an easy, gravel road ride through a spectacular wind farm.

Grade 1+ **Time** 2–4 hours **Distance** 25 km

Start from the summit of the Pahiatua Track, which connects Palmerston North to Pahiatua, 17 km southeast of Palmerston North. There is a signpost at the summit: 'North Range Road – No Exit'. Follow North Range Road as it traverses the northern tip of the Tararua Range. The gravel road climbs gently for most of the first 5 km, then there is a drop and another climb before the road heads onto the wind farm.

After traversing the range, either head back the way you came or make it a round trip by descending steeply to Hall Block Road. Turn right at Ballance Gorge Road and ride back to the Pahiatua Track. Refer to any good map of the area.

Kahuterawa Loop ★ ☆ ☆ ☆

This once popular mountain biking area was being logged in 2011, but three new tracks are planned. They should be finished in 2012.

Grade 3 **Time** 1–2 hours **Distance** 11-km loop

From Palmerston North, head southwest out of town for 3 km, past the university on Tennant Drive, until you hit Old West Road (Highway 57). Turn left, and then straight away right, onto Kahuterawa Road. Head down this road until you are 4 km past Kahuterawa Reserve – there's a car park on the right, 100 metres before the road ends at an old wooden bridge.

Hopefully, by the time you visit, the new tracks will be built and signposted. Refer to the Manawatu MTB Club (www.mmbc.co.nz). This area is being logged through to May 2013 – access is restricted during the working week.

Sweet climbing at Kahuterawa.   Raewyn Knight

Santoft Forest   ★★☆☆

Flat, sandy forest tracks, open to Manawatu Mountain Bike Club members only.

Grade 2+   **Time** 1–2 hours   **Distance** 14 km

Located 40 km west of Palmerston North, these sandy tracks are good in the wet, and you can easily make up a 10-km loop. But before you can ride there, you have to join the Manawatu Mountain Bike Club. For more details check out www.mmbc.co.nz/tracks

Waitarere Forest   ★☆☆☆

A once popular race destination, Waitarere Forest is now seldom visited. Only a few of the single tracks remain, leaving mostly flat forestry roads to explore.

Grade 2   **Time** 30–60 minutes   **Distance** 4–12 km

Turn off Highway 1, 7 km north of Levin at the 'Waitarere' sign and cruise 6 km down to the township. There are toilets and a nice picnic area at Waitarere Domain (a left turn off the main street).

At the old petrol station building on the corner of Forest Road, head left to the south block of the forest, where (in 2011) there were still a few single tracks left as well as forestry roads.

To get your bearings, head straight out to the coast along Waitarere Coast Road and then turn left and ride along the beach for several hundred metres. Keep an eye out for marker posts half buried in the sand dunes. Walk inland past the right post and you'll strike single track within a couple of minutes. Head south until you run out of single track and then head back on the forestry roads that lie just a little further inland.

Waitarere Forest is owned by Rayonier NZ Ltd – no permission needed, but watch out for logging trucks. The single tracks are firmer after recent rain. The beach is not suitable for riding during high tide.

Tangata Maunga   ★ ☆ ☆ ☆

A good old-fashioned, there-and-back hill climb.

Grade 4   **Time** 3–4 hours   **Distance** 22 km return

From Otaki, drive towards the hills up Rahuia Street for 3 km. Turn left onto Ringawhati Road. After 2 km, turn right at a T-intersection, and 700 metres later, turn right and park just before the Waitoha Quarry entrance gate.

Hop over the gate and cycle up the road for a minute before veering right across a concrete bridge and along a farm road to a 'Tararua Forest Park' sign. Just past the sign, turn right, cross the paddock, and follow a 4WD track up into the bush.

Stay on the main track all the way, climbing past an old steam boiler and along the main ridge. Don't take any turn-offs. The 4WD track ends a few hundred metres past the last major turn-off. Leave your bike and follow a vague walking track through the forest for 15 minutes, to the scrubby tops. There is a hydrology station nestled on a flat spot beside Tangata Maunga (912 m). Head back the way you came, giving yourself around an hour for the full descent.

Wairarapa

1 **Mikimiki Track**
2 **Rimutaka Pylon Track**
3 **Aorangi Crossing**
4 **Cape Palliser**
★ Plus two other rides

WAIRARAPA HIGHLIGHTS

Wairarapa, the home-away-from-home for Wellingtonians boasts some fine backcountry riding. Flanked by the Tararua Range to the west and the Pacific Ocean to the east, riders can choose from a range of farmland, forest, and coastal mountain biking.

1 Mikimiki Track

ADVANCED

Also known as Kiriwhakapapa Tramline

22 km northwest of Masterton

This hard-core ride covers 7.5 km of semi-ridable single track on the eastern side of the Tararua Range.

Grade 4+
Time 2–3 hours
Distance 7.5 km one way
Track conditions 20% 4WD track, 80% single track

Maps NZTopo50 BP34 Masterton and BN34 Shannon or Tararua Parkmap 274-02.

How to get there Drive 11 km north of Masterton on Highway 2 before turning left onto Mikimiki Road and driving another 6 km to a large mapboard on the right.

Route description

From the road-end mapboard, head up the old tram track. Veer left up the hill past the 'No Buses' sign. Follow the orange triangle markers into the bush.

Unridable sections become more frequent as the track climbs over a 200-m saddle and descends steeply to the Kiriwhakapapa Valley on the other side.

Cruise down to the road-end picnic area and shelter on the old Kiriwhakapapa tramline. After a well-deserved breather, turn round and follow your tyre prints back.

Alternatively, if you're sick of bike pushing, and don't mind 4 km on Highway 2, loop back via the road.

Notes There are many slippery sections that are unridable when wet; this ride is best done at the end of summer after a prolonged dry spell. Please don't skid, and give way to walkers.

Passing through on the way to Kiriwhakapapa.

2 Rimutaka Pylon Track ★ ★ ☆ ☆

EXPERT

Featherston to Kaitoke

This is the nastiest climb in the lower North Island. It's long and extremely steep. Endorphin addicts love it. At the Kaitoke end, there is a brilliant technical single track to finish with. For an honest day out, pack an extra sandwich and make this a full loop trip by riding the Rimutaka Rail Trail as well.

Grade 5

Time 2–3 hours

Distance 15 km

Track conditions 15% sealed road, 20% single track, 65% 4WD track

Maps NZTopo50 BP33 Featherston and our Rimutaka map in the Wellington chapter.

How to get there From Upper Hutt, you can ride over the Rimutaka Rail Trail to get to the start of this track (see Wellington chapter). Alternatively, drive or catch the commuter train to Featherston. A third option is to park at the YMCA camp near Kaitoke (signposted off Highway 2, 3 km north of the 'Rimutaka Rail Trail' sign and 2 km up Marchant Road) and ride to the start of the Rimutaka Rail Trail.

Route description

From Featherston, ride west on Highway 2 for 3 km. Nip across the highway onto a 4WD track behind several large concrete blocks on your right (it's just before the double bridges over Abbots Stream). From there, follow the main pylon road, across a small stream and then up, up, up. This 4WD track climbs from 100 m up to almost 800 m in less than 5 km. In 2011, it had been graded recently and was in better condition than ever. Don't be distracted by any of the turn-offs; they dead-end at pylons.

At the top, you will sidle through some native bush to reach a solid steel gate. Squeeze around the side and begin a long descent of the main ridge. Keep a sharp eye out for the old 'Horse Track' sign tucked up on a bank on the left of the 4WD track about three-quarters of the way down the hill. If it is hard to spot, then do everyone a favour by stopping and pulling away the weeds in front of it. Opposite the sign, you'll find a technical single track that bucks its way down to the YMCA camp at Kaitoke; it's mostly ridable downhill, in the dry. Just as the track opens out to buildings and farmland, you'll see two gates. Squiggle up to the one on your right and go through it to the main YMCA building and the car park.

Rob Lancaster leads the stable up the old Horse Track.

Jonathan Kennett

If you need to get back to Featherston, the most satisfying option is to complete a loop via the Rimutaka Rail Trail. From the YMCA camp car park, cruise 1 km down to Marchant Road, turning left and riding 2 km to Highway 2, then turning right and riding 3 km to the Rail Trail (well signposted on your left).

Notes Expert riders keen for a challenge may wish to do this ride in reverse, from the YMCA camp, grunting their way up the Horse Track, followed by the Pylon Track. There is a private car park at the YMCA, and a donation for parking is expected (pop your coins in the red box at the car park). Ride around the right side of the main YMCA building to a gate 10 metres from the back corner of the building. Once through the gate, do a quick right-left squiggle to enter the bush on the old Horse Track (which was opened up by the YMCA in 2010).

3 Aorangi Crossing ★ ★ ★ ★

ADVANCED

Martinborough, Southern Wairarapa

The full loop is a gung-ho combination of mountain biking and cycle touring, with plenty of great scenery thrown in for good measure. This is a classic from way back.

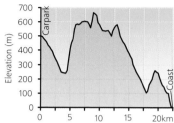

Grade 4

Time 1–2 days

Distance 24–104 km

Track conditions 60% sealed road, 20% gravel road, 20% 4WD track

Maps NZTopo250 16 Wellington is helpful for navigation.

How to get there From Wellington, ride/drive/train to Featherston and then head southeast along Highway 53 to Martinborough, 17 km away. Another alternative is to catch the train to Upper Hutt and cycle via the Rimutaka Rail Trail (see Wellington chapter).

Route description

Head southwest from Martinborough on Jellicoe Street. Turn left onto White Rock Road after 2 km, then right after another 7 km onto Ruakokoputuna Road. Blink and you won't realise you've passed through Ruakokoputuna.

After 25 gravelly kilometres, you'll pass through a gate and climb 4 km to a small car parking area and a 'Sutherland Track' and 'Haurangi Forest Park' sign.

From the car park, descend on a fast 4WD track to the first of several stream crossings. After 1.5 km in the valley, you'll come to a left-hand fork at the base of a humongous hill. Sutherlands Hut is another 200 metres down the valley.

The main obstacle of the ride starts from this fork – a teeth-gritting granny-gear climb. It's at least an hour to the top, often involving walking, sometimes defying gravity, up a super-steep 4WD track.

From the top (just above a large slip), the track generally undulates along the ridge west towards the sea for about 9 km before dropping steeply to Hurupi Stream. It then climbs up on the other side to a gate beside a park boundary map.

From here, take the 1-km diversion to the Putangirua Pinnacles. Some of these gigantic alluvial towers are capped with castaway islands of bush. This is where Peter Jackson shot one of his first films, *Brain Dead*.

Grinding to the top of the Aorangi Crossing.

Return to the gate beside the park boundary mapboard and descend through farmland on the obvious 4WD track to the Palliser Bay coast. Just ignore the minor turn-offs and follow the orange markers around the last paddock. From the coast road, return via either Cape Palliser or the roads to Martinborough.

Notes There is a pub and motor camp at Lake Ferry. This is a hunting area, so wear all your fluoro gear. The Aorangi Range catches the full brunt of southerly storms, so go prepared.

4 Cape Palliser ★ ★ ☆ ☆

Martinborough

INTERMEDIATE

A little bit of rough stuff, lots of good scenery and quiet back-country roads make this the quintessential fat-tyre touring trip.

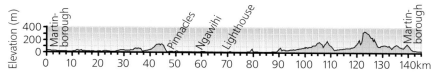

Grade 3- **Time** 2 days **Distance** 145-km loop

Track conditions 60% sealed road, 33% gravel road, 6% 4WD track, 1% unridable sand

Maps NZTopo250 16 Wellington is helpful for navigation.

Landowners There is a section of private land northeast of Cape Palliser. Phone Haami Te Whaiti, (06) 307 8230 for permission to go through.

Route description

From Martinborough, ride south via Pirinoa (which has a dairy) to the coast about 45 km away. Five hundred metres after reaching the coast, you'll pass the Aorangi Forest Park entrance and a DOC camping area. If you have a spare hour or two, check out the Putangirua Pinnacles, New Zealand's answer to the Grand Canyon.

Continue round the coast to the tearooms at Ngawihi, which offer good views of this little fishing village. It's only 6 km from here to the Cape Palliser lighthouse, from where a 4WD track continues along the coast, passing a large seal colony en route.

About 6 km on from the lighthouse, you'll have to walk a short sandy moonscape stretch before dropping down to the DOC hut at Te Rakauwhakamataku Point. There are good camping spots between the lighthouse and the hut, and also at White Rock. The hut, however, is the only spot with a reliable water supply and one of the few places sheltered from the prevailing wind.

Pedalling along the wild south coast of Cape Palliser.

From White Rock, follow the main road inland back to Martinborough, 55 km and a couple of huge hills away.

Notes Ngawihi has more bulldozers per head of population than anywhere else in the world! Be warned: this route is hellishly exposed to strong winds. You can take your bike for free on the train from Wellington to Featherston and start the ride from there.

Two Other Rides

Carterton MTB Tracks ★ ★ ☆ ☆

4 km northwest of Carterton

Grade 2 **Time** 30 minutes **Distance** 2-km loop

There are a couple of short, easy loops starting from Dalefield Road, 4 km northwest of Carterton. It's all fairly flat, windy single track on land provided by Carterton District Council. There are a couple of wooden skills features to play around on, too.

This is stage one of the plans for a much larger MTB area, which would include some big climbs and descents on DOC land on Mt Dick.

Toratora Mountain Bike Track ★ ★ ☆ ☆

34 km southeast of Martinborough

Grades 3–4 **Time** 1–3 hours **Distance** Up to 30 km

You can now explore an interesting corner of the Wairarapa on a privately owned mountain bike track that runs through an 18 hectare block of native forest. There is also a coastal ridgetop ride out to a popular surfing beach called Tora.

Toratora is a farm with interests in outdoor tourism activities. They have built an excellent 16-km mountain bike track and also allow riding in other areas around the farm.

The tracks cost $25 per adult and $15 per child to ride. They are open from 8 am to 4 pm daily (except from 20 December to 10 January, when they are closed).

Toratora is one-and-a-half hours' drive from Wellington. Make sure you phone the owners before going out, as sometimes the track can be closed. You must book in before noon, and your booking gives you track access and a map. For more information, go to www.toratora.co.nz or phone (06) 307 8151.

Wellington

1 **Karapoti Classic**
2 **Karapoti Challenge**
3 **Rimutaka Rail Trail**
4 **Belmont Regional Park**
5 **Wainuiomata MTB Park**
6 **Skyline Track**

7 **Makara Peak**
8 **Sanctuary Fenceline**
9 **Polhill to Hawkins Hill**
10 **Hawkins Hill**
11 **Mt Victoria**
★ Plus fifteen other rides

WELLINGTON HIGHLIGHTS

For over a decade now the hills around Wellington have been alive with the sound of picks and shovels crafting fine single track. Most locals head to Makara Peak, the undisputed hub, but some sweet new single track has also been built at Polhill. The Karapoti Classic is a 'must do' for expert riders, and the Rimutaka Rail Trail is an excellent beginners' trail.

1 Karapoti Classic ★ ★ ★ ☆

Akatarawa Forest, 10 km northwest of Upper Hutt

The famous Karapoti has thrashed more racers, over a longer period of time, than any other track in New Zealand. The course is physically and, in places, technically very demanding – it's not called the 'Classic' for nothing.

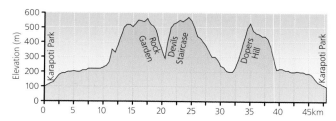

Grade 4+ **Time** 4–8 hours **Distance** 48-km loop

Track conditions 30% gravel road, 55% 4WD track, 10% single track, 5% unridable

Maps You must take the Greater Wellington Regional Council's 'Akatarawa Forest' map, NZtopo50 BP32 Paraparaumu or a guide with you.

Other users Motorbikes, forestry vehicles, hunters, horses

How to get there From Brown Owl (3 km north of Upper Hutt), head up Akatarawa Road for 6 km till you reach Karapoti Road. Turn left and follow Karapoti Road for 2 km to a large car park. We often catch the train to Upper Hutt and ride from there.

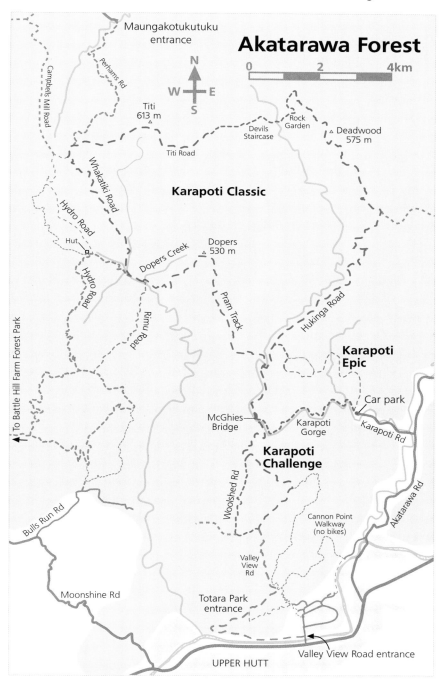

Akatarawa Forest

Blood is thicker than mud. The authors racing up Karapoti Gorge.

Route description

From the car park, the road turns into a 4WD track that leads you through the Karapoti Gorge. About 6 km from the car park (and 2 km past a concrete bridge on your left), there is a forestry road branching off on the right. This is the start of the main 32-km loop.

Take that road on the right and head northeast, always staying on the main track. After 4 hilly kilometres and a short sharp descent, the track appears to end at a stream. Follow the stream bed to your right for 100 metres, and you'll pick up the track again. Ride (if you can) uphill for about 2 km till you reach a T-intersection, then turn left towards Deadwood.

After 5 km of a roller-coaster 4WD track, you should spot a small clearing with a track on your left signposted the 'Rock Garden'.

This gnarly downhill has some intimidating drop-offs and lots of – you guessed it – rocks. At the bottom, veer right for 30 metres and cross the stream. On the other side, a rutted boggy track leads to the Devils Staircase, the second major hill climb. Carry or push your bike up for about 1.5 km to a pleasant clearing at 520 m elevation.

From there, an old gravel road undulates west past Titi (613 m) towards Paekakariki. Stay on the main track until you reach an intersection by a small stand of pine trees. Turn left at Whakatiki Road and ride on to the Pram Track (both signposted).

The downhill continues for 4 km before ending at a stream crossing. This is followed by a 1-km flat section (where you must veer left). This takes you to Dopers Creek at the foot of the last major hill. After a steep climb to 547 m, it's all downhill-ish to the clearing at the top of Karapoti Road where you started the 32-km loop.

From the clearing, it's a cruisy 6 km back down the Karapoti Gorge to the car park.

Notes Riders get lost in the Akatarawas every year, sometimes having to spend the night out. Start early and take warm clothing and plenty of food. Motorbikers can't hear you, so be cautious, especially in the Karapoti Gorge.

In 1986, the Karapoti Classic was New Zealand's inaugural national championship race. It now attracts well over a thousand riders in the first weekend of every March. See www.karapoti.co.nz for more info. In any weekend throughout January and February, you will meet other mountain bikers training for the big race.

2 Karapoti Challenge ★ ★ ☆ ☆

INTERMEDIATE

Akatarawa Forest, 10 km northwest of Upper Hutt

If the Karapoti Classic sounds a bit too hardcore for you, try the Challenge first – it's a fun ride with only one big climb.

Grade 3
Time 2 hours
Distance 20-km loop
Track conditions 50% forestry road, 50% 4WD track

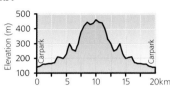

Maps Take the Greater Wellington Regional Council's 'Akatarawa Forest' map or NZtopo50 BP32 Paraparaumu.

How to get there Follow the directions for the Karapoti Classic write-up.

Route description

From the car park, ride up the gorge on the main 4WD track until you reach the major concrete bridge (McGhies Bridge). Cross the bridge and follow the major forestry road over a medium-sized hill, and down to a three-way intersection. This is the start/end of the challenge loop.

From the intersection, head left and ride up a large hill. Turn right at the top, ride along a flattish road for a few kilometres, and then turn right again for a fast, sometimes slippery, downhill back to the three-way intersection. Then retrace your tyre tracks back to the concrete bridge and down the gorge to the car park.

Notes Expect trail bikes in the gorge.

3 Rimutaka Rail Trail ★ ★ ★ ★

BEGINNER

Between Upper Hutt and Featherston

This historic trail is the most interesting and scenic beginners' ride in the Wellington region. The gradient is generally gentle, and there are old bridges, tunnels and railway stations to keep the interest piqued.

Grade 1+
Time 2–4 hours
Distance 18 km one way
Track conditions 90% wide smooth rail trail, 10% single track

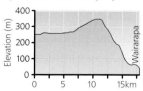

How to get there From the Upper Hutt railway station, follow Highway 2 northeast for 10 km before turning right onto the signposted Rimutaka Rail Trail.

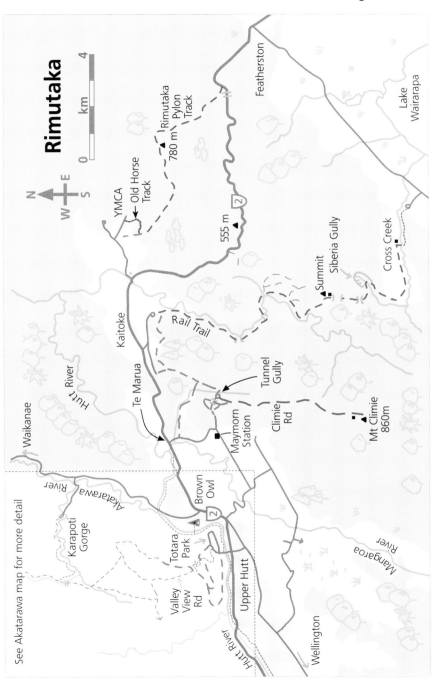

Rimutaka

N
W + E
S

0 km 4

Featherston

Lake Wairarapa

Rimutaka Pylon Track

780 m

YMCA

Old Horse Track

2

555 m

Summit

Siberia Gully

Cross Creek

Kaitoke

Rail Trail

Te Marua

Tunnel Gully

Mt Climie 860m

Climie Rd

Maymorn Station

Hutt River

Waikanae

Akatarawa River

Karapoti Gorge

Brown Owl

2

Totara Park

Valley View Rd

Upper Hutt

Hutt River

Wellington

Mangaroa River

See Akatarawa map for more detail

Route description

There is a car park at the first locked gate about 1 km up the road. Past the gate, a gravel road climbs gently to Rimutaka Summit 10 km away. You'll find a picnic area at the summit and the longest of four tunnels. If you haven't got a torch, just concentrate on the speck of light at the end of the tunnel almost 600 metres away and keep your elbows out to act as feelers.

At Siberia Gully (1 km on from the summit tunnel), you'll encounter the most technical section of track. This gully is famous for its gale-force winds – in the 1890s, a 10-tonne locomotive was blown off the tracks here! From the other side of the gully, you can relax and coast 5 km down to Cross Creek.

When you reach the Cross Creek shelter, ride over the footbridge on your right and cycle through manuka forest on weaving single track to another little shelter at a car parking area. From here, either backtrack or head down the gravel road to the Wairarapa plains and left onto the sealed road to ride to Featherston.

Notes This trail was once the main railway line to the Wairarapa, hence the gentle gradient, tunnels and station shelters along the way. Most family groups just ride up to the summit tunnel and back. The last bit of single track on the

Start 'em young on the Rimutaka Rail Trail.   Jonathan Kennett

Featherston side was improved half a grade in 2011 and is now grade 2. A 2.5-km 4WD track called Station Road now connects the Rail Trail (at the Kaitoke end, close to Highway 2) with Tunnel Gully (see Mt Climie under Other Rides) and Maymorn Station.

4 Belmont Regional Park ★ ★ ★

Western hills, Hutt Valley

Belmont Regional Park is a huge area with many great riding options. The route we've described below is a great first-time trip. After that, check out the other options listed below the notes. All tracks are best ridden when dry. The pine forest around DANZIG is due to be logged – be prepared to detour around that part of the park.

Grades 3–6
Time 2–4 hours
Distance 17 km

Track conditions 35% 4WD track, 65% single track

Maps You can download pamphlets with good maps covering the area from www.gw.govt.nz/belmont and there are mapboards at the track entrances.

How to get there The main entrance for biking is Stratton Street. Turn off Highway 2 near Lower Hutt at the 'Belmont Regional Park' sign and head up to Maungaraki. Stay on the main road until you reach Stratton Street. Then turn left and ride down to the very end of the road.

Route description

From the end of Stratton Street, follow the 'Old Coach Road' sign. Within a few hundred metres, you'll pass a wool shed and will have to squeeze around a gate. Ten metres later, veer right, and after another 20 metres, you'll pick up a single track on your left. This track, called DANZIG, was built by the Hutt Valley MTB Club. It climbs at an intermediate grade for 2 km. Be warned though, this track may be logged in the near future.

At the top of DANZIG, turn left. Now follow the Old Coach Road and orange markers to Round Knob. All the main intersections are signposted. From Round Knob, ride to Cannons Head. There are several concrete bunkers here to shelter in on a breezy day.

Now ride from Cannons Head to Belmont Trig. Some of this is untracked pasture and requires a little walking. The trig is the highest point in the ride. It's a spectacular spot – well worth the pilgrimage.

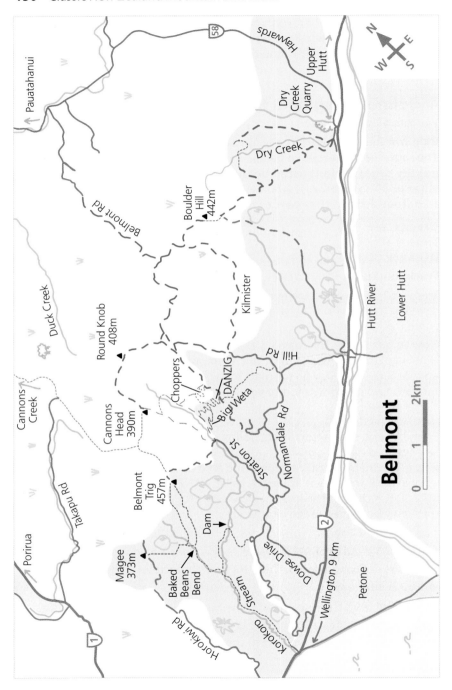

From Belmont Trig, follow the narrow track towards Wellington harbour. This is an awesome track, technical and scenic, but watch out for walkers; it's a popular area.

On the way down, turn left at a 'Korokoro' sign. Then at the next intersection, turn right to ride out to Cornish Street via the Korokoro Track or left to ride up to Oakleigh Street (not far from Stratton Street).

Notes Bikers are welcome on most tracks in the park as long as they don't skid. Much of Belmont Regional Park is closed during lambing (August through to October). Dogs are not allowed on the farmland. Other popular rides in the park are listed below.

Trig Short Cut

If it's a really windy day, or you simply want to take the shortest route to Belmont Trig, ride into Stratton Street and stop at the first car park with a mapboard. The map shows a farm track starting 100 metres down the road. Its gradient is punishing up to the trig, but the ride down the other side (described above) is ample reward.

Dry Creek Loop

This is a grade 3, 1–2 hour loop. It starts from the regional park buildings, 200 metres south of the Haywards turn-off, just beside Highway 2. From the information board at the car park, follow orange markers up through farmland, into an area of regenerating native bush and then back down to the car park. Best ridden in a clockwise direction.

Boulder Hill

This grade 3 track starts with a climb up the gravel road 200 metres south of the Haywards turn-off, beside Highway 2. Follow the orange track markers to Boulder Hill (442 m). From the top, keep following the markers down to Belmont Road.

From Belmont Road, the best routes out are either via Hill Road or round to DANZIG via Old Coach Road. It takes 2–3 hours to ride the full 13-km track.

The Slide

This slippery downhill track starts from the top of DANZIG and is the fastest way to lose altitude in this part of the park, taking about 3 minutes from top to bottom. The first half down to the green hut is grade 5; the second half is grade 6. Ride only when dry.

Big Weta

This is a fun, grade-4 alternative to the second half of The Slide or DANZIG. It starts just south of the green hut and is also only recommended when dry. After 3-4 minutes, you'll pop out near the bottom of DANZIG.

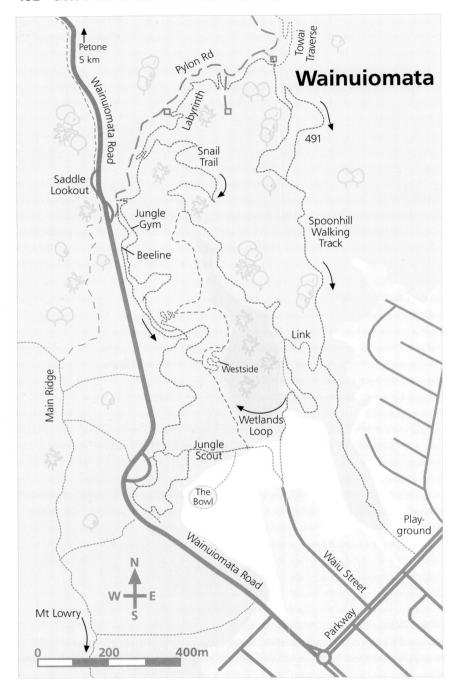

5 Wainuiomata MTB Park ★ ★ ★

INTERMEDIATE   ADVANCED

7 km southeast of Petone

This relatively new mountain bike park is developing fast. It already has seven tracks through native forest that provide some excellent loops.

Grades 3–4+ **Time** 1–2 hours **Distance** 10 km

Track conditions 100% single track

How to get there From Petone, head along the Esplanade to Gracefield and follow the 'Wainuiomata' signs up the Wainuiomata hill. Stop at the top of the hill.

Alternatively, head over the hill and turn left at the first roundabout, then left up Waiu Street – the main park entrance awaits at the end of the street. From this entrance you'll start this ride with Jungle Gym.

Racing through Wainuiomata native forest.

Jono Baddiley

Route description

From the top of the Wainuiomata hill, head left through a large steel gate and plug up the gravel pylon road for 50 metres. Then take the obvious right turn and ride into the bush on a cruisy single track.

After another 30 metres, this track splits in two. This is the top of Jungle Gym, which you will ride back up later to complete a loop. Head left at this fork and follow Labyrinth, which climbs gently to a pylon.

From the pylon, a technical track called Spoonhill (grade 4+) follows the spur down to a park on the edge of Wainuiomata. If you find the start of the track too difficult, then part way down hang a left at an obvious intersection to take the easier route (491) down.

At the park at the bottom of the track, head right and out to Waiu Street. At the end of Waiu Street, check out the mapboard and follow signs to the bottom of Jungle Gym, a 2-km, grade-3 climb back to the top of the Wainuiomata hill – that's a 6-km loop.

There are four other tracks to stretch the chain on.

Beeline: A steep downhill track going from near the top of Jungle Gym down to the end of Waiu Street.

The Wetland Track: An excellent 3-km loop for families that circumnavigates the wetland near the end of Waiu Street.

Jungle Scout: An extension to Jungle Gym, which leads to Waiu Street.

Snails: An excellent, relatively easy downhill track from Labyrinth. It leads down to the back of The Wetland Track.

Notes There are mapboards at the top of the Wainuiomata Hill and at the end of Waiu Street. Most of the tracks have temporary signs. In 2011, the Wainui Trail Project crew were beavering away on an eighth track, the Towai Traverse – a long single track heading north from the top of Spoonhill. Definitely worth a look if you are hankering for some adventure off the beaten track.

6 Skyline Track ★ ★ ★ ☆

INTERMEDIATE   ADVANCED

Wellington

The Skyline Track is Wellington's ultimate point-to-point ride. It traverses the hills bordering the western side of Wellington on a mixture of farm and single track.

Grades 3–4
Time 5–8 hours
Distance Up to 36 km
Track conditions 10% sealed road, 55% 4WD track, 35% single track

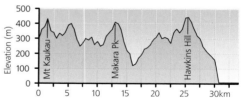

How to get there From Wellington railway station, catch the commuter train to Johnsonville. Bikes are free on Wellington commuter trains, but space is limited to two bikes. From Johnsonville station cycle up to Carmichael Street.

Route description

In a nutshell, the Skyline Track starts from the Old Coach Road in Johnsonville and follows the Outer Green Belt southwest all the way to the south coast, near Island Bay. On the way, it traverses Mt Kaukau, Makara Peak, Wrights Hill and Hawkins Hill. We have marked every intersection with a fluoro disc on a warratah.

The Skyline Track can be tackled in several ways as there are numerous side tracks connecting it with various Wellington suburbs. It provides excellent links with Makara Peak.

Here is a breakdown of the ride:

1. Johnsonville to Makara Peak (2–3 hours). From the end of Carmichael Street, in Johnsonville, take the Old Coach Road track to a signpost on the ridgeline (a few hundred metres away).

Follow the ridge south (to the left) to Mt Kaukau. Several short sections used to be unridable, but we have re-routed all of them and it is now 100% ridable

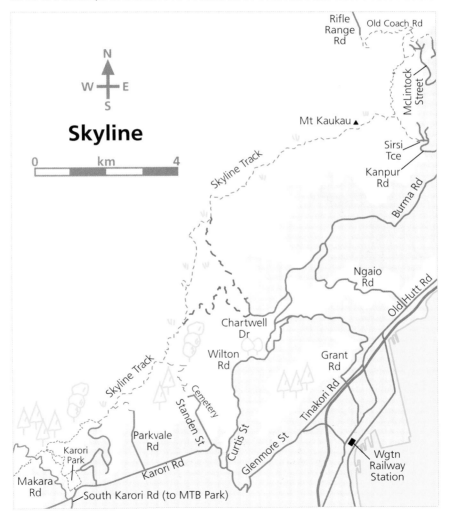

Another beautiful day on the Skyline Track.

in dry conditions. On a fine day, the views from the lookout platform on top of Kaukau are magnificent. From the top, marker poles lead you south along grassy sheep tracks to a farm track above Chartwell. Veer right to carry on along the main ridge following marker poles to Makara Peak. The last kilometre to Makara Peak Mountain Bike Park is fun single track. This section ends at Makara Road.

2. Makara Peak to Wrights Hill (1–2 hours). Cross Makara Road and take the following single tracks to traverse Makara Peak: Varley's, Zac's, North Face, and Lazy Fern. They lead you to the main car park on South Karori Road. Head out of the car park and turn right, then after 300 metres turn left up Hazelwood Avenue and then right into Fitzgerald Avenue. At the end of Fitzgerald, follow the track on your left up a moderate 3-km climb (known as Salvation). When you reach a sealed road, you are almost at the top of Wrights Hill.

3. Wrights Hill to the Coast (2–3 hours). From Salvation, climb up the sealed road for 100 metres, then turn right onto a gravel road. The main route from here leads you to the Karori Sanctuary Fenceline (see 8 Sanctuary Fenceline below). Head right and follow the fence for a few kilometres. After climbing solidly for about 10 minutes, you will see a narrow sealed road on your right. Hop onto it and turn right to ride almost to the top of Hawkins Hill. Now follow the Hawkins Hill to Red Rocks description (see 10 Hawkins Hill below) to reach the coast and Owhiro Bay.

Notes Some sections of the track above Chartwell are still being farmed and over winter become trashed by cows.

The Skyline Track is dual-use; be prepared to meet walkers and other cyclists around any corner. Most of the track is exposed to the wind.

7 Makara Peak ★ ★ ★ ★

Karori, 8 km from downtown Wellington

The hub of Wellington's vast track network is the popular Makara Peak Mountain Bike Park. Eight kilometres of sweet single track lead to the 412-metre-high summit. After taking in the views, there are several great options for your homeward run, ranging from easy to extreme.

Grades 2–5
Time 1–6 hours
Distance Up to 40 km

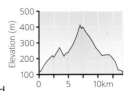

How to get there From the cenotaph near Parliament in downtown Wellington, follow the trolley bus cables up Bowen Street and all the way to the end of Karori Road, 7 km away. When you reach the bus turnaround area, veer left and ride down South Karori Road for 800 metres to the main car park.

Alternatively, there are great options for riding to Makara Peak via Wrights Hill or the Skyline Walkway (see 6 Skyline Track above).

Route description

The map below shows the single track that has been built since 1998. The tracks are connected by an 8-km network of 4WD pylon roads. Track building is ongoing, so check out www.makarapeak.org for updates.

The best **easy ride** is to trundle up Koru and down Lazy Fern. This is a 5.5 km, grade 2+ loop. You can detour to the Skills Area on the way for a bit of extra fun.

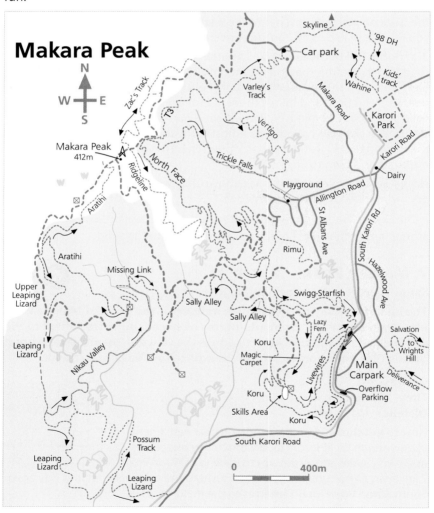

The best **intermediate introduction** is the following 14-km loop: ride up Koru, along Sally Alley (grade 3), through Missing Link (grade 3+), up Aratihi (grade 3+) to the summit. Take in the views, then head down the steep 4WD track towards the city for 100 metres, before turning right onto the North Face (grade 3), Smokin (grade 3), and onto Ridgeline Extension (grade 3+). Finish off with SWIGG (grade 3+) or Lazy Fern (grade 2).

The best **expert tracks** all start from the top of Makara Peak. Try them in the order of difficulty: **Ridgeline** (grade 5-, 1.5 km, exposed to the wind), then **T3 and Vertigo** (grade 5, 2.3 km descent to the bottom of Trickle Falls, steep and gnarly with several tricky obstacles to keep it interesting), and finally, if you enjoyed them, **Trickle Falls** (grade 5+, 2 km downhill track, the hardest track in the park; not suited to hardtails).

Notes The less popular tracks out the back of the park are sometimes lacking in maintenance, which can make them a grade harder than listed. Don't forget to drop a donation into the box at the car park. The car park is often full in the weekend. Consider riding to/from the park along the Skyline or one of the sweet single tracks described overleaf.

Ridgeline Track, Makara Peak.

Murray Drake

WARNING DAPPLED LIGHT CONDITIONS AHEAD

Diving down Deliverance, Wrights Hill.

Connecting tracks:

Wahine (Makara Peak to Karori Park) ★ ★ ☆ ☆

Grade 3   **Time** 20 minutes   **Distance** 1 km

From the bottom of Varley's Track, cross the road and ride around the council gate onto a gravelly 4WD track. Veer right at the first fork, and then 50 metres later turn hard right onto the Wahine single track. This is a primo route down to Karori Park. This area is heavily used by walkers, so be ready to stop quickly. Wahine also makes for a good honest climb.

Deliverance (Wrights Hill to Makara Peak) ★ ★ ★ ☆

Grade 5-   **Time** 10 minutes   **Distance** 2 km downhill only

From the lower car park on Wrights Hill, 500 metres from the summit, there is a gnarly track called Deliverance, diving down through native bush into a valley that leads out to the end of Fitzgerald Avenue in Karori. It starts 50 metres from the car park and is signposted (turn left off Skyline). At the bottom, follow your nose down to Makara Peak, 200 metres away (take the first left, then turn right at South Karori Road).

Salvation (Makara Peak to Wrights Hill) ★ ★ ★ ☆

Grade 3   **Time** 30 minutes   **Distance** 3 km

This sweet track climbs from the bottom of Deliverance to the top (i.e., from the end of Fitzgerald Avenue almost to the top of Wrights Hill). It is part of the Skyline Track (see above) and is a two-way, dual-use track.

8 Sanctuary Fenceline   ★ ★ ☆ ☆
INTERMEDIATE

Wellington city

Although this is a big loop around the wildlife sanctuary (Zealandia), most people don't do it as a loop. They use parts of it to ride from one area to another, often on their way to town, Hawkins Hill or Makara Peak. An added bonus to this ride is the kaka that can often be heard and seen overhead.

Grade 3+
Time 1.5–2.5 hours
Distance 10–12 km

Track conditions 70% 4WD track, 30% single track

How to get there You can start this ride from the wind turbine, George Denton Park (Highbury), Wrights Hill or Campbell Street scout hall (Karori), and it's good in either direction. We'll describe it from the city end, as it's the best way to ride from the city to Makara Peak. George Denton Park is at the end of Highbury Road, in Highbury, 30 minutes ride from downtown Wellington.

Claire Pascoe and Ashley Burgess on a roller-coaster ride for two.   Simon Kennett

Route description

Pass through the big gate beside the park and follow the 4WD track up hill to the fence and continue south along the fenceline. The sanctuary fence will be your guide for the next half hour as you ride up the Roller Coaster to the wind turbine, down to the southern end of the sanctuary and then up again to Wrights Hill.

A word of warning: the downhill to the southern end of the sanctuary has some heinously off-camber corners that have claimed many a speeding rider.

On your way up to Wrights Hill, about 500 metres from the top, the main 4WD track actually peels off to the left and sidles around the summit. Turn left and follow it if you want to ride down Deliverance (see above).

Otherwise, simply continue following the fence for a few hundred metres until you reach a 'To Campbell Street' sign. The single track to Campbell Street in Karori zigzags down through forest and is well worth checking out. It leads to a scout hall.

However, to get to the top of Wrights Hill, you should turn left 10 metres before the 'Campbell Street' sign and follow a single track up to a small bridge, turn left and continue climbing up to the lookout at the top. The view is a stunner on a fine day.

From the top of Wrights Hill, you can take the sealed road down into Karori (boring), try Deliverance (exciting) or head back the way you came and take the single track down to Campbell Street (fun).

Once at the scout hall on Campbell Street, you can follow the fence for another kilometre and then turn left (don't go straight ahead) onto a single track signposted 'Birdwood Steps'.

It takes you either to the long set of steps above Birdwood Street Karori, or there is a right-hand fork (just before a bridge) leading down to St Johns Pool and on up to Waiapu Road near the main entrance to Zealandia. This last section of track is grade 4 – very narrow and steep with extremely tight corners (not recommended when wet).

Straight across Waiapu Road, the perimeter track continues up a concrete path, past some houses and back into the bush. Although some of this last section is too steep to ride up, it is the most direct route back to George Denton Park.

Notes Be prepared to meet other bikers or walkers around any corner as this is a popular area.

9 Polhill to Hawkins Hill ★ ★ ★ ☆

INTERMEDIATE

Wellington city

Over the last three years, some of the best tracks in Wellington have been built closest to the city. They make for ideal lunchtime loops, or great connecting tracks to Hawkins Hill and the Sanctuary Fenceline.

Grade 3
Time 1.5–3 hours
Distance 6–18 km

Track conditions 15% narrow sealed road, 15% 4WD track, 70% single track

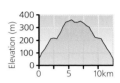

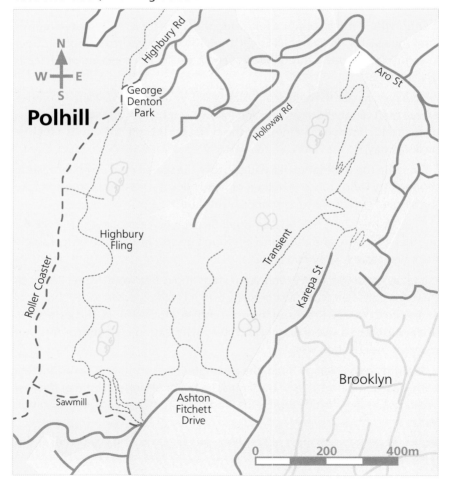

How to get there You can start this ride from the centre of Wellington. Ride up to the top of Aro Valley, and look for a track at the back of a small grass area southeast of a bus stop. Alternatively, ride up to the top of Polhill via Ashton Fitchett Drive in Brooklyn, or Highbury Road in Highbury.

Route description

From the back of the grass area behind the bus stop at the top of Aro Valley, Transient enters the bush and leads up to Ashton Fitchett Drive in Brooklyn. It's a 3.5-km-long track purpose built for bikers, but open to walkers as well. It actually meets another purpose-built track called Highbury Fling just before Ashton Fitchett Drive. Highbury Fling sidles from Brooklyn across to the Roller Coaster, 50 metres above George Denton Park in Highbury.

From either end of Highbury Fling, you can ride up to the Brooklyn wind turbine car park en route to Hawkins Hill. The fastest way is to ride left along Highbury Fling, to Ashton Fitchett Drive, and then turn right and ride up the sealed road to the turbine. The off-road way is to head right along Highbury Fling, and then left up the Roller Coaster (beside the sanctuary fence) to the wind turbine.

From the turbine, squeeze around the gate at the southern end of the car park and ride up the narrow sealed road until you have gone 50 metres past a putrid pink castle on your right and reach the signposted top of the Tip Track. Head left down the Tip Track for 200 metres and keep an eye out for a new single track on your left called Barking Emu.

Barking Emu is 2.4 km long and sidles down to Car Parts (3 km long), which takes you back to the Roller Coaster (1 km long), Highbury Fling (2 km long), and Transient (3.5 km) – that's at least 15 km of single track for a primo loop!

Notes Polhill, in particular, is a popular area with walkers and runners; take it easy on the way down. An uphill single track alternative to Car Parts will be started in 2012 (it will be called Windmill).

10 Hawkins Hill

Te Kopahou Reserve, South Wellington

This is one of the largest mountain bike destinations within riding distance of Wellington city. The tracks are well signposted with mapboards and marker posts.

Grades 3–4   **Time** 1–4 hours   **Distance** 10–30 km

Track conditions Mostly 4WD track with a couple of tasty single tracks

Maps See our map, or refer to NZTopo50 BQ31 Wellington.

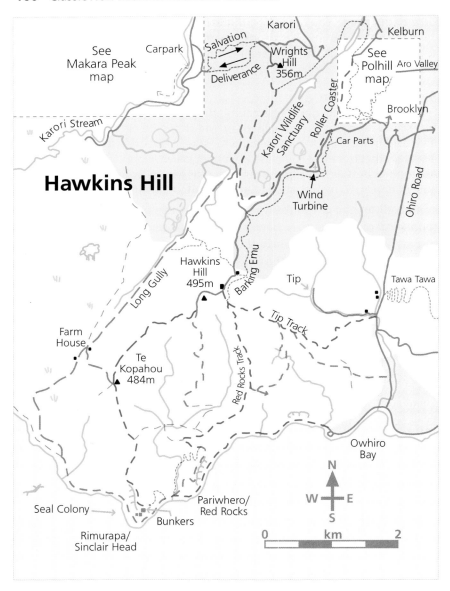

Hawkins Hill to Red Rocks ★ ★ ★ ☆

Grade 4   **Time** 2–4 hours   **Distance** 15 km

From the Brooklyn shops, follow the signs to the wind turbine. At the southern end of the car park, squeeze around the gate.

Once past the gate, continue along the sealed road nearly all the way to the top of Hawkins Hill – the one to the south with the large golf ball on top.

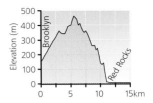

As you approach the top, you'll pass a building on your left, followed 250 metres on by a castle-type building on your right. Go a further 100 metres and turn left down a 4WD track called The Tip Track (see below). Ride down this rough route for 200 metres before turning right uphill (off The Tip Track).

This track leads to the coast and is signposted all the way. About 1 km before the coast there is a single track off to your right (it should be sign posted by now). This was built for mountain biking and is more fun than the 4WD track that goes straight ahead, especially if you like switchbacks. Be careful with the killer drop about 50 metres from the coast.

Once you reach the coast, turn left and head past Red Rocks and the old quarry site to Owhiro Bay.

The Tip Track ★★☆☆

This is the shortest possible route to the top of Hawkins Hill. In other words, it's damn steep, which is great if you're after a lung-searing hill-climb workout.

Grade 3+   **Time** 30–60 minutes   **Distance** 4.5 km, 400 vertical metres

Start at the large steel gate beside the turn-off to the Happy Valley Tip (aka Southern Landfill). There is a council mapboard at the bottom, and from there you can see a pukey-coloured castle-type building way up on the ridgeline – that's the top! This much-loved/hated climb is 100% ridable (on a good day).

There are three common ways down from the top:

1. Scoot down to Red Rocks (see above).

2. Ride to the south coast via the bunkers (see below).

3. Head north on the new Barking Emu single track (see 9 Polhill to Hawkins Hill above) and continue along Car Parts (see 9 Polhill to Hawkins Hill above). At the end, cross the road and follow the Roller Coaster (beside the Sanctuary Fenceline) down to George Denton Park, Highbury.

Hawkins Hill Bunkers ★★☆☆

Grade 5-   **Time** 2–4 hours   **Distance** 11 km from the top

Ready for an adventure? Ride up to the golfball-like radar on the top of Hawkins Hill and continue south on the sealed road for 1 km before veering left onto a 4WD track (signposted). After a few hundred metres, this track becomes very rutted, and some riders may have to walk a bit. When the 4WD track turns sharply to the left, go straight ahead, following an even rougher track heading south. After a short climb, the track drops steeply down a really, really rough grass slope to the concrete bunkers that can be seen in the distance to the south. As you approach them, you'll see the head of a small valley on your left.

After checking out the bunkers, follow a barely discernible track down into that valley (we marked it with warratahs in 2011). It soon becomes unridable as it drops to the coast beside a very steep stream. After grovelling down to the coast, turn left and follow the gravel road round past Red Rocks to Owhiro Bay.

11 Mt Victoria　

Wellington city

The tracks on Mt Victoria provide the closest riding to the central city. First timers can do the figure-of-eight loop that was marked out in 2009, with its series of newer low-gradient detours offering gentler options.

Grades 2–3
Time 1–2 hours
Distance Up to 8 km
Track conditions 25% 4WD track, 75% single track

Route description

Mt Victoria encompasses a fair chunk of Wellington's town belt and is used extensively by walkers and runners. There is a maze of tracks traversing the sun-soaked city side of the hill, just east of downtown Wellington. We recommend you start with the following signposted route.

Ride along Courtenay Place and then straight up to the end of Majoribanks Street. From the flat grassy area (just above the car park), ride past an MTB code sign, and follow the main gravelled track to your right. You are now on the signposted 'Intermediate MTB Track'. Every intersection is signposted from here on.

After 10 minutes, you'll cross Alexandra Road and start the 'Easy MTB Track'. We recommend you veer left and follow the easy gradient 'Hataitai Zigzag' single track downhill for the next 3–5 minutes. There are two junctions – a sharp left and a straight-through. As soon as you reach a building, head straight past and ride round the velodrome. After 10 minutes, you'll see the kids' skills area that we built in 2009. From there, the track turns right again and climbs beside the road for a while. The signs lead back to the start of the easy track, from where you can follow the intermediate track uphill for a few hundred metres and then back down to Majoribanks Street.

That will take about an hour. Head back in and explore if you have more time.

Notes Remember, a cheery 'hellooo' tends to disarm even the most fervent anti-biker.

Fifteen Other Rides

For a lot more detail on any of the following rides, pick up a copy of *Wellington's Best Bike Rides* from any local bike shop, or order online from www.kennett.co.nz

Queen Elizabeth Park ★ ★ ☆ ☆

In 2011, there were three short walking tracks open to bikes in this iconic coastal park and a mountain bike loop across the road in Whareroa Farm.

Grade 3 **Time** 1–2 hours **Distance** 7-km loop

If you are driving, head for the main entrance to the park at McKays Crossing, 3.5 km north of Paekakariki.

From wherever you start your ride, it is easy to do a loop using the Inland Track and the Coastal Track, and there are connector tracks between the two

Murray Drake

Easy riding at Queen Elizabeth Park.

if you're looking for a bit of variety. There are also lots of picnic areas, and the beach is popular on a hot summer's day.

We recommend you head south to north on the Coastal Track and north to south on the Inland Track. The tracks are mostly 2 metres wide and well gravelled, although there are a few short steep sections that some riders walk up.

One other track, which is ideal for beginners, is the 1.8-km long Whareroa Stream Track. It branches off the Inland Track and heads back to Whareroa Road near the main park entrance.

Notes This park is hugely popular for walking, horse riding and picnicking. Please be considerate of other users. For more information, including a map, check out www.gw.govt.nz/parks/

Whareroa Farm ★ ☆ ☆ ☆

As far as mountain biking tracks are concerned, this area is a work in progress. It has potential, so we will be back, for sure.

Grades 3–4 Time 1 hour Distance 6 km

Across the road from the McKays Crossing entrance lies Whareroa Farm, recently purchased by DOC. They developed an intermediate grade, 6-km mountain bike loop there in mid 2011 and downhill tracks are on the way with the help of the Kapiti Mountain Bike Club. Also, the farm can be used to access the Akatarawa Forest via old Campbell's Mill Road. For more info, check out: www.doc.govt.nz/parks-and-recreation/places-to-visit/wellington-kapiti/kapiti/whareroa-farm/

Waiotauru Valley ★ ★ ☆ ☆

This is one tough trip, but the scenery is great. If you're fit, and don't mind a few kilometres of tramping, you'll love it.

Grade 5 Time 5–10 hours Distance 45 km

Take NZTopo50 BP32 Paraparaumu and BP33 Featherston, and a compass/GPS, along with your normal epic survival kit.

From the saddle of Akatarawa Road (22 km north of Upper Hutt), climb north up the 4WD track deep into the Tararua Forest Park. After 9 km, you'll descend to Waiotauru Hut. Soon after the hut, the 4WD track deteriorates into a narrow single track. After crossing a swing bridge, things get really gnarly, with lots of bike carrying and a couple of epic slips to negotiate. If you're lucky, you'll make it through to the Otaki Forks road end in one piece. In 2009, a massive slip wiped out 100 metres of track shortly before the road end. In 2010, when the river wasn't in flood, we found it easiest to descend and follow the river flats for a couple of hundred metres, rather than crossing the slip.

Notes In 1986, this was almost the route for the first mountain bike race Paul organised, but people told him it would be too tough, so he settled on the Karapoti Classic instead.

Mt Climie ★★

Back in the good ole days, this ride was used for both uphill and downhill national championship races.

Grade 3+   **Time** 1–3 hours   **Distance** 12 km return

If you want to explore other tracks around here, check out the Greater Wellington Regional Council map of the Tunnel Gully area at www.gw.govt.nz/parks/

This ride hits the dirt at Tunnel Gully Reserve, located at the end of Plateau Road, 10 km northeast of Upper Hutt. Go to the last car parking area, take a deep breath and start toning those *musculus quadriceps femoris*. From the top of Mt Climie (860 m), you'll be treated to fantastic views. Once you've got your breath back, enjoy an exhilarating and extremely loose descent.

Keep an eye open for walkers and service vehicles.

Karapoti Epic ★★

A classic 'jungle ride' involving many natural obstacles, both ridable and unridable. The navigation is also challenging.

Grade 5   **Time** 3 hours
Distance 12-km loop

Maps Our map on page 143 is the best available.

From Karapoti car park, ride up the gorge for 6 km to a large clearing. Turn right and after another kilometre, where the main forestry road swings left, continue for a further 600 metres before turning hard right.

Ride up hill for about 1.2 km on a gravel road, and when it flattens out, take a left turn up a minor old forestry road – very old, but the bench will be obvious after a minute or so.

Murray Drake

Stay on the old track until eventually you reach a sharp left-hand bend. Stop and look! To the left, the track is rutted and climbs steeply; you need to go right. Within 30 metres, you'll be on an obvious track that drops down to a stream. Go down stream for a few hundred metres and pick up a benched route on the true left.

Follow your nose to a cliff face. There is a 12-metre length of rope dangling at the cliff, but it looks very old. We didn't trust it. Better to take your own if you haven't got good rock climbing skills. From the cliff, navigation is straightforward all the way back to the car park.

Cannon Point ★ ★ ☆ ☆

The Cannon Point Walkway and Karapoti Challenge loop combine to create an excellent introduction to the Akatarawa Forest.

Grade 3   **Time** 1–3 hours   **Distance** 17 km

Refer to the map in the Greater Wellington Regional Council's 'Akatarawa Forest' pamphlet.

From Tulsa Park (in Totara Park, Upper Hutt), ride up the Cannon Point Walkway for a few hundred metres and then turn left to continue your climb on a gentle old pylon road. After a couple of kilometres, veer right onto the gravel Valley View Road and keep climbing up to a major intersection by Cannon Point (345 m). Stay on Valley View Road for another 1.5 km, then turn left onto Airstrip Drive (you are now on the course used for the Karapoti Challenge, the easier version of the Karapoti Classic).

A few minutes later, turn right onto Woolshed Road – a major downhill. At the bottom, veer right to rejoin Valley View Road and climb back to the main ridge to complete the loop. Then drop back to Cannon Point and follow the walkway down to Tulsa Park.

Major intersections are signposted. Logging operations periodically close some areas during weekdays.

Battle Hill ★ ☆ ☆ ☆

Twenty kilometres north of Porirua, this is an OK place to go for a spin before (or after) having a family picnic.

Grades 3–4   **Time** 2–4 hours   **Distance** 4–14 km

There are two tracks here – the short Battle Hill Loop and the vertically challenging, 10-km-long Transmission Gully loop. If you are looking for something more adventurous, Battle Hill also provides access to the Akatarawa Forest. For general information and maps, refer to www.gw.govt.nz/parks/

Whitireia Park ★ ☆ ☆ ☆

An easy family trip with coastal scenery and good picnic spots.

Grade 1+   **Time** 30–60 minutes   **Distance** up to 9 km

Start and finish from the end of Onepoto Road, off Titahi Bay Road in Porirua. Ride north round the coast for a few kilometres until the track ends at a road. At that point, you can turn around and head back the same way or climb up the road, over a farmed hill, and down into the suburb of Titahi Bay via Transmitter Street.

Eastern Hutt Hills ★ ☆ ☆ ☆

Old service roads provide a good training ride through the regenerating forest on the hills beside the Hutt Valley.

Grade 3   **Time** 1.5 hours   **Distance** 10 km

From the top of the Wainuiomata Hill Road, head north on a gravel road to Fitzherbert (377 m) – the knob with a radio mast right out of a NASA garage sale. After taking in the view, backtrack from Fitzherbert for 5 minutes and turn right down the wide Summit Road firebreak. Keep on the main firebreak track and you should pop out to Summit Road, Epuni, Lower Hutt.

Hutt River Trail ★ ★ ☆ ☆

This is a fine 'family ride'. The trail covers over 30 km of single tracks, 4WD tracks and sealed cycle paths from Te Marua (just north of Upper Hutt) to Wellington Harbour at Petone. There are plenty of picnic spots and swimming holes en route, and countless start and finish options.

Grades 1–2+   **Time** 2–4 hours   **Distance** Up to 30 km

The main route is well described in the 'Hutt River Trail' pamphlet available from the Upper Hutt information centre or online at www.gw.govt.nz/parks/

The two best start options are, either drive to Harcourt Park near Upper Hutt, or catch the commuter train to Upper Hutt. If you catch the train, then just ride through the shopping centre and out to the Hutt River. The river trail is between Highway 2 and the river, but to avoid crossing the busy highway, you can follow the obvious path on top of the floodbank for the first 2 km. Either way, you'll be staying on the eastern side of the river all the way down to within 400 metres of Wellington Harbour. Here it ducks under and then loops back to cross a large river bridge. On the other side, hang left and follow the track round to Hikoikoi Reserve McEwan Park, on the Petone foreshore. From here, you can continue west along the Petone Beach reserve.

Notes As well as walkers and runners, keep an eye out for the odd equestrian. Harcourt Park, near the northern end, is an excellent picnic spot.

Mt Lowry ★ ★ ☆ ☆

Some of the old bush tracks in the East Harbour Regional Park provide slow, technically demanding riding that expert riders drool over. Avoid when wet.

Grade 5-   **Time** 1–2 hours   **Distance** 7 km one way

Maps Check out www.gw.govt.nz/eastharbour for a map of the tracks in the East Harbour Regional Park.

Follow the directions to get to the Wainuiomata MTB Park, except, from the top of the Wainuiomata hill, head south on the Main Ridge Track all the way to Mt Lowry (373 m). From there, the track veers east and passes a couple of lookouts before descending in earnest to Wainuiomata. You have a choice of two tracks, the Firebreak Track or the Rata Ridge Track to get you down.

From the bottom of either track, it's a 20-minute ride back to the top of the Wainuiomata hill on the main road or 10 minutes to the Wainuiomata MTB Park.

Long Gully ★ ☆ ☆ ☆

Long Gully is a privately owned farm 6 km southwest of Wellington. It provides access on a farm road from the Karori Sanctuary fenceline to the south coast.

Grade 3   **Time** 2–3 hours   **Distance** 27 km

Long Gully is privately owned and provides access on a farm road from the Karori Sanctuary fenceline to the south coast. Phone Steve Watson on 027 442 7334 or (04) 476 5296 for access permission and remember to leave all gates as you find them.

There are also a number of downhill tracks starting from just south of the Hawkins Hill summit, which are managed by the Wellington Mountain Bike Club (www.wmtbc.org.nz). Contact the club for permission to ride in that area.

Opau Loop, Makara wind farm ★ ☆ ☆ ☆

This is a short track at West Wind, the wind farm near Makara.

Grade 4   **Time** 1 hour   **Distance** 6 km

Head out towards Makara Beach, and you will see Opau Road leading up to a public car park at the start of the ride. The track is a 6-km loop, starting behind the big old post office building. It should be well signposted by the time it opens in late 2011. The area is farmed, so be prepared for some gates and cow shit. As you might expect, much of this ride is very exposed to strong winds!

Miramar Track Project   ★ ★ ☆ ☆

This is a tiny area, but what it lacks in quantity is made up for in quality.

Grade 4   **Time** 1 hour   **Distance** 2 km

From the Miramar shops, head up Park Road, Weka Street, then Darlington Road. Two hundred metres up Darlington Road, you'll reach a grassy area, just before a bend in the road.

Cross the grassy area and start riding up Conviction. It writhes through the forest, climbing steeply in a couple of places. After 1 km, cut across the hillside for a few hundred metres, on a track called Boot Leg, to meet a sealed road.

Either return the same way, or ride down the road to Jail Brake – a short, sweet downhill track.

Track work is ongoing – check out www.facebook.com/MiramarTrackProject for the latest news. There is a skills area going in near the top of Jail Brake and a new track called Repeat Offender (connecting the bottom of Jail Brake to Conviction).

Pencarrow Head   ★ ☆ ☆ ☆

On a fine weekend day, this completely flat ride is popular with families and beginner riders.

Grade 1   **Time** 2–3 hours   **Distance** 20 km return

Follow the main road all the way through Eastbourne until it ends at a gate. From there, a gravel road leads round the coast for 5 km to Pencarrow Head and then another 5 km to Baring Head. The last 200 metres to the rocks at Baring Head are too sandy to ride. Most people return the same way.

For a more adventurous ride, explore the signposted Lake Kohangapiripiri and Cameron Ridge tracks, east of Pencarrow Head. They'll add up to 5 hilly km and some big views to your trip. Pick up a copy of the 'East Harbour Regional Park' pamphlet from your local Greater Wellington Regional Council office or log on to www.gw.govt.nz/eastharbour for more information.

In 2011, the Greater Wellington Regional Council purchased Baring Head Station with plans to improve recreation facilities. For the latest details on how things are progressing, see www.gw.govt.nz/eastharbour

Wellington's Skyline Track after the big snow of 2011.

Nick Boyens

The Greater Wellington Regional Council has produced regional cycling maps, which show some of the rides around Wellington. These maps are available free from Wellington region bike shops and information centres.

The council also provides a 'journey planner' web service, which can estimate ride times around the city (see www.journeyplanner.org.nz).

Nelson

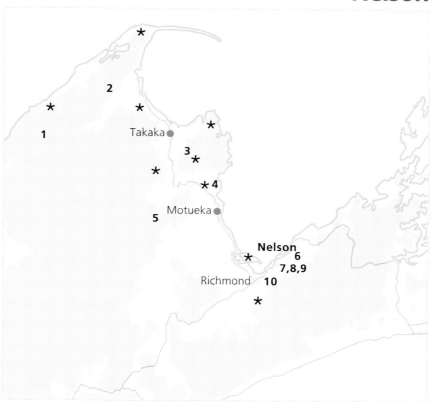

1 **Heaphy Track**
2 **Aorere Goldfields**
3 **Rameka Track**
4 **Kaiteriteri Mountain Bike Park**
5 **Flora Saddle to Barrons Flat**
6 **Hira Forest MTB Park**

7 **Codgers MTB Park**
8 **Dun Mountain Trail**
9 **Peaking Ridge**
10 **Involution, Barnicoat Range**
★ Plus nine other rides

NELSON HIGHLIGHTS

Nelson has it all, the lucky buggers! From downtown cafes you can ride out to primo purpose-built single tracks or awesome back-country tracks. The quantity and quality of tracks makes Nelson one of the top mountain biking destinations in the country. In 2011 alone, several brilliant tracks were built, the Dun Mountain Trail was upgraded and extended, and the magnificent Heaphy Track was reopened to bikes.

1 Heaphy Track ★ ★ ★ ★

Kahurangi National Park, Golden Bay to the West Coast

The Heaphy is open for a trial period, from 2011–2013, between 1 May and 30 September – the coldest, wettest months of the year. In fine weather, it's the greatest back-country ride in New Zealand. In bad weather, it's an epic. For experienced back-country riders, the Heaphy remains a classic among classics for its stunning scenery, amazing wildlife, and the satisfying sense of accomplishment it engenders.

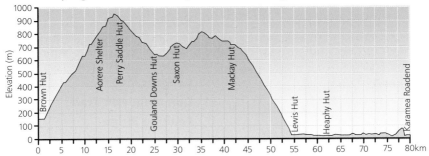

Grade 4   **Time** 2–3 days   **Distance** 80 km

Track conditions 95% single track, 5% unridable.

Maps NZTopo50 BP22 Heaphy and BP23 Gouland Downs

Which direction? Most grade 4 riders prefer biking the Heaphy from east to west because in that direction the Mackay–Lewis downhill is challenging fun. Grade 3 riders, however, will enjoy the track more by travelling west to east – you'll have to walk up the grade 4 climb to Mackays Hut, but you'll get to enjoy riding down the less technical stretch to Brown Hut.

Heading north, an hour from the Karamea Road end.

Jonathan Kennett

How to get there From Nelson, drive over to Golden Bay and through to within 1 km of Collingwood before turning left at a T-intersection onto Collingwood-Bainham Main Road, which becomes Aorere Valley Road just after passing the Bainham store. After another 30 km, you will reach the first of three fords. These are unpassable after heavy rain. The track starts another 3 km up the road.

From the west coast side it's 16 km from the road end to the township of Karamea. There are a variety of shuttle services available. Contact the Karamea Information Centre (www.karameainfo.co.nz) or Google 'heaphy shuttle'.

Route description

From the car park at the end of Aorere Valley Road, ride a few minutes to Brown Hut (16 bunks). From there, the Heaphy Track crosses Brown River and climbs steadily for a good hour or more to Aorere Shelter where there is water and a toilet.

From the shelter, the track continues much the same – good gradient and good surface – to the highest point on the Heaphy Track, Flanagans Corner at 910 m (800 m above Brown Hut). From the corner, a 3-minute walk takes you

Cave Brook near Gouland Downs Hut, Heaphy Track.   Jonathan Kennett

to a stunning lunch spot. Beyond Flanagans Corner, the track sidles to Perry Saddle Hut (24 bunks, fully serviced, good views).

From Perry Saddle, the track is rough and rocky down to Gouland Downs Hut (8 bunks, no cookers). There are some fantastic views of the vast Gouland Downs, and you pass the famous 'boot tree' on your way down to the hut.

The track is in very good condition from Gouland Downs Hut along to Saxon Hut (16 bunks), which lies in the open among tussock. If the track is saturated, which it is most of the time over winter, we recommend doing an about-turn here and enjoying the fantastic riding back to Golden Bay. If you have an appetite for mud and bike carrying, continue west.

From Saxon Hut to James Mackay Hut, the track deteriorates and, when we rode/walked it in May 2011, there were many boggy and rutted sections. There is also plenty of 600-mm-wide boardwalk – durable, but on the narrow side for some riders. Sections below James Mackay Hut are penciled in to be upgraded before the 2012 season.

The toughest section of the whole track is from James Mackay Hut down a massive hill to Lewis Hut beside the Heaphy River. The track is well endowed with rocks, ruts and roots, interspersed with short easy sections. Grade 5 riders will have a ball. Grade 3 riders should expect a lot of walking. Note that DOC are planning on upgrading this section in late 2011. It might be fine in 2012!

From Lewis Hut down to Heaphy Hut, the track runs parallel to the huge Heaphy River. There are three difficult swing bridges and many boggy sections to negotiate.

The final stretch from Heaphy Hut out to the Karamea track end is mostly ridable, but there are a couple of walking sections along the coast where the track has been swallowed up by the sea. Then it is an easy 16 km ride to Karamea, where there is good accommodation and food.

The entire route is surrounded by magnificent scenery – beautiful rivers, pristine forest, distant mountain views, and wild West Coast beaches. The notorious sandflies are far less of a problem in winter. Instead, be prepared for wind, rain and cold; plenty of it.

Notes This is a track of two halves. The Golden Bay side, which has been well built and maintained, is 99% ridable for grade 3 riders; the West Coast side is poorly built most of the way and is getting chewed up. At the time of writing, there was talk of fixing the West Coast side, and some work was imminent.

Riding after dark or in groups of more than six riders is prohibited on the Heaphy. Attempting to blast through in a day is simply a waste of stunning, world-class scenery. All the big huts have billies and gas cookers, so it's easy to travel light, but don't skimp on clothing.

A stop at the character-filled Bainham store should be compulsory, for an ice cream and look-see at the very least.

Takaka and Westport have the only bike shops close to the track.

2 Aorere Goldfields ★ ★ ★

11 km southwest of Collingwood

INTERMEDIATE

On a dry day, this is one of the best rides in Golden Bay. Some of the single track is excellent, and it's an interesting area both historically and scenically.

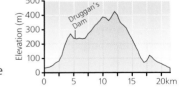

Grade 3+
Time 2–5 hours
Distance 21-km loop

Track conditions 60% 4WD track, 38% single track, 2% unridable

Maps Take NZTopo50 BN24 Collingwood if you want to do the full loop.

How to get there From Collingwood, head west on the Collingwood-Bainham Main Road towards Rockville for 10 km. Go straight onto Devils Boots Road and park at Devils Boots (large upside down boot-shaped limestone formations).

Route description

You can do the full 21-km loop or ride up to Druggan's Dam and back (11 km return). There is a cave, old gold workings and a dam to visit on this ride.

From the boots, ride up the rough road for 15 minutes before turning left up a steep 4WD track at the 'Aorere Goldfields' signpost.

What follows is a tough climb that will require the odd bit of walking. Turn right at the 'Goldfields Walk' sign and then veer left at the 'Caves 5 min' sign.

For an interesting 20-minute diversion, we walked down to the Ballroom Cave and climbed through to the Stafford Cave (torch essential) before walking back to our bikes.

From the caves, a water-race track leads on to Druggan's Dam. It's technical in places, so don't race it on your first time through. The dam is a common resting spot, as is the lookout spot 5 minutes past it.

For a great 2–3 hour ride, turn around at the dam (or lookout spot) and enjoy the single track you rode up.

Alternatively, complete the grand loop by riding round to Red Hill and down towards Plain Road on a wide fast 4WD track. At the bottom, hop over a gate, coast down to Plain Road, then turn left to return to Devils Boots.

Notes The ride is best done in dry weather.

3 Rameka Track ★ ★ ★ ☆

INTERMEDIATE

36 km from Motueka or 47 km from Takaka

The Rameka Track is an old classic with exciting new tracks at both ends – Canaan Downs and Project Rameka.

Grade 3+

Time 3–4 hours

Distance 33 km

Track conditions 15% sealed road, 15% gravel road, 5% 4WD track, 65% single track

Maps Take NZTopo50 BP25 Motueka and BP24 Takaka.

How to get there Most people get dropped off at the start of Canaan Road, which is near the top of the Takaka Hill. Alternatively, drive 11 twisty km along Canaan Road to a car parking and camping area, with toilets. The shuttle from Canaan Downs to Takaka is so long (1 hour) that Golden Bay locals often prefer to ride up and down from Takaka.

Route description

Near the top of Takaka Hill, turn north onto the twisty, gravel Canaan Road. Cycle to the road end 11 km away (there is a toilet there). At the far end of the camping area, hop over a gate and head up past an 'Abel Tasman National Park' sign on a grassy 4WD track.

One kilometre from the camping area, turn left at a 'Rameka Track' signpost. In the next few kilometres, you'll wind down through native bush on an excellent single track with many technical challenges.

Just before you break out of the bush, the track steepens, and there is a short rocky section that requires walking. The track officially ends at a flat grassy clearing, from where people used to follow a gravel road down to Takaka. Not anymore!

Cross the grassy clearing and you will find a new single track diving down to an old Pack Track, which leads all the way to Project Rameka.

Enter Project Rameka and follow the old Rameka Trail, and then Great Expectations, down to Rameka Creek, 3.5 km away. It's well signposted and leads all the way to another clearing (the Mill Site) beside Rameka Creek Road.

From the Mill Site, you can cruise down the road, and into Takaka (follow the orange markers) or turn left to take Two Klick – a technical grade-4 single track running beside the road for 1 km. After being spat back onto the road for a short spell, you will reach One Klick, another 1 km stretch of single track.

Takaka township is only 15 minutes from the end of the single track. At the bottom of the Rameka Creek Road, you'll reach a T-intersection with several letterboxes. Turn left and left again, following orange markers to Central Takaka Road, and then right to coast to Highway 60, about 5 minutes away. Go straight across the highway to take Dodson Road (to avoid highway traffic) around to Takaka township, only 2 km away.

Notes There is a 30-minute walk (no bikes allowed) from Canaan Road car park to Harwoods Hole, a 176 m deep tomo that is popular with cavers. Local riders have also developed a series of mountain bike tracks at Canaan Downs that are worth exploring (see Nine Other Rides at the end of this chapter).

Harriet Harper flying down to Kaiteriteri.

Project Rameka

In 2008, Jonathan and his partner Bronwen bought a large chunk of land halfway down Rameka Road to create a carbon sink. They soon discovered that the original Rameka Track (built in the 1850s) actually runs right through the property! So it's been cleared and a new track (Great Expectations) built right down to Rameka Creek. Naturally, it's open to walkers and cyclists.

This is a two-way track, so if you're based in Golden Bay, you will be able to ride from the bottom up to Rameka Track rather than do a huge shuttle.

If you would like to assist with Project Rameka, drop into The Quiet Revolution Cycle Shop in Takaka or check out projectrameka.carbonsink.org.nz

4 Kaiteriteri Mountain Bike Park ★ ★ ★
14 km north of Motueka

This is a great little mountain bike park situated in the forest beside the popular beach resort of Kaiteriteri.

Grades 2–5   **Time** 1–3 hours   **Distance** 5–15 km

Track conditions Some forestry road, but mostly sweet single track.

Maps Before your ride, pick up a map from Coppins Outdoor Store in Motueka, or the motor camp store in Kaiteriteri.

How to get there From Motueka, you can either drive to the main entrance or ride to the closer entrance. If driving, head north through Riwaka and turn right at the 'Kaiteriteri' sign. Park by the beach, and ride to the park entrance just a few minutes away from the motor camp store. There is no parking on Martin Farm Road.

If riding to the park, use the cycle path to Riwaka (5 km from Motueka), then cycle on the main road towards Kaiteriteri. Just over 5 km from Riwaka, on the left side of Riwaka-Kaiteriteri Road, you will see the start of Easy Rider, heading into the park.

Route description

From the Kaiteriteri motor camp store, ride south on the main road for a couple of hundred metres, then turn right onto Martin Farm Road and ride for another couple of hundred metres before turning left up into the mountain bike park.

With the map in hand, you can choose from several tracks. The best intro loop is to head up Salivator, along Sidewinder, Swamp Monster, Glade Runner and Revelation, then up Ziggy, Big Airs and Skullduggery, along a new track (un-named in 2011) then down Bay View and Swish before cruising back along

Easy Rider and down Half Pipe. That fun circuit took us 1.5 hours and was almost completely on purpose-built single track!

The black tracks up the ridges are old forestry roads – not so hot, and you need a permit from the motor camp to get to the top of some of them.

Notes This park is a work in progress, but it's developing incredibly fast. Suffice to say, the area is worth a whirl every time you holiday at Kaiteriteri.

5 Flora Saddle to Barrons Flat ★ ★ ☆ ☆
34 km southwest of Motueka

EASY   ADVANCED

This ride runs through stunning beech forest in Kahurangi National Park.

Grades 2–4   **Time** 2–6 hours   **Distance** 15 km return or 37 km right through to Cobb Valley Road, Upper Takaka

Track conditions 25% 4WD track, 75% single track

Maps NZTopo50 BP24 Takaka and BQ24 Tapawera.

How to get there From Motueka, head southwest on Highway 61 for 18 km to Ngatimoti.

Cross the Motueka River and head west along Motueka West Bank Road, then follow the Mt Arthur track signs all the way up Graham Valley Road to the car park. This gravel road gains 850 m altitude and is so steep in parts that concrete slabs have been laid down for traction.

Route description
From the road end, it's an easy 1 km on a 4WD track to Flora Saddle (975 m). Now veer right to head to Flora Valley. In a matter of minutes, the track reaches Flora Hut. Veer left at the 'Flora Track to Takaka Valley' sign to follow a beautiful, leaf-littered 4WD track towards Takaka Valley. Another cruisy 5 km will bring you to 'Gridiron Gulch – Population 2', an impressive rock bivvy. Shortly after this, veer right at Upper Junction. Now the sweet, sweet single track starts, and things get technical. Either take a short single-track fix and then return the way you came, or gobble an extra muesli bar, tighten your pack straps and prepare for a slog.

If you continue beyond Upper Junction, you'll find the track deteriorates fast. The former stock route over Barrons Flat may require some walking in places, especially if wet. Eventually you'll descend an old 4WD track and pick up a marked easement through farmland to Cobb Valley Road, in Upper Takaka, Golden Bay.

Notes Be prepared for rough weather at any time. This is a remote back-country ride.

Beyond Gridiron Gulch.

Simon Kennett

6 Hira Forest MTB Park ★ ★ ★ *

2 km east of Nelson   ✳ really fun!; Didn't get a permit

INTERMEDIATE   EXPERT

Hira Forest is within easy riding distance of town and has purpose-built as well as old-school tracks. Most are awesome fun.

Grades 3–5

Time 2–5 hours

Distance 15–37 km

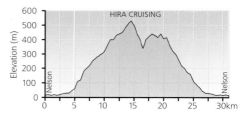

Landowners Hancock Forests Ltd. Riders need an access permit. Pick up a temporary access permit from any bike shop in Nelson, Stoke or Richmond. Membership of the Nelson MTB Club includes an annual permit.

How to get there Ride up Maitai Valley Road for 2 km and turn left into Sharland Road.

Route description

This is one of the main riding areas in Nelson. The tracks are marked on a mapboard up Sharland Road. In 2011, locals showed us R 'n' R, which is an awesome alternative to the Slingshot and Scottwood Wiggles described below. Either way, you'll have a long climb followed by a lot of fun.

Murray and Stew checking out Waterloo Track in Hira Forest.   Jonathan Kennett

Ground Effect Slingshot and Scottwood Wiggles

Grade 3+   **Time** 2 hours   **Distance** 31 km

First timers should start with these excellent, purpose-built single tracks. Climb for almost an hour up Sharland Road and Bobs Fern Road (the second Bobs Fern Road, not the first one) to reach the 'MTB Track' sign near the trig at the top. There are few tracks in New Zealand that return as much for your hard-earned elevation as Ground Effect Slingshot. It weaves back and forth on its way down the valley, providing a long, flowing ride. After 15 minutes, it connects with Scottwood Wiggles, which is a bit steep and more difficult in places and leads out to Sharland Road at the '5 km' sign.

Now you have three options:

1. Cruise down the road and back to town (grade 1, 30 minutes).

2. Carry on taking new single tracks following the river and the main road back to the car park (grade 4, 30 minutes).

3. Tackle the Supplejack Track (grade 5, 1 hour). Coast down Sharland for 5 minutes and then turn off up Bobs Fern Road. Within 2 minutes, turn left onto the first 4WD track you see. When you reach the main ridge, turn right and climb a bit more. You're aiming for a lookout next to a skid site (spot height 388 on the topomap). The track is signposted 'Rimu and Matai Trail' at the far side of the skid site. After 5 minutes, you will meet a 4WD track and should nip up to the signposted 'Supplejack'.

This technical downhill will test your cornering ability to the max. Please don't skid or cut the corners. Supplejack leads back to Sharland Road.

Notes The Nelson MTB Club maintains and builds tracks here. Keep an eye on the mapboard for changes. These tracks are a grade harder when wet.

7 Codgers MTB Park ★ ★ ★

1 km south of central Nelson

INTERMEDIATE   ADVANCED

Codgers Connection, the overgrown and lost part of the Dun Railway between Tantragee Saddle and Brook Street was rediscovered and cleaned up by a group of 'old codgers' early this century. This popular trail now forms the backbone for an expanding MTB trail system that networks seamlessly between public recreation reserve and plantation forest.

Grades 3–4
Time 1–2 hours
Distance 5–30 km

Track conditions 25% sealed road, 30% gravel road, 15% 4WD track, 30% single track

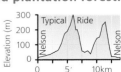

Landowners Hancock Forests Ltd. Riders need an access permit. Pick up a temporary access permit from any bike shop in Nelson, Stoke or Richmond. Membership of the Nelson MTB Club includes an annual permit.

The Nelson MTB Club has negotiated 24/7 access to the area bounded by Brook St, Maitai Valley, Groom Rd and Tantragee Saddle so these trails can be enjoyed any time with only minor logging operations affecting selected areas.

Route description
Head onto the Codgers Connection, on your left just past 135 Brook Street. On your way up toward Tantragee Saddle branch off onto the trails of your choice. Everything leads back to Codgers, or across to Fireball Road and Tantragee Saddle. The Fireball Loop is a local favourite as are P51 and Pipilini on the other side of the valley, and the famous Turners off Fireball Road.

At the time of writing, there were 15 trails ranging from 500-metre-long link tracks, to the 8-km Fireball Loop. The expansion of this trail network is happening rapidly – trail updates can be found in the recreation section of the council's mapping website www.topofthesouthmaps.co.nz or on www.nelsonmountainbikeclub.org.nz

Notes If you live in Nelson we recommend you join the impressive Nelson MTB Club, see www.nelsonmountainbikeclub.org.nz

8 Dun Mountain Trail ★★★★ ✱ Great ride
1 km south of Nelson

This much-loved ride follows a historic tramline deep into beech forest, and then out across alpine mountain slopes before a long descent to Maitai Valley. If you are new to Nelson, there's no better place to start. The first half of the ride up to a shelter called Third House is a gentle grade 2. Beyond Third House the track becomes a grade 3 as it climbs to Coppermine Saddle.

Grades 2–3+
Time 2–6 hrs
Distance Up to 42 km

Track conditions 5% sealed road, 5% gravel road, 50% historic rail trail, 40% single track

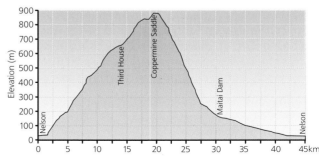

Maps NZTopo50-BQ26 Nelson.

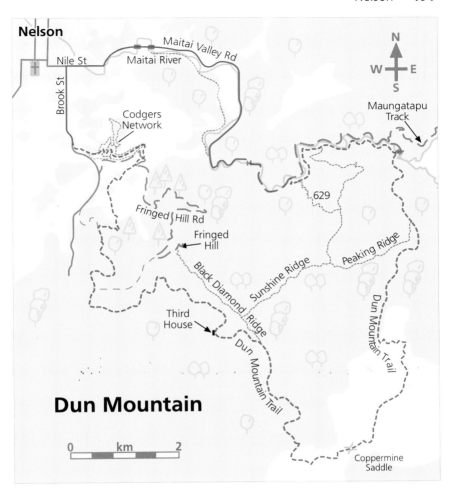

Route description

Only 1 km from downtown Nelson, you'll find the start of the Dun Mountain Walkway signposted on your left just past 135 Brook Street. The first section of the walkway is also known as (Old) Codgers Track. Follow the easy climb for 20 minutes till you pop out onto the gravel Tantragee Road. Ride up the road for 300 metres until you see another 'Dun Mountain Walkway' sign heading off to your right.

After about an hour's riding on an easy gradient, you'll come to a well-signposted four-way intersection. Follow the Dun Mountain trail straight ahead – it just gets sweeter and sweeter, all the way to Third House. Sitting at the top of a grassy clearing, this shelter overlooks Nelson Bay and is a rewarding goal.

From Third House, you can turn around and return the way you came for a nice easy ride, or carry on and complete the full loop.

If going the full distance, continue up the Dun Mountain Trail, climbing above the treeline to Windy Point (signposted).

Windy Point is a good place to reassess the weather – you've got another hour of exposure above the bushline to complete this marathon.

If the weather looks good, then carry on to Coppermine Saddle. From the sign at the saddle (with your back to the sign) go straight ahead and follow the well formed trail down, down, down … for a very long way.

Eventually you'll reach, and cross, the Maitai River South Branch on an arched wooden bridge. From here, there's even more sweet smooth riding to a T-intersection above the main Maitai River. Turn left to follow another 3 km of new single track beside a pipeline and down to the gravelly Maitai Road.

Finally, it's 40 minutes pedaling, gently downhill, back to the centre of Nelson.

Notes Check out www.nzcycletrail.com for updates on the track and www.coppermine.co.nz if you are interested in racing this mighty ride.

9 Peaking Ridge
1 km southeast of Nelson

This is a ruggedly technical route down from Fringed Hill, guaranteed to keep expert riders on the edge of their seats. It's a gnarly alternative to the Dun Mountain Trail.

Grade 5   **Time** 4–8 hours   **Distance** 30-km loop from Nelson

Track conditions 10 % sealed road, 5% gravel road, 15% 4WD track, 70% single track

Maps Check out the map in this book.

How to get there From downtown Nelson, ride up the bottom of the Dun Mountain Trail to Tantragee Saddle and then up to Fringed Hill (810 m) on a major forestry road.

Route description
From the Fringed Hill radio masts, take the Black Diamond Ridge single track. After 30 minutes of challenging riding, turn left at the 'Maitai Caves' sign, and 15 minutes later, you'll come across another 'Maitai Caves' signposted turn-off that includes a small 'to Peaking Ridge' sign. Follow that sign along Sunshine Ridge, and after another 30–40 minutes, you'll reach an obvious 'Peaking Ridge' sign, which points to the right.

Heading up towards Coppermine Saddle, Dun Mountain.

The first 500 metres is loose and steep and has a boardwalk with a drop-off at the end. After 30 minutes of diving down a rough and rooty, minimalist single track, you'll drop out onto a smooth 4WD track that runs alongside the Maitai River South Branch.

Turn left and take the 4WD track to the main Maitai Valley, and then turn left again to follow the pipeline track (this is the end of the Dun Mountain Trail). After a few kilometres, it descends to the Maitai Valley Road.

Take a breather as you pedal the 30 minutes down valley back to the centre of Nelson.

Notes Some local riders, impatient to get their Peaking fix, are starting from Maitai Dam and following steep (barely ridable) forestry roads up to a track called 629, and then accessing a new track (un-named in 2011) to the top of Peaking Ridge. This loop took us just over 2 hours.

10 Involution, Barnicoat Range
3 km east of Stoke

An honest workout is rewarded with great views and a long, long downhill.

Grade 3+
Time 2 hours
Distance 11 km
Track conditions 30% gravel road, 10% 4WD track, 60% single track
How to get there Ride up Marsden Road, off Main Road, Stoke, to the quarry gates.

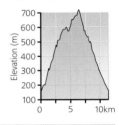

Route description
From the quarry gates, take the little bridge on your right, then, after 100 metres, take another bridge on your right. Now climb on a good 4WD track for around 40 minutes. Hang a left when you hit the ridge and follow the small signs along a humpy ridge, climbing some more to get to a high point, where there is an 'Involution' sign. This is a good place to regroup with your riding buddies.

Involution is a lot of fun, but dial it back the first time down – it's easy to overcook some of the corners. When you reach a 4WD track, go straight across it and you'll find a bit more single track. The second time you roll onto a 4WD track, it's all over rover, and you'll be rolling on down to the gate beside Marsden Road.

Notes Please don't ride this track when wet.

Involution is now one of the longest and most popular tracks in Nelson.   Jonathan Kennett

Nine Other Rides

Puponga Farm Park ★ ☆ ☆ ☆

This isn't a long ride, but if you're checking out Cape Farewell, it's worth it.

Grades 3–4 **Time** 1 hour **Distance** up to 10 km

From Collingwood, Golden Bay, drive up to Farewell Spit and park at the Paddle Crab Cafe. Here you can buy a DOC pamphlet on the area, which shows the tracks that are open for riding. Backtrack a little to Puponga and head along Wharariki Road, up to the woolshed in Puponga Farm Park and then east to Pillar Point Lighthouse. From there, head up past the high point, Old Man (155 m) and soon after, veer left and drop down to a farm track on Triangle Flat that leads back to the cafe at the spit.

You can also explore further west on the Green Hills Route. After crossing Green Hills Stream, the track splits in two – go right (the left branch is poxy!).

Kahurangi Lighthouse ★ ★ ☆ ☆

This is a remote and beautiful part of New Zealand. The cycling is on gravel roads, beaches and a little bit of single track.

Grade 2 **Time** 1–2 days **Distance** Up to 120 km return

Maps Refer to NZTopo50 BN22 Kahurangi Point and BN23 Paturau River and/or drop in to The Quiet Revolution Cycle Shop in Takaka to get information and a pamphlet of rides in the Bay.

Ride north out of Collingwood, Golden Bay, past Pakawau, then west over to the remote and beautiful West Coast beaches. The roads are quiet, and generally you can have the beaches and glorious sunsets all to yourself. An excellent overnight trip is to head south from the Anatori River mouth to the lighthouse at Kahurangi Point. To get there, you must cross Big River one hour either side of low tide.

There is an old farmhouse to stay at hidden in the trees 1 km east of the lighthouse. The farmhouse is managed by DOC and has beds but no cooking equipment.

You should also drop into the DOC office in Takaka for hut tickets if you intend staying overnight.

Ye Old Mill Road ★ ☆ ☆ ☆

A pleasant uphill workout to a good lookout over Golden Bay.

Grade 2+ **Time** 1 hour **Distance** 6 km return
Start from a nondescript driveway 19 km northwest of Takaka, Golden Bay, on Highway 60. Four hundred metres after passing Tukurua Road on the way to Collingwood, you'll reach two letterboxes on the left near the top of a small hill. This is where the ride starts.

Take the driveway 10 metres before the letterboxes and follow the gravel 4WD track up into the hills for half an hour. Regroup at the park bench (290 m) for a brilliant vista of Golden Bay.

You can continue climbing for another few minutes to a 'Private Property' sign before turning around and enjoying the downhill. After about 10 minutes downhill, at the end of a long flattish section, take a sharp left-hander for a more challenging descent. Later, after crossing a ford, just go straight ahead, then turn right at the major gravel road. This leads back to Highway 60, 1 km west of where you started.

Gibbs Hill ★ ★ ☆ ☆

This ride through Abel Tasman National Park is only open to cyclists from 1 May to 1 October.

Grade 3 **Time** 3–4 hours **Distance** 23-km loop
From Takaka in Golden Bay, drive out towards Totaranui. On the far side of Wainui Bay, turn left onto McShane Road and drive to the road end.

From the road end car park, follow the Inland Track north to the first saddle, then turn hard right and settle in for 20-minutes of steep climbing. Near the next small saddle 100 metres from the top, a narrow track leads off to the summit trig.

The downhill from that second saddle to Totaranui is both fast and dangerous. You've really got to keep your wits about you and control your speed. After 1 km, there is a sharp left and the track becomes quite rough in places. It takes 30 minutes to get from the top down to Totaranui – one of Golden Bay's most popular camping grounds. From there, it's a spectacular 13-km dirt road ride back to the Wainui Bay car park.

This ride has only been opened up to cyclists as a trial. Please support the cause – respect other users and avoid when wet. Take NZTopo50 map BN25 Totaranui.

Kill Devil and Waingaro Forks ★ ★ ☆ ☆

This tough ride, 18 km south of Takaka has fantastic scenery, and countless technical challenges, with 57 switchbacks packed into a 900-m climb.

Grade 5   **Time** 4–8 hours   **Distance** 24 km return
Buy a copy of NZTopo50 BP24 Takaka before your ride.

From Upper Takaka, head north for 6 km, turn left at Uruwhenua Road and head south for almost 3 km to the signposted start of the track.

Follow a farm road for a few hundred metres to the base of the hills, then triangle markers will lead you across a stream and up a steep spur on a challenging single track. After about 2 hours of riding and walking, you'll reach the top of the climb at almost 1000 m. The next part of the ride involves quite a bit of walking – most people turn back at this point.

Riordans Hut is still another 1–2 hours away. Ride along the rocky ridge for 4 km until you reach a '15 min' signpost. This is the turn-off to the historic hut, 1 km away. Alternatively, you can carry on straight ahead and down to the Waingaro Forks Hut. The track to the forks is harder than anything you've ridden so far, but it leads to a beautiful spot, and we wished we'd had longer to spend there: a night would have been great.

Most people just go to Riordans Hut though. From there, take in the views before tackling the short climb back to the ridge and then the tough descent back to Uruwhenua Road.

Descending to Riordans Hut.

Andrew McLellan

Canaan Downs ★ ★ ☆ ☆

There are several biking options at Canaan Downs. The grade 4, 13-km loop we describe here is a fine introduction to this vast area.

Grades 2–4   **Time** 3–4 hours   **Distance** Up to 24 km

Follow the directions to the top of the Rameka Track (see Rameka Track on page 182). At the car park at the end of Canaan Road, there is a large information board showing the tracks around Canaan Downs. The biggest loop heads up past the start of the Rameka Track to Wainui Saddle (3 km). From the saddle, head to your right to a fence 50 metres away. Veer left and follow markers on a long sidle track that dips in and out of creeks as it heads south and gradually downhill to Gold Creek.

From the bottom, follow markers across Gold Creek and up to a lookout at the highest point on Canaan Downs. After taking in the view, start the tricky downhill that zigzags through the Downs and across to the gravel Canaan Road. On the way back to the car park, watch out for a new track on your left that provides a car-free option for your return.

There is also a grade-3 loop starting from the car park, which takes about an hour.

Marble Mountain ★★☆☆

You get one chance a year to ride the Marble Mountain. Don't miss it!

Grade 4-   **Time** 2–3 hours
Distance 35 km

Each April, landowners above Kaiteriteri give permission for an event to be run over their properties. After skirting around the coast for a while, the route climbs farm tracks and crosses some funky marble limestone landscape before diving back down to Kaiteriteri. See www.marblemountainclassic.org.nz

Jonathan Kennett

Bruce's surprise tackle. Rugby was the winner on the day.

Rabbit Island ★★☆☆

This sandy forested island has two elements: a small area of spaghetti-like mountain bike tracks, and a new track crossing the island and connecting with a ferry to Mapua.

Grade 1+   **Time** 30 minutes or 1 hour   **Distance** 2 km or 7 km

Rabbit Island is a flat, forested recreation reserve about 40-minutes drive west of Nelson. You can also ride there from Nelson on the Nelson/Tasman Trails, which is a part of the New Zealand Cycle Trail project. The island's a great place for a picnic at the beach.

The Tasman District Council have built a 2-km network of easy mountain bike tracks here – great for kids and beginner mountain bikers. There is a mapboard but no signs on the tracks, so riding can become a bit aimless.

Also, in 2011, a wide, easy 7-km track was built from the entrance to the island, across to a ferry landing, where a ferry called the Flat Bottomed Fairy can take you across to Mapua village for an ice cream.

Aniseed Valley ★ ★ ★ ☆

There are three, good back-country trips heading up the Aniseed Valley from a large picnic area.

Get a copy of NZTopo50 BQ26 Nelson before your ride. Head south from Richmond on Highway 6 for 4 km then turn left at the 'Hackett Picnic Area' sign. After another 12 km on Aniseed Valley Road, you will reach Roding River Recreation Reserve. This is the starting point for the following three rides:

Whispering Falls

Grade 2 **Time** 1 hour **Distance** 8 km return

Cross the bridge and pass the 'Hackett Hut 2 hours' sign. After 30 metres of single track, veer left onto a gravel road and follow it up valley for 10 minutes to a swing bridge (ignore a climb off to the left). Once across the swing bridge, follow a grade-2 single track to a signposted fork. Keep left to head up to a bridge, from where you can view the Whispering Falls.

Hackett Hut

Grade 3 **Time** 2 hours **Distance** 12 km return

On the way to Whispering Falls, there is a signposted fork where you can veer right and ride a grade-3 track to Hackett Hut, 30 minutes away. There is one short-ish steep climb and descent to tackle before reaching the hut at an idyllic picnic spot. The hut lies just across a stream. Head back the same way.

Browning Hut

Grade 5 **Time** 3–4 hours **Distance** 18 km return

From Hackett Hut (or from the signposted fork 10 minutes before Hackett Hut), a difficult grade-5 track leads to Browning Hut. It's one of those pay-before-you-ride type tracks. In other words, there's lots of bike carrying on the way up, but riders who have a few trials skills will love the ride back down. Hot tip: This ride is only worth doing after a long dry spell.

These tracks are popular with elderly walkers and families; treadle with care.

Marlborough

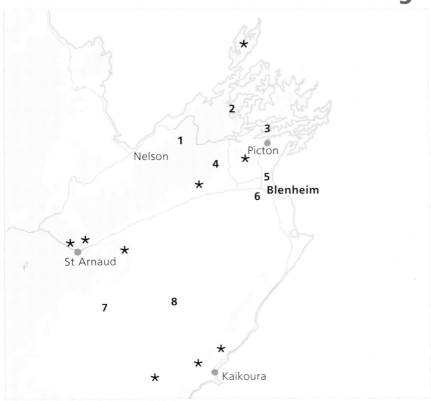

1 **Maungatapu Track**
2 **Nydia Bay**
3 **Queen Charlotte Track**
4 **Wakamarina**
5 **Whites Bay – Mt Robertson Loop**
6 **Wither Hills**
7 **Rainbow**
8 **Molesworth**
★ Plus nine other rides

MARLBOROUGH HIGHLIGHTS

Marlborough is a back country track rider's dream. Queen Charlotte Track, Wakamarina and Nydia Bay are some of the best single track adventures in the country, although, being clay based, are best avoided when wet. Further south, the Rainbow and Molesworth road trips cover the sort of BIG country that helps put city life in perspective.

1 Maungatapu Track

Pelorus Bridge to Nelson

This popular 'short cut' to Nelson crosses the Bryant Range on a steep 4WD pylon track. It's now better than ever because it's been closed to motorised through traffic and upgraded on the Nelson side.

Grade 3+
Time 4–6 hours
Distance 35 km

Track conditions 20% sealed road, 45% gravel road, 35% 4WD track

Maps Refer to any good road map, or NZTopo250 13 Nelson.

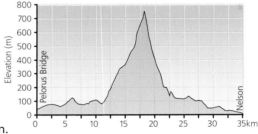

How to get there Pelorus Bridge is 53 km from Picton via Queen Charlotte Drive and 57 km from Nelson via Highway 6.

Route description

Turn west off Highway 6 at Pelorus Bridge and ride up Maungatapu Road. There are two major forks in the road – both are well signposted. The gravel road turns into a 4WD track 12 km from the highway and climbs steadily out of the Pelorus Valley. Carry on straight ahead at a four-way intersection. The last few kilometres up to Maungatapu Saddle (740 m) are very steep and, depending on the condition of your legs, may be unridable in places.

At the saddle, check your brakes before heading straight down past the 'Water Catchment Area' sign on an even steeper 4WD track.

The track is in fine condition as it heads down into the Maitai Valley. Don't take any of the turn-offs to pylons – stick to the main track. A long way down,

Matt Gerstenberger on his way to Nelson, Maungatapu Track.   Jeff Lyall

when you think you are at the bottom of the hill, the track splits in two, and you must turn right to follow an obvious 4WD track up a steep but short hill.

After passing the Maitai Reservoir and climbing another minor hill, you coast down into the Maitai Valley again. Follow the valley road for about 10 km, then turn right at the first intersection in Nelson to go to the town centre.

Notes Pelorus Bridge has a shop/cafe and camping ground.

2 Nydia Bay ★ ★ ★

ADVANCED

96 km northwest of Blenheim

If this ride weren't so hard to get to, it would be one of the most popular technical rides in the country. If you've got great riding skills and an eye for fine scenery, you'll love it.

Grade 4

Time 4–7 hours

Distance 34 km

Track conditions 25% 4WD track, 75% single track

Maps Take Parkmap Marlborough Sounds.

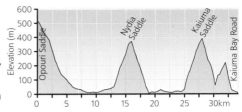

How to get there Head 26 km northeast from Rai Valley on Opouri Road to the top of Opouri Saddle (500 m). If shuttling this ride, we recommend you have someone in your group who would be happy riding the much shorter Archers Track (see below) then driving to the finish of the Nydia to pick you up.

Route description

From Opouri Saddle, experienced single-track riders can head down the gnarly Opouri Saddle Track to the right, while intermediate riders should descend via Tennyson Inlet Road. At the bottom, turn right and cruise 3 km to Tennyson Inlet settlement. Carry on around the bay to the start of the Nydia Bay Track.

This rock- and root-riddled track will lead you over Nydia Saddle (370 m) and down to Nydia Bay. At the far end of the bay, head inland through farm paddocks, then up and over a second saddle, Kaiuma (387 m). Overall, the ride is technical and rewarding. If you can average 7 km per hour, you'll be doing well. Part of the track follows the route of a 1910 timber railway line.

The track finishes on Kaiuma Bay Road, a gravel road 23 km from Highway 6 and another 3 km from Canvastown.

Notes In dry weather, it's 98% ridable north to south, much less from south to north. In wet weather, it's mostly unridable either way. Intermediate riders will enjoy this track more in the reverse direction from the above description.

There's a groovy backpackers' hostel and DOC lodge at Nydia Bay but no shops.

Opouri Saddle Track and Archers Track   ★ ★ ☆ ☆

INTERMEDIATE ADVANCED

Grades 3–4   **Time** 2–3 hours   **Distance** 16 km return

Following the how-to-get-there instructions above, to Opouri Saddle, either ride the technical, grade 4 downhill single track (signposted 'Opouri Saddle Track 3 km', on your right) or cruise down Tennyson Inlet Road. The track rejoins the road just before the bottom of the hill. A minute later, turn north onto Archers Road and follow it for 6 km to Penzance Bay.

Now follow the grade 3 Archers single track around to Deep Bay and beyond. Eventually the single track turns into a 4WD forestry road that goes through to Elaine Bay.

John Randal finding his roots, Nydia Bay.

Simon Kennett

Return to Penzance Bay the same way and back up to Opouri Saddle (500 m) via the track (Grade 4 uphill) or the road.

3 Queen Charlotte Track ★ ★ ★ ★

INTERMEDIATE

Picton, Marlborough Sounds

This is one of the longest single tracks in the country. Add to that lovely coastal scenery, good cafes and accommodation stops along the way and a brilliant beech forest section at the end, and you have a recipe for one of the best weekend rides in New Zealand.

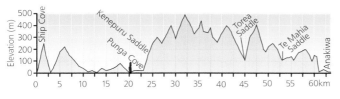

Stunning! Started at Pung cove. Beautiful ride. Lots of really steep climbs but all ridable. Rode back on the road from Anakiwa - Picton.

Grade 3+   **Time** 2–3 days   **Distance** 63–86 km

Track conditions 2% gravel road, 96% single track, 2% unridable

Maps   Refer to Parkmap Marlborough Sounds.

When to ride   The northern third of the track, from Ship Cove to Punga Cove/ Kenepuru Saddle (much of it on private land) is closed to mountain bikes during the peak walking season – 1 December to 28 February. The track is best ridden when dry.

Track access pass   You need a $12 four-day pass to cross the private land on the Queen Charlotte Walkway; this pass pays for track maintenance. It can be purchased from several places listed on the landowners website (www.qctlc.com), including the Picton I-Site and several businesses along the track.

Other users   This track is very popular with walkers – be ready for them to appear around any corner.

Accommodation   Punga Cove resort, phone (03) 579 8561; Portage hotel resort, phone (03) 573 4309; Portage Bay shop, phone (03) 573 4445; Te Mahia resort, phone (03) 573 4089. There are also many good camping areas. There is a shop and camping ground at Momorangi Bay, 9 km from Anakiwa on Queen Charlotte Drive, en route to Picton.

How to get there   Catch the Beachcomber, phone (03) 573 6175 and www.mailboat.co.nz, or Arrow Water Taxi, phone (03) 573 8229, from Picton to Ship Cove. Or you can get dropped off/picked up at any one of several bays along the way to shorten your trip. The trip costs $58 per adult plus $5 for your bike and $5 for bag transfers.

Route description

The first 26 km of the track to Punga Cove (Camp Bay) is generally quite ridable and fills the first day nicely. Either start from Ship Cove, or 3 km along the track at Resolution Bay. DOC have upgraded the track from Resolution Bay, so we recommend you start from there, especially if it's wet, or you don't like semi-ridable up-hills.

From Punga Cove (Camp Bay), things get hillier, and many riders choose to avoid the middle section by riding along the road from Kenepuru Saddle to Portage or Te Mahia. If you stick to the track, be aware that it's very exposed in places (i.e., it has awesome views) and drinking water is scarce. Those who take the road generally make it back to Picton on the second day; those who go over the top often stop at Te Mahia for the night and finish the ride the next day.

The last section from Te Mahia to Anakiwa (the Anakiwa Track) is biking at its best – exhilarating single track through beautiful native forest.

Picton is 23 km from Anakiwa via Queen Charlotte Drive; a meandering and scenic route that rates as one of the best sections of road riding in the country.

Another beautiful day on the Queen Charlotte.   Andy Cotgreave

Notes The percentage of this track that is unridable increases dramatically when wet. A DOC survey found that while most people are happy to share the track with bikes, they don't appreciate large groups of bikers – spare a thought when planning your trip. Also, DOC are steadily making improvements to this track – it's nowhere near as hard as it was in the 1990s.

5 Wakamarina ★ ★ ★ ★ *Check this one out if you can!*

25 km northwest of Blenheim

We suggest two options for this once-busy goldminers' track: a fun trip to the tops and back or the full hardcore crossing of the Richmond Range from Onamalutu to Canvastown.

Grades 3 or 5-

Time 2 or 5 hours

Distance 13 km or up to 35 km

Track conditions 5% sealed road, 45% gravel road, 45% single track, 5% unridable

Maps Take NZTopo50 BQ27 Rai Valley or Parkmap Mt Richmond.

When to ride In 2011, access to the southern end of the track was open in the weekends only, due to logging.

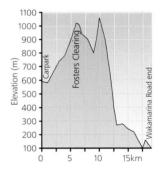

Other users Trampers

How to get there From Renwick (just west of Blenheim), follow Highway 6 for 4 km. Then turn left onto Northbank Road and after 5 km veer right onto Onamalutu Road. You will pass Onamalutu Reserve and after another 7 km of climbing hang a sharp left turn at the 'Wakamarina Track' sign. The road end is 100 metres away.

Route description

The two great options for the Wakamarina are:

There and back Ride up to Fosters Clearing for the views and an endorphine hit. DOC has upgraded this section of track, so it is now grade 3 when dry. There is a 10-minute, grade 4+ diversion to Fosters Hut, where the views are breathtaking. Head back the same way. That will take 2–3 hours. Some fit locals lengthen this ride by starting from Onamalutu Reserve.

The full crossing Ride up to Fosters Clearing for your first rest stop (there is a water supply at the clearing). Next, descend and sidle about 2 km before walking to the top of the crossing (at 1066 m). This is rugged country, and you will have earned every metre of elevation. Now fine-tune your brakes and clear

Early winter on the Wakamarina.   Martin Langley

your mind in preparation for switchback-city Arizona. You're about to descend over 800 m in 2.5 km of twisting, turning single track.

Near the bottom, turn right at the turn-off to 'Stone Huts'. Shortly after, you'll reach Devils Creek Hut turn-off. Pop down for a squizz at the hut, then sidle down the Wakamarina River Valley. Four kilometres on, after the Doom Creek Hut site, veer left down to the footbridge, cross Doom Creek and veer left again. The Wakamarina Road end is 2 km further on. From there, it's 15 easy km to Canvastown.

Notes This track has a clay surface – avoid when wet.

There's a motor camp in the Wakamarina Valley, 10 km before Canvastown. Canvastown itself has a pub, and that's it; it's half an hour's ride to Pelorus Bridge or Havelock.

5 Whites Bay – Mt Robertson Loop ★ ★ ★ ★

ADVANCED

20 km northeast of Blenheim

Most of this ride involves physically and technically challenging single-track riding through native bush.

Grade 4+

Time 2–3 hours

Distance 12–26 km

Toughest climb I've ever done! Ridable though! The descent is worth the hard climb.

Track conditions 10% sealed road, 3% 4WD track, 87% single track

Maps Take NZTopo50 BQ29 Waikawa.

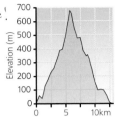

How to get there From Blenheim, take Highway 1 north to Tuamarina, turn east and go past Rarangi to Whites Bay.

Route description

Park your car at the historic cable station in Whites Bay, then ride back to the road and north up the hill for 2.5 km. On the left side of the road, 50 metres past the crest of the hill, is a pylon track signposted 'Whites Bay Loop Track'. That's where you want to head.

Expect some bike carrying towards the top of Mt Robertson.

Zane Smith

After 1 km, you'll pass a pylon and then the track narrows to single track. It takes about an hour to ride and push your bike to a signposted fork on top of the ridge.

From there, you have two choices, carry on up to Mt Robertson or turn left and drop down to Whites Bay.

If heading for the top, go straight ahead, and after roughly half an hour, the track will become steep and loose in places. You'll feel the burn as you ascend the 1036-m Mt Robertson. When you reach a radar station, you're there.

Back down at the fork in the track, you should head south and follow a tight squiggly downhill through native bush. At the end, follow a pylon track down to a fork, turn sharp left and you'll soon reach the road between Whites Bay and Rarangi. Turn left to return to your car, 2 km away.

Notes You'll need to carry plenty of water as there are no streams along the way, and this region can be extremely hot and dry.

6 Wither Hills ★★
Blenheim

This mountain bike park in Blenheim will keep you fit and prepare you for the longer trek to Mt Vernon (see below).

Grades 2–4

Time Up to 3 hours
Distance 5–20 km
Track conditions 100% single track

Maps Pick up a copy of the Marlborough District Council's Wither Hills map from the informaton centre at the railway station.

How to get there Ride south out of Blenheim on Maxwell Road (it becomes Taylor Pass Road). The Wither Hills Mountain Bike Park is well signposted 2 km south of the hospital. It's 1 km south of the main walkway car park. The council has developed a track from central Blenheim along the Taylor river bank out to the mountain bike tracks car park; it's a lot more fun than the road.

Route description
At the mountain bike car park, there is a mapboard that shows all the main tracks. The layout is very

clear, so it's easy to plan your trip. Try starting off with the 'Main Track'. It's a 20-minute, grade-2 loop that climbs to the top of the park and back. You'll then know what the whole area looks like.

Next, move onto the grade-3+ technical single track. It's narrow and off camber in places. There are many bus stops beside the main track and a technical downhill in the main valley.

Wither Hills.   Simon Kennett

Mt Vernon Loop

INTERMEDIATE

Grade 3-   **Time** 1–3 hours   **Distance** Approx 15 km

This ride climbs almost to the top of Wither Hills just south of Blenheim. From near the centre of town, follow Redwood Street south right to the last house. There you'll see a sign introducing the ride. Follow the markers up to the top of Mt Vernon (422 m) for some great views.

Form the top of Mt Vernon, either carry on around the Taylor View Track to the Wither Hills Mountain Bike Park or head downhill via the Cob Cottage Track followed by a cruise along Mapp Track back to Redwood Street. The tracks described here are nearly all farm tracks.

Notes Mt Vernon is extremely exposed to the elements – go prepared for freezing conditions.

7 Rainbow ★ ★ ★

Hanmer to St Arnaud

The Rainbow follows a pylon road through mountainous country, along the original stock route from Marlborough to Canterbury. It's now one of New Zealand's best mountain bike touring rides.

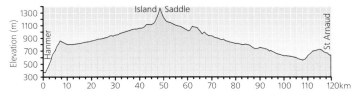

Grade 3 **Time** 1–2 days **Distance** 120 km

Track conditions 10% sealed road, 70% gravel road, 20% 4WD track

Maps Take NZTopo250 18 Murchison.

Landowners The Rainbow Road is open for a toll of $2 per bike between 26 December and 25 April, payable at the Rainbow Cob Homestead, near the northern end of Rainbow Road. Outside this season, permission to cross Rainbow Station must be obtained from Star Holdings Ltd, phone (03) 545 7600.

Route description

Hammer out of Hanmer up Clarence Valley Road. Cycle over Jacks Pass (869 m) and down to the Clarence River Valley, then turn left onto Tophouse Road. From here it is 32 corrugated kilometres to the turn-off to Lake Tennyson (a 3-km detour). Lake Tennyson is as exposed to bad weather as it is beautiful. You may want to camp near the Clarence River Bridge or even head over Island Saddle (8 km further on) to Coldwater Creek where there are more pleasant camping areas. The last few kilometres up to Island Saddle (1372 m) are steep and unrelenting, but even if you walk, the rewards of a great downhill and excellent views make it worthwhile.

About 5 km on from Island Saddle and 400 metres before reaching the Wairau River, a 4WD track on your left leads to a hut 400 metres away, which can't be seen from the road. It has four bunks, a toilet and space for camping next to it.

From Island Saddle, it is another 50 km passing through tussock, then beech forest, to Highway 63. Continuing down the valley, there are several fords that may be impassable after heavy rain. About half an hour after crossing Rough Creek, veer left at the 'Rainbow Forest Park' sign and climb the last few kilometres to the highway.

Simon struggles across a flooded ford, Rainbow Valley.

Once you reach Highway 63, it's an easy 10 km west to St Arnaud where you will find the tranquil Lake Rotoiti, a general store, a motor camp, a backpackers' hostel and lots of sandflies.

Notes Doing the ride in the direction we've described is great for linking up with the Molesworth ride (see below), but if you do this ride the opposite way, from St Arnaud to Hanmer, there is often a tail wind, making it an excellent day's riding.

Another option is to tie this in with the St James Cycle Trail – making it a 3 day ride from St Arnaud to Hanmer.

Go well equipped and be prepared for snow at any time of year. No fires are allowed in the precious remnants of native bush north of Coldwater Creek. Leave all gates as found.

8 Molesworth ★ ★ ☆ ☆

INTERMEDIATE

Blenheim to Hanmer

This ride passes through the country's largest farm, Molesworth Station and runs alongside the massive Inland Kaikoura mountains.

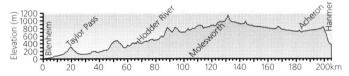

Grade 3   **Time** 2–4 days   **Distance** 205 km

Track conditions 15% sealed road, 85% gravel road

Maps Take NZTopo250 18 Murchison and 19 Kaikoura.

Landowners Molesworth Station is open to the public from 7am to 7 pm, 28 December to 3 April. Outside this time, permission is required from DOC South Marlborough Area Office, phone (03) 572 9100.

The station is closed in winter because of deep snow and sometimes in summer because of high fire risk. Recently it's also been closed over Easter for a goose shoot.

Route description

From Blenheim, ride south on Maxwell Road and head over Taylor Pass on a gravel road. This takes you to the main sealed road heading southwest up the Awatere Valley.

After about an hour's cycling, the road climbs high above the Awatere River before dropping down to Jordan. There are several newly sealed stretches, but the road is still very hilly – try to travel light and pace yourself.

At the Hodder River Bridge (72 km from Blenheim), there is a public toilet and some good trees to rest under on a hot day. Cyclists and mountain climbers often camp here for the night. There is also a reasonable camping spot among trees further on near Upcot. Not far past Upcot, you must tackle the formidable Upcot Saddle – a steep, crank-bending, knee-grinding, granny-gear climb.

From Hodder River, it takes 3–5 hours of riding to reach the old Molesworth Homestead, which has a pleasant DOC camping area (but no safe water supply) and is the entry point to the massive Molesworth Station. Within Molesworth Station, camping is only permitted here and at the historic Acheron Accommodation House, a good 5 hours away.

After climbing to the top of Wards Pass, it's downhill all the way to the Acheron River. From Isolated Saddle, undulate along to the Acheron Accommodation House, at the confluence of the Acheron and Clarence rivers, where there is more good camping and a drinkable water supply.

It's about an hour's cycling from Acheron Accommodation House to the Hanmer Springs turn-off. Those who are heading back to Blenheim via the Rainbow Valley (see above) can carry on straight ahead at this fork. Otherwise, cycle over Jollies Pass down to Hanmer about an hour away. Hot pools, ice creams and a camping ground await at the bottom of a long fast downhill.

Notes This is BIG country. Gigantic hills and valleys are guaranteed to make even the most confident rider feel very, very small. Take a gas cooker as open fires are not allowed on Molesworth Station. Also take an extra water bottle; summer temperatures often rise into the 30s, and the river water is not always palatable. Leave all gates as you find them.

Go well equipped and be prepared for snow any time of year. Further information can be obtained from DOC in Renwick, phone (03) 572 9100.

Due reverence should be paid to Kennet Peak between Upcot and Molesworth (even if it is spelt wrong).

Nine Other Rides

D'Urville Island   ★ ★ ★ ☆

This remote island perched in the northwestern tip of Marlborough Sounds is a great place for a few days' holiday. The riding is technically easy but requires some fitness.

Grade 2   **Time** 2 cruisy days   **Distance** 53+ km
Maps Take NZTopo50 BP28 Te Aumiti and BN28 Port Hardy.

From Rai Valley, halfway between Picton and Nelson, head north to French Pass, at the end of a windy 60-km road (it takes 2 hours to drive). From there, a 10-minute boat trip gets you to D'Urville Island. Contact French Pass Sea Safaris (www.seasafaris.co.nz), phone (03) 576 5204, or French Pass Sea Link, (03) 576 5337, to book a trip across.

From Kapowai Bay, follow Main Road up onto the spine of D'Urville. After about 45 minutes climbing, turn right. It's another 2 hours to the D'Urville Island Community Hall – an ideal lunch spot and base for exploring.

In the afternoon, head west to Greville Harbour. If you appreciate good views but don't like hard climbs, stop just past the bush edge. The sunsets from here can be stunning. Return to the hall for the night.

The next morning, ride up to Mt Ears for more great views as far as the lower North Island.

In the afternoon, ride south from the hall for 1 km before turning left onto a 4WD track signposted 'Wilderness Resort'. This track follows power poles down to Catherine Cove. A few hundred metres from the bottom, there is a fork in the track – turn right. Then, after another 100 metres, turn left.

At Catherine Cove, you can catch the boat back to French Pass or stay the night and enjoy swimming, short walks and the fine restaurant.

The trip described here is only 53 km long, so you'll have time to explore.

There is accommodation at French Pass, D'Urville Island Community Hall in the middle of the island, Greville Harbour (DOC house) and the Wilderness Resort at Catherine Cove. Camping is also available at French Pass and Catherine Cove. Accommodation can be booked through French Pass Sea Safaris.

Notes There is a total fire ban on D'Urville. Most of the 4WD tracks on the island end up on private land. Check with your transport provider to the island if you plan to explore beyond the trip described above.

Mt Patriarch   ★ ★

Another essential trip for mountain biking peak baggers.

Grade 3   **Time** 4–6 hours   **Distance** 66 km return

Maps Refer to Parkmap Mt Richmond.

About 4 km north of Renwick on Highway 6, turn left (just north of the Wairau River Bridge) and follow Northbank Road for 33 km, to Top Valley Road. In 2011 logging was restricting access to weekends only.

Ride up Top Valley Road for 6 km, turn left onto Staircase Stream Road and climb through forest, then alpine scrub for 12 km to the Lake Chalice car park.

From the car park, continue for another 12 km to the road end on the flanks of Mt Patriarch. At an altitude of 1460 m, there are stunning views of the Wairau Valley and inland Marlborough.

You can leave your bike and walk the last 3 km to the summit of Mt Patriarch (1656 m) by negotiating a demanding rocky ridge and then sidling across a shingle slope. The route is marked with poles, and there is a trig at the top. This is a very exposed area.

Waikakaho Track ★★☆☆

Also known as Linkwater Long Cut

This is the long way from Tuamarina (10 km north of Blenheim) to Linkwater. It is enjoyed by jungle riders who are willing to walk for the satisfaction of a technically demanding downhill.

Grade 4+ **Time** 4–6 hours **Distance** 33 km

Take NZTopo50 BQ28 Havelock and ride from Tuamarina (10 km north of Blenheim on Highway 1), west on Bush Road and then Kaituna–Tuamarina Road for 6 km. Turn north up the Waikakaho Valley gravel road and ride for another 12 km. Pass the farm buildings and continue for 3 km. The track starts on the left of the river soon after the road peters out (100 metres past a hay barn) and climbs steadily up a spur.

The track up to the saddle (800 m) is a granny-gear grind and will take 1–2 hours. Allow some extra time to check out the mining relics on the way up.

The following 2-km section along the top of the ride to Cullens bush edge is rutted, rooty and largely unridable. From here, follow the zigzag track down to the valley floor on the other side. If you plan to ride from north to south, this steep section will require a fair bit of bike carrying. From the valley floor, it's a further 5 km on sealed road to the Linkwater store.

Teetotal Trails ★★☆☆

Mountain biking isn't the main attraction at St Arnaud, but if you are there with a bike on a fine day, these tracks are worth riding.

Grades 2 and 4 **Time** 1–3 hours **Distance** Up to 35 km

Ride from St Arnaud towards Murchison for 1 km, then turn right at the 'Teetotal Mountain Bike Trails' sign. There is a car parking area 30 metres off the highway, but the sandflies there are terrible (better to ride from town and just keep moving).

The three main loops are:

Teetotal Flats Loop (5 km long, easy loop)
From the car park, follow the DOC signs around this easy loop. It twists across farmland, through a few stands of manuka and past a lake.

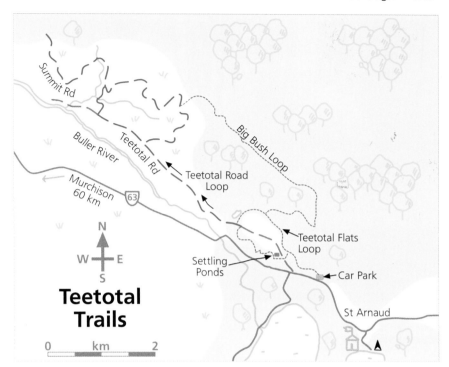

Teetotal Trails

Teetotal Road Loop (16 km, easy-ish loop)

This is a good trip for those who want to stretch their legs on an easy trail. Start with the first half of the Flats Loop Trail and then head west when you hit the farm road (it's signposted). At the far end of this loop, you can nip up the signposted 'Teetotal Summit' road for a decent workout and some good views. Give yourself up to half an hour for this return trip to the summit.

Big Bush Loop (13 km, difficult loop)

This loop also branches off the Flats Loop Trail and is well signposted. The initial climb is getting rutted out by 4WDs – you may have to walk a bit. After half an hour climbing, you should reach a subtle high point (856 m). Check your brakes and let the fun begin. But beware: the track becomes steep, fast and narrow!

When you hit Teetotal Road, turn left for the quick route back to St Arnaud or right to lengthen your ride by 5 km off-road. There are signposts to guide you back to the highway.

Michelle Ducat and Sarah Drake on the Teetotal Flats Loop Trail.

Beebys Knob ★ ★ ☆ ☆

Looking for a BIG hill to test your lungs and then your brakes? Then Beebys Knob is for you. The summit vista is spectacular!

Grade 4 **Time** 2–5 hours **Distance** 15+ km return

Head out of St Arnaud on Highway 63 towards Blenheim. After 8 km, turn left, then follow Tophouse Road for 800 metres; DOC signs show the bottom of the track on your right.

Hop over the gate by the signs and change down. This is a very tough 4WD track up to the tops at 1400 m (alongside the Beebys Knob TV transmitter). Beebys Hut is another 1.5 km beyond the Knob, descending along the ridge. We turned around at the hut, but you can carry on along the ridge for another 5 km before turning back.

Keep an eye out for 4WDs and other riders on the descent.

This ride is covered in one of DOC's two pamphlets about local MTB tracks, available from the St Arnaud information centre. Best avoided in winter (when it is likely to be under snow). Be prepared for freezing alpine conditions any time of the year. The 4WD vehicle access season is 1 December to 30 April.

Branch and Leatham Valleys   ★ ★ ☆ ☆

These two valleys 70 km west of Blenheim offer riders the chance to get into the base of some remote mountains without taking on anything particularly technical or mountainous.

Grade 2   **Time** ½–1½ days   **Distance** 30–95 km

Turn south off Highway 63 onto Leatham Road, 70 km west of Blenheim, and look for a place to park. Ride along the gravel Leatham Road for 7 km to the confluence of the Branch and Leatham rivers (a new footbridge over the Branch River was built in 2008). This spot is another option for parking.

There are 4WD tracks heading up both of these mountainous, bush-clad valleys. Allow half a day to explore the Branch Valley as far as Greigs Hut and back (a total of 30 km). From the hut, Tourist Track is ideal for those in search of their new maximum heart rate.

Give yourself a day to explore the Leatham Valley – it's over 50 km to the Lower Gordon Hut and back. The scenery is more of a mixed bag up this valley, with farmland early on, but it's spectacular up the top end. The track becomes unridable shortly after the hut.

Notes If you want to spend the weekend exploring these valleys, you can stay overnight at one of the huts (with a DOC hut pass/ticket) or camp at the confluence of the Branch and Leatham (7 km from Highway 63). Take NZTopo250 maps 18 Murchison and 19 Kaikoura.

Okiwi Bay–Half Moon Bay   ★ ☆ ☆ ☆

This is a good ride for locals looking for borderline granny gear climbing to push their fitness.

Grade 3   **Time** 4–5 hours   **Distance** 20-km loop

Okiwi Bay is 98 km south of Blenheim, or 31 km northeast of Kaikoura, and the track is signposted 'Okiwi Bay Walkway Tracks' on Highway 1.

The route is well signposted all the way up to a grassy saddle and fence line. A further 20 metres on, go straight through another fence opening (the gates have been removed) and head towards Kaikoura.

From here, just follow the main 4WD track through multiple fence lines down, up and then down again to Half Moon Bay and Highway 1. Turn left and ride the 7 km back on Highway 1 to Okiwi Bay.

This track is used mainly by hunters on 4x4 quad bikes, so it's a bit rutted.

David Drake negotiates a slip beyond Lower Gordon Hut, Leatham Valley.

Mt Fyffe ★★☆☆

Mt Fyffe is the pinnacle of hill climbing in New Zealand.

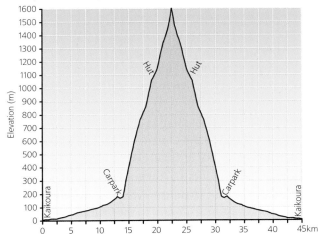

Grade 4   **Time** 3–5 hours   **Distance** 16 km return from the car park

Head out of Kaikoura on Ludstone Road, turn right onto Mt Fyffe Road, left at Postmans Road, then follow the DOC signs to a picnic area 12 km from town. There was a sign or two missing when we last did this, so a map came in handy.

From the car park, the 4WD track ahead climbs from 180 m to 1602 m in 8 cruel kilometres. There is a DOC hut shortly after the halfway mark (1100 m), beyond which the track deteriorates and a significant bike push is necessary (but only on the ascent).

The view from the top is fantastic, but it will get chilly up there, even on a fine day. Take extra clothes as well as food and water.

Walkers and 4WD vehicles regularly use this track.

Clarence Expedition ★★☆☆

25 km west of Kaikoura

Wedged between the Seaward and Inland Kaikoura Ranges, with a breathtaking mountainous landscape, good campsites and DOC huts, the Ka Whata Tu o Rakihouia Conservation Park provides great scope for exploration. Unfortunately, this is a there-and-back trip.

Grade 3+   **Time** 1–3 days   **Distance** 54–158 km

Maps NZTopo50 BT26 Mount Clear and BT27 Mount Northhampton are essential. Also check out the DOC pamphlet Clarence Visitor Information, from the Kaikoura I-Site, or www.doc.govt.nz

The track starts from the northern side of the Kahutara River Bridge (the topomap marks this incorrectly), on Highway 70, 25 km west of Kaikoura township. Almost straight away, you'll have to tackle the formidable climb up to Blind Saddle (1200 m).

On the way down the other side, you'll pass Tentpoles Hut (rough but quaint), some weird rock formations, and near the bottom, Warden Hut (12 bunks) and the nearby historic Bluff Dump Hut. Another kilometre down valley, on your left, you'll see an unusual, small hill. Behind it is hidden the historic Black Spur Hut.

After carrying on down valley for a few kilometres, you'll reach a signposted intersection. Continue straight ahead to the Clarence River (via a 200-m hill) where you'll find Seymour Hut (10 bunks) at Quail Flat.

From Quail Flat, beside the Clarence, follow the markers 20 km down the Clarence River Valley to Goose Flat Hut (6 bunks). You can also ride up the Clarence River Valley for the same distance (26 km) to the historic Willows Hut and the newer Palmer Hut (12 bunks).

After exploring as much as you like, head back out the way you came!

For more information, contact DOC in Renwick, phone (03) 572 9100. Access beyond the conservation area is currently verboten!

West Coast

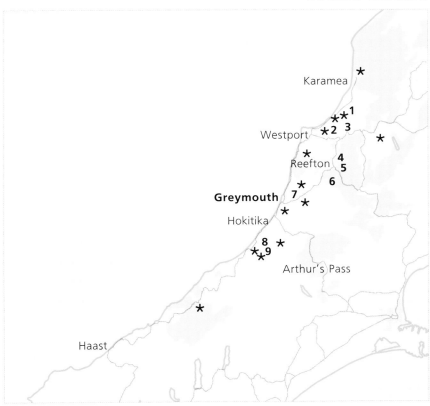

Karamea

Westport

Reefton

Greymouth

Hokitika

Arthur's Pass

Haast

1 **Charming Creek**
2 **Denniston Short Cut**
3 **The Old Ghost Road**
4 **Kirwans Track**
5 **Blacks Point**

6 **Big River**
7 **Croesus Track**
8 **Tunnels Tracks/Blue Spur**
9 **Kaniere Water Race**
★ Plus thirteen other rides

WEST COAST HIGHLIGHTS

The Ghost Road is the most exciting new track on the West Coast, but for a mountain bike base, you can't beat Reefton, which has several fantastic forest rides along old mining trails. This is just the beginning of what the West Coast has to offer. If the weather is fine, you'll think you're in mountain bike heaven.

1 Charming Creek ★ ★ ★ ☆

INTERMEDIATE

30 km northeast of Westport

This is a very cool ride through native bush on an old railway line. There are tunnels, bridges, waterfalls, huge trees, the works. You'll love it; we did!

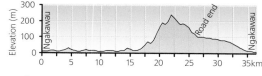

Grade 3
Time 3–5 hours
Distance 36 km

Track conditions
45% sealed road, 30% gravel road, 25% single track

Maps NZTopo50 BR21 Granity shows most of this ride.

How to get there From Westport, head north on Highway 67, past the small settlement of Granity, for 32 km to reach the small settlement of Ngakawau.

Route description

From Ngakawau, continue north on Highway 67 for 13 km before turning right to go through Seddonville. After another 3 km, turn right again at the 'Charming Creek' signpost. This road soon turns into gravel and climbs steadily among scrubby bush. Follow the main road, passing several turn-offs, to the road-end car park 10 km from Seddonville.

Carry on over a bridge and past old coal-mining machinery to a tunnel. Follow the old railway line track into the bush, and you'll soon reach a large mill shelter with a logbook to sign; it's a good place for a break. Navigation from here is a piece of cake. The track follows Charming Creek down through native forest, past historic sites (with shelters), through more tunnels and over swing bridges.

There are also lots of bumpy railway sleepers to rumble across, and bird life abounds in the area. The track ends at a car park at the edge of Ngakawau.

Notes Remember, parts of this track are also a walkway – give way to those on foot. There is still some of the original wooden centre rail (used for braking) along some of the old rail route – best try and avoid riding on it as it is fragile in places. If the weather is terrible, locals just ride from Ngakawau up the old rail line to the Seddonville Road end and back as this section is sheltered most of the way.

2 Denniston Short Cut

24 km northeast of Westport

This remote ride follows a pylon road through subtropical rainforest from Denniston Plateau to the Iron Bridge on the Buller River. It was pioneered by hardcore cycle tourers in the 1980s.

Grade 4

Time 4–6 hours

Distance 33 km

Track conditions 80% gravel road, 20% 4WD track

Maps Take NZTopo50 BR21 Granity and BR22 Lyell.

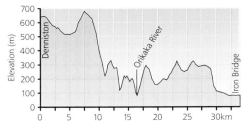

Landowners The ride passes through private land at the Buller River end. Contact DOC Westport for current access conditions. In 2011, you needed to phone the landowners on (03) 789 0098 for permission to pass through.

Other users Mining trucks , occasional 4WD vehicles and motorbikes

How to get there Ride 16 km northeast of Westport on Highway 67 to Waimangaroa. Then tackle the character-building 8-km climb to Denniston.

Route description

A maze of rough gravel roads and 4WD tracks traverses Orikaka State Forest to Iron Bridge on the Buller River.

From Denniston, ride inland on the main sealed road towards Burnetts Face. Do not turn right towards Sullivans Mine. The seal soon ends, and you descend to Burnett Stream. At the bottom, keep left on the main road and take the bridge across Burnett Stream. The gravel road will lead you past a burning coal mine, across a surreal 'Dr Who' type landscape and into the forest.

The mine (marked on the topomap) has been burning underground since it was accidentally lit in 1953. About 5 minutes past the mine, you'll cross Cedar Stream. Take the next right turn, about 200 metres away. It's a 4WD track that takes you up a short steep hill. When you're almost at the top, turn left at the four-way intersection. At the next fork, by the pylons, turn right then right again after 50 metres. Now just stay on the main gravel road and enjoy a fast downhill to the hut at Stevenson Stream.

Just after the top of the next steep hill, turn right down a gnarly gravel road to Mt William Stream. Cross it, climb steeply for another 15 minutes, then cruise along a short flat section to a T-intersection. Head left over a gate and down to Orikaka River (also known as Mackley River).

The Orikaka River is deadly when in flood. On the other side, tackle another 15-minute hill climb. At the top, navigation becomes tricky – there are pylon tracks and roads heading off all over the place. Two sets of pylons head south to the Buller River, while another set (the one you should follow) heads east towards New Creek.

At the first intersection after the hill climb, veer right (south) away from a tin hut. Cruise along on the main gravel road for 500 metres until you drop to a major T-intersection. Turn sharp left (back towards your pylons) and, within 50 metres, you'll start descending fast. Stay on the main road and, in 5–10 minutes, you'll reach an intersection by a 'Blue Duck' sign. Veer left and meander up to a saddle where you'll veer left again. Then cruise to Iron Bridge on Highway 6.

Notes Shuttling this ride is a real drag. It's better to get fit enough to do the whole 118-km loop or tackle it as part of a West Coast cycle tour.

Didn't get to ride – heard good things!

3 The Old Ghost Road ★ ★ ★ ☆

ADVANCED

Buller Gorge, 16 km northeast of Inangahua Junction

This ambitious track is one of the New Zealand Cycle Trail projects. When finished, it will rival the Heaphy Track as the best multi-day backcountry ride down under. From the Buller Gorge, it follows an old mining trail up to Lyell Saddle, traverses the tops and, in the future, will descend Mokihinui Gorge to the coast.

Grade 4
Time 1–3 days
Distance Up to 120 km return

Track conditions 100% single track

Maps Take NZTopo50 BR22 Lyell.

How to get there The ride starts from Lyell camping area beside Highway 6 in the Buller Gorge. That's 34 km west of Murchison and 16 km northeast of Inangahua Junction. There are no shops at Lyell.

Jonathan scoping out the route along the Lyell tops for the Old Ghost Road trail.

Route description

The Old Ghost Road team have already opened up the first 18 km to Lyell Saddle, following a mining track built in the 1880s to a hut built in 2011.

From the camping area, cross the Lyell Creek and ride up the other side of the valley (don't take the obvious walking track on the camping area side of the valley). The track follows a steady gradient up past Eight Mile Point (an old mining camp) to the saddle. The hut is 100 metres off the main track, a few minutes before the saddle. Allow 2–3 hours to reach the saddle.

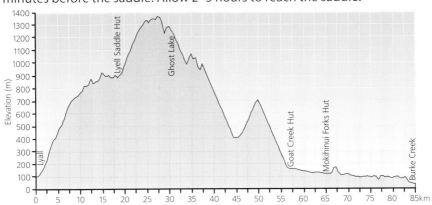

At the time of writing, the track team were forging ahead, from the saddle up onto the Lyell Range where they plan to build a second hut at Ghost Lake (a tarn at grid reference 301 834). The track will be above the bushline for most of the way – stunning views but also totally exposed to wind, rain and snow. We estimate this section will take 3–4 hours riding.

In the future, from the Ghost Lake, the track will descend to Mokihinui Forks Hut, 30 km away. Ghost Lake Hut to the forks will probably take 4–5 hours down, and 5–6 hours back up.

The rough track from Mokihinui Forks down the gorge to Seddonville is only 50% ridable (see below). Unless you have a raft in your backpack, or enjoy tramping with your bike, ride back out the way you came. The 18-km downhill from Lyell Saddle will make a fantastic end to your trip.

Notes Lyell camping area is a magnet for sandflies. For more information on trail building progress, check out www.nzcycletrail.com

Mokihinui Track

Be warned! The eastern half of the Mokihinui Gorge Track, between Mokihinui Forks and Seddonville, is in a dilapidated state. Meridian are proposing to dam the Mokihinui River, and in the process, drown this historic track and the beautiful gorge. Because of this, the track, which is planned to form the last 18 km of the Old Ghost Road, has not been upgraded. Until it is, we advise avoiding the eastern half.

Riding high above the stunning Mokihinui Gorge.

Jonathan Kennett

Heard good things about this - didn't get to ride.

*4 Kirwans Track ★ ★ ★ ☆

19 km northeast of Reefton

This rates as one of the most enjoyable masochistic ride
The track is so fascinating that the prolonged slog
direction is actually fun; views from the top are stunning,
downhill lasts for over an hour.

Grade 5+

Time 5–8 hours

Distance 26 km return

Track conditions 100% single track

Maps NZTopo50 BS21 Reefton and BS22 Shenondoah.

How to get there Head north out of Reefton on Highway 69 for almost 12 km, turn right onto Boatmans Road and then Capleston Road to ride another 6.5 km to the DOC road end.

Route description

Kirwans Track is signposted from the road end. Cross the rickety bridge and follow markers across the paddock to pick up the track as it enters forest. The track follows the valley for 4 km before climbing a massive hill to Kirwans Reward Mine at 1220 m.

About 10 minutes (1.5 km) from the road end, you have to turn right, cross a bridge, then scuttle through a tunnel to your left and scamper across a swing bridge. Next comes a mostly unridable section, but after half an hour, the track improves slightly. Frequent dismounts are still required.

Climb steadily for 2–3 hours to an intersection near the top. Follow the signposts to 'Kirwans Hut 30 min' (not to be confused with the 'Old Hut Site'). The last few hundred metres to the hut are unridable, but the views are great.

Then tighten those brakes up for a mega-technical downhill back the same way. Allow 1.5–2.5 hours to return to the car park.

Notes Watch out for walkers, as this is a popular tramping track. Sandflies at the road end have no mercy!

Over time, this track has suffered from erosion and sadly can no longer rate as a four-star ride.

ᴊacks Point ★ ★ ★ ★

tahu Valley, Reefton

INTERMEDIATE

ᴊeech forest, mining remains and vintage single track make this an excellent outing.

Grade 3

Time 1.5–4 hours

Distance 27 km

Track conditions 33% sealed road, 30% 4WD track, 37% single track

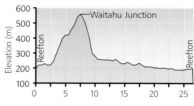

Maps Take NZTopo50 BS21 Reefton.

How to get there From Reefton, ride east on Highway 7 for 2 km before turning left at the 'Murray Creek' sign.

Route description

Hop over the gate and head up the mellower of the two climbs. Continue following the obvious old mining trail to 'Energetic Junction', turn left to 'Murray Creek Track' and 10 minutes later dip down to cross the bridge on to the true right of the stream.

Carry on to 'Cementown Junction' and past Chandlers mine to the top of the hill at Waitahu Junction. The climb is well graded and in good condition. For an easy ride, turn around here and head back the way you came.

The alternative descent to Waitahu Valley is described by DOC as a 'tramping track'. At the beginning of 2011, it was upgraded and a swing bridge put in over the Waitahu River, making the full loop a much more enjoyable trip for intermediate riders.

If you plan to continue down, turn right at the 'Waitahu Junction Tramping Track' signpost. This next section of track is grade 4 in places and requires your full attention! It drops down through the odd bog and washout, with some serious exposure to big falls.

Near the bottom, climb briefly (following the orange track markers) before taking a tight new descent to the swing bridge.

Across the river lies the Waitahu 4WD track. Turn left and follow this good track out to Gannons Road. From the end of the 4WD track, it's a cruisy 8-km ride back into Reefton.

Notes Avoid the area during high rainfall.

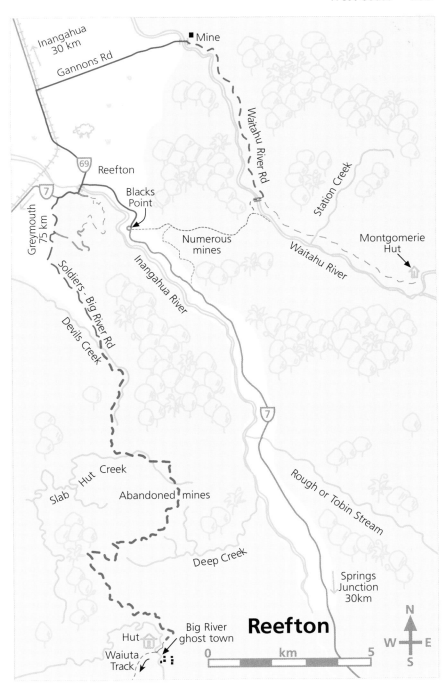

Inangahua
30 km

Gannons Rd

Mine

Waitahu River Rd

Station Creek

69

Reefton

7

Blacks
Point

Greymouth
75 km

Numerous
mines

Montgomerie
Hut

Inangahua River

Waitahu River

Soldiers - Big River Rd

Devils Creek

7

Rough or Tobin Stream

Slab   Hut   Creek

Abandoned   mines

Deep Creek

Springs
Junction
30km

Reefton

Hut

Big River
ghost town

Waiuta
Track

0   km   5

N
W   E
S

6 Big River ★ ★ ★ ☆

Reefton

Historic mining road + native bush scenery + gnarly single track likely to destroy numerous bike parts = a classic old-school ride.

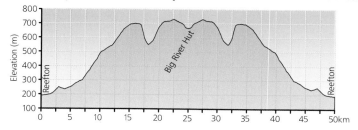

Grade 3   **Time** 4–8 hours   **Distance** 50 km return

Track conditions   A mix of gravel road and 4WD tracks

Maps   Refer to NZTopo50 BS21 Reefton and BT21 Waiuta.

Route description

Ride south from Reefton on Highway 7 and cross the Inangahua River bridge. After 1 km, turn left onto Soldiers Road. This soon becomes a gravel road and climbs up Devils Creek Valley for 9 km to the 'Alborn Coal Mine' car park. One hundred metres further on, Big River Road veers off to the left.

The ride continues for another 2–4 hours, through native bush, on a rocky but ridable 4WD track, to Big River (impassable in flood).

Various sites in this area were extensively mined for gold in the 1800s. Some old machinery remains and huge piles of mullock (waste rock) stand as testimony to the environmental effects of mining.

The luxurious Big River Hut ($10 per night) is perched about 50 metres above the river, overlooking the Big River township site and surrounding countryside. It's worth staying overnight to explore various side tracks and the abandoned gold workings. Remember, this is a 4WD track – give way to those with a smaller brain-to-weight ratio.

Waiuta Track Option

The walking track from Big River to Waiuta, a mining ghost town, is now open to cyclists! DOC did some major maintenance here in 2011. It's still 12 km of grade-4 riding: expect a fair bit of walking with some long sections of dream-like single track. From Waiuta, there are 10 km of gravel and 27 km of sealed road to ride on back to Reefton. Give yourself 2–4 hours to get to Waiuta and another hour and a half pedalling from there back to Reefton.

Simon swings into action over Waitahu River.

Simon Kennett

Heard good things - didn't get to ride

7 Croesus Track ★ ★ ★ ☆

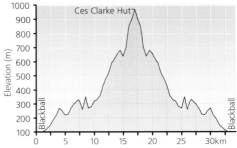

ADVANCED

Blackball, 25 km northeast of Greymouth

A big dose of rugged pre-cycling single track, up to the alpine zone, makes this one of New Zealand cycling's unpolished gems.

Grade 4+
Time 1 day
Distance 35 km return

Track conditions 30% gravel road, 70% primo single track

Maps To make sure you stay on route, take NZTopo50 BT20 Ahaura and BT19 Runanga.

Seasonal restrictions Because this track is so popular with walkers, it is closed to bicycles from 25 December to 25 January and during the Easter break.

How to get there Head northwest out of Blackball and follow Blackball Road for 6.5 km to the road end where the Croesus Track starts. It's signposted.

Route description

From the road end, an interesting old mining trail snakes through the forest. A few bits are rough and steep, but generally it is well graded and ridable – if it's dry! If it's wet, head somewhere else.

At a steady pace, it will take you 3–4 hours to reach Ces Clarke Hut, just above the bushline. The hut is lovely, and the views are stunning. After a wee rest, it's worth wandering up to Croesus Knob, 2 km away, for even better views, but the track up there is mostly unridable.

From the hut, the ride back down to Blackball is fantastic. Beautiful forest, challenging riding, good friends; what more could you ask for?

If you have time, it's worth making a diversion to Garden Gully Hut (a shack) and the abandoned mine beyond it. It is clearly signposted 3.5 km down from Ces Clarke Hut and offers great single-track riding.

Notes The place to stay in Blackball is the famous Formerly The Blackball Hilton.

8 Tunnels Tracks/Blue Spur ★ ★ ☆ ☆

Hokitika

INTERMEDIATE   ADVANCED

The Hokitika MTB Club has built a fun network of tracks on the Blue Spur Range, only 5 km ride from town. A couple of tunnels, a granite rock drop, a spectacular vista and a few river crossings give the tracks a distinctive West Coast feel.

Grades 3–4   **Time** 1–2 hours   **Distance** 10–20 km

Track conditions 20% gravel road, 10% 4WD track, 70% single track

Maps Pop into Hokitika Cycles for a rough photocopied map.

How to get there Ride out of town on Hampden Street, which turns into Hau Hau Road, which turns into Blue Spur Road. At a 4-way intersection by a hotel and an information board, turn right down Reg Cox Drive. After another 300 metres, take an obvious gravel road uphill. After 200 metres, hop over a gate and carry on uphill. You will soon start seeing red signs marking the mountain bike tracks.

Tom Hopkins in the zone on Stags Drop.

Route description

For a good 1-hour loop head up the gravel road for 15–20 minutes until you see the start of Stags Drop on your left. This takes you back to the gravel road, and you can go straight ahead onto Bad Boys and The Cutting. Slow Girls is another track to look out for, and the more adventurous will enjoy The Sea Saw. The actual see-saw is gone now, but the track still offers a fun downhill to a stream, followed by a 10-minute climb back onto the gravel road.

Once you have had your fill of those tracks, head down the gravel road until you see The Tunnels Track. This is a great way to end the ride and will bring you out onto a gravel road after 10–15 minutes. Head right, and right again after about 300 metres and you will be back on Hau Hau Road; follow it back into town.

Notes The club is still building new tracks, so expect some changes.

9 Kaniere Water Race ★ ★ ☆ ☆

INTERMEDIATE

Kaniere, 19 km southeast of Hokitika

This is one of the better rides around Hokitika. Most of it is flat and easy.

Grade 3
Time 1–2 hours
Distance 10 km

Track conditions 10% 4WD track, 90% single track

How to get there Head southeast of Hokitika to Lake Kaniere (about 19 km). There is a little parking area at the start of the track (it's 20 metres past a 'Kokatahi' sign, just over a bridge).

Route description

Head into the bush on the narrow track that follows the water race. The first 4 km are scenic and easy. Then you'll cross a gravel road, and the track will become more difficult and dangerous. Less confident riders should turn left and follow the gravel road out to Lake Kaniere Road.

Those who stick to the water-race track will soon find they have to dismount to walk half a dozen gulches. The riding in between makes up for this inconvenience though. At the end of the single track, you'll ride onto a 4WD track, where you should turn right and, a few hundred metres later, left. You'll soon pop out onto Lake Kaniere Road.

Turn left to ride back to the start of the track (7 km away) or right to cruise back to Hokitika (12 km away).

Notes This track is also popular with walkers. The track may be upgraded and incorporated into the Westland Wilderness Trail (part of the New Zealand Cycle Trail project). If this happens, then the gulches will be bridged, and the last steep bit rerouted; the result will be an easy trail, 100% ridable by everyone.

Thirteen Other Rides

K Road

Even on a fine day, this is a miserable excuse for a mountain bike track.

Grade 4-   **Time** 1–2 hours   **Distance** 6 km

Just north of Karamea loads of dosh have been poured into providing a toilet, car park, mapboard and promotion for K Road. Only one thing is missing – a half decent track. Instead you get to ride a steep, grovelly dead-end forestry road. In an area renowned for outstanding scenery, this ride offers virtually none. It's a logged-over, weed-infested landscape that might look good in a few decades, but the steep forestry road will still be 'K' for krap.

Britannia Track   ★ ★

This well-graded historic mining track climbs deep into native forest.

Grade 3   **Time** 2 hours   **Distance** 12 km return

From Waimangaroa, 16 km north of Westport on Highway 67, drive 2 km north and turn right at the DOC sign. A gravel road heads inland to a car park 2 km away.

From the car park, a signposted track heads across paddocks and onto a lovely old benched track that climbs through native forest to a waterwheel stamping battery about 1 hour away.

There are half a dozen short walking sections, but it's worth taking your bike up to the end of the bench – the ride back down is a hoot.

Denniston Plateau Tracks   ★ ★

The bizarre landscape around Denniston has been adopted by the Buller Cycling Club. In partnership with DOC, they have signposted several mountain bike routes along old 4WD tracks.

Grades 2–4   **Time** 1–12 hours   **Distance** Over 50 km of track

Drive 16 km northeast of Westport on Highway 67 before turning right at Waimangaroa and heading up the hill to Denniston. After 7 km, turn right at a T-intersection and drive a further 1 km to the 'Friends of the Hill' museum (first driveway on your right after turning right at the top Y-intersection), where there is an MTB tracks information board. Fit locals ride up the hill in 30 minutes!

The best way to explore the area is with a copy of the "Denniston Plateau Mountain Bike Tracks" pamphlet. It costs a gold coin and is available from DOC offices and selected shops in Westport and Waimangaroa. There are also track details on the Buller Cycling Club website (www.cyclebuller.co.nz). Ten tracks are marked on the ground, and shown on the DOC pamphlet. We explored some of them, and our favourite was Mt Rochfort (described below).

The tracks' surfaces are suitable for riding in all weather conditions, even after a typical West Coast deluge. However, be careful not to stray from the marked routes. Decades of mining have left hidden dangers such as underground fires, poisonous gases and collapsing terrain.

This is an alpine environment, so fill your riding pack with suitable clothing and don't attempt to cross flooded creeks.

Mt Rochfort   ★ ★ ☆ ☆

Stunning views and a unique landscape make this 1040 m peak well worth the climb.

Grade 3   **Time** 2–3 hours
Distance 18 km return

From Denniston, a tough 500-m vertical climb up the 4WD road deposits you at the communications tower on top of Mt Rochfort.

On a fine day, this ride provides the best views for miles around. In foul weather, it can be hair-raisingly wild. Return the same way, only much faster. The route is shown on NZTopo50 BR21 Granity.

Jonathan Kennett

Tiropahi Tram Track   ★ ★ ☆ ☆

As long as you don't mind an hour of road riding, the single-track sweetness makes this ride well worthwhile.

Grade 3+   **Time** 2–4 hours   **Distance** 25-km loop

Tiropahi Tram Track car park is signposted 8 km south of Charleston on Highway 6. Don't forget to take NZTopo50 BS20 Charleston.

From the car park, ride north on Highway 6 for 5 km before turning right onto Four Mile Road. Follow old forestry roads inland for 12 km. Turn right at all four intersections. The road becomes a 4WD track before dropping down to a pakihi swamp and an orange triangle marker.

From here there are two ways to go:

1. The original route continues along the forestry road for 1 km, then heads left at a purple track marker, dropping down to the Tiropahi Tram Track.

2. The new way to go is to bike and hike across the swamp to the Tiropahi Tram Track – this involves a fair bit of walking but no gorse bashing.

The Tiropahi Tram Track heads west for 4 km, to the Tiropahi River. The car park is on the far side, and like all rivers on the coast, it is uncrossable after heavy rain.

Pioneer Heritage Trail   ★ ★ ☆ ☆

This is a classic, fat-tyre touring route from Nelson Lakes to Springs Junction.

Grade 3   **Time** 2–3 days   **Distance** 135 km

From St Arnaud, head northwest up Highway 63 until you reach Howard Valley Road on your left. Ride up the valley and over the precipitous Porika Track (signposted 'Porika Road') to Lake Rotoroa.

Next, head across the Gowan River and over the Braeburn 'Track' (a gravel road). Turn left when you hit Tutaki Road North and cruise into Murchison township via Mangles Valley.

From Murchison, head south on Fairfax Street, which turns into the gravel Matakitaki Road. Eventually this turns into Maruia Saddle Road. Follow this road through beech forest over the saddle (580 m) and glide down to Highway 65 just north of Maruia.

From the highway, ride south to Springs Junction about 40 km away.

Moonlight Track   ★ ★ ☆ ☆

This half-day, technical single track is similar to the Croesus Track, but not as ridable.

Grade 5-   **Time** 4–6 hours   **Distance** 32 km return

From Blackball, head south on the Taylorville Blackball Road, then northeast on Atarau Road. About 10 km later, turn left onto Moonlight Road. Park at the picnic area with the old sluicing cannon.

Head north on the rough Moonlight Road. After the bridge over Moonlight Creek, take the track on your right and climb up the river terrace.

Half an hour after the picnic area, you'll reach a car park and the start of Moonlight Track. You can drive to here if your car has reasonable ground clearance, but it's a better ride.

The benched single track follows Moonlight Creek through numerous old mining claims and hut sites.

Beyond the hut, the track is mostly unridable. Head back the same way for a rip-snorting downhill. Crashing aside, you'll easily make it back to the car park within an hour. Refer to NZTopo50 BT20 Ahaura for more details.

Napoleon Hill ★ ★ ☆ ☆

This bizarre track will have you totally baffled as it swoops down narrow canyons, across several streams and through improbable tunnels.

Grade 4+ **Time** 2.5–5 hours **Distance** 23 km

Landowners This ride crosses private property. If considering this route, call Malcolm Smith or Robyn Curtis-Smith on (03) 732 3849 or 021 131 4632 to apply for access and arrange payment of your $5 access fee (used for occasional road maintenance). They will be able to tell you of changes to the track network that will affect your navigation.

NZTopo50 BT20 Ahaura and BT21 Waiuta don't show the entire route but will indicate roughly where you are. Just remember you're doing a big figure of eight and you'll be fine.

From Ahaura, 35 km northeast of Greymouth on Highway 7, head inland on Orwell Creek Road. Turn left after 9 km to stay on Orwell Creek Road and drive another 3 km before parking at a four-way intersection just before the end of the pines.

Follow the main gravel road up Orwell Creek Road and round onto Napoleon Hill. At NZTopo50 grid reference 921 092, turn off the track marked on the map to head north and follow a 4WD track down into Nobles Creek. This becomes a canyon that finally closes over completely. Expect to spend a fair bit of time in the stream bed. After passing through the second tunnel, head right and follow a farm track up a large stream for about 1 km and then right again to ride up Mosquito Creek.

Follow the Mosquito Creek track back up to grid ref 921 092 and then follow another 4WD track down to Orwell Creek Road where it crosses Smythes Creek. Cruise back down to your car.

Westland Wilderness Trail   ★ ★ ★ ☆

This New Zealand Cycle Trail project began construction in 2011 and will be the West Coast's version of the Otago Rail Trail. The trail goes from Greymouth to Ross, via Kumara and Hokitika.

Grade 2   **Time** 2–4 days   **Distance** 120 km

From the Greymouth railway station, head over to the Grey River stopbank 40 metres away. On top of it is a wide smooth cycle trail heading out to the coast via a lagoon. The first stage of the trail is 22 km long and heads south along the coast to the Taramakau Road/Rail Bridge, and then inland to Kumara on the Kumara Tramline.

The second stage will be 31 km long, and head further inland via lakes, rivers and forest to Cowboy Paradise. This stage, once complete, will be incredible as it passes through true West Coast wilderness. Cowboy Paradise is a replica western town, complete with saloon and boardwalks.

The third stage, 32 km, will weave down to the coast via Lake Kaniere, an historic water race trail and the Kaniere-Hokitika Tramline to Hokitika.

The final stage, 34 km, will head south to the scenic Lake Mahinapua, and then along an old railway line to the small town of Ross. For more details, refer to our 2012 book *Classic New Zealand Cycle Trails*.

Noname/Kumara Mud Plug   ★ ★ ☆ ☆

This old classic features a mix of scenery alongside old logging tracks and gravel roads.

Grade 3+   **Time** 2–4 hours   **Distance** 33 km from Marsden

Maps Take NZTopo50 BU19 Kumara.

From Greymouth, the quickest way to Marsden is to head south on Highway 6 for 5 km, then turn left at the 'Shantytown' sign and ride to Marsden another 8 km away. A scenic alternative is to ride through Boddytown and on down Marsden Road.

From Marsden, head to the right and cross the bridge a few hundred metres away before turning right at Noname Road. During the next kilometre, ignore all tracks that branch off the original road (including the big driveway at the 'Noname 0152' sign).

After about 5 km, you'll drop down a small hill and reach a T-intersection (with a left turn that may be overgrown by now). Turn right, and before long, you'll reach a four-way intersection. Ride straight ahead onto the 4WD track.

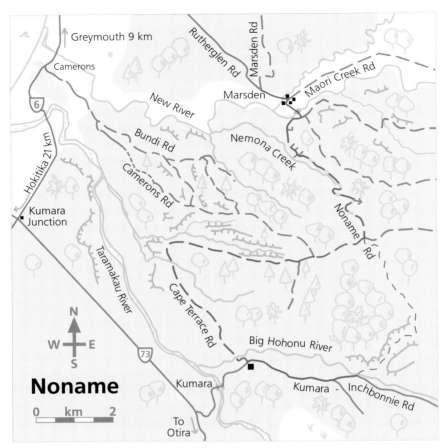

After a few kilometres, this track becomes quite rough and nips back and forth across Blackwater Creek a few times before reaching the Big Hohonu River.

Cross the Big Hohonu and head for the Kumara Inchbonnie Road, a stone's throw away. Turn right and follow this road for 3 km before turning right again at Cape Terrace Road, opposite some large old buildings. Head down to the river, go downstream for 100 metres and then cross the Big Hohonu River again. Continue on Cape Terrace Road for another 10 km. About 1.5 km after passing the Bundi Road turn-off, you'll reach the four-way intersection at the start of the loop. Turn left and follow Noname Road back to Marsden. If it's been raining, choose another ride as the Big Hohonu River will be uncrossable.

LakeKaniere   ★ ☆ ☆ ☆

This lake loop ride is a mixed bag: half of it is cruisy gravel and sealed road riding, and the rest is semi-ridable technical single track.

Grade 5   **Time** 2 hours   **Distance** 21-km loop

From Hokitika, head east on Kaniere Road for 4 km, then turn left onto Lake Kaniere Road and drive to the lake a further 13 km away. At the lake, there is a fork in the road. This is the start of the lake loop. If you ride it in a clockwise direction, then you can warm up on the 10 km of sealed road. You will pass a whole bunch of baches and then travel onto a narrow gravel road. The Lake Kaniere Walkway is signposted on your right. It starts off easy enough but soon becomes very difficult as it climbs over a hill, past a lovely viewing platform, and then back down to the lake. There are several walking sections, but also some brilliant on-the-edge ridable sections. The trail ends at a car parking area 1 km from the start of the loop via Sunny Bright Road.

DOC are upgrading this single track; it might be more ridable by the time you get there. The track is shown on DOC's Hokitika Walks pamphlet.

If you are riding back into Hoki', make sure you take the Kaniere Water Race Track (see page 238).

Mahinapua Walkway Loop   ★ ★ ☆ ☆

An old tramline, 7 km south of Hokitika, provides the destination for a scenic 20-km loop.

Grade 2+   **Time** 2–3 hours   **Distance** 27 km

From Hokitika, ride south across the highway bridge, using the footpath on the western side. Two-hundred metres on from the end of the bridge, turn right on to Golf Links Road, which ends only 20 metres from the highway. Continue south down the highway again for 2.5 km, or, if it's been built already, take the new trail beside the highway and Mahinapua Creek. Turn left off the highway at the Mahinapua tramline/walkway sign and follow the old tramline east through bush and across a wetland. It leads to the old highway (Woodstock–Rimu Road).

When you reach the old highway, turn left and ride 8 km north to cross the Hokitika River at Kaniere. On the other side of the bridge, turn left onto Kaniere Road, and after 300 metres, left again onto Hokitika-Kaniere Tramway. This is planned to be part of the New Zealand Cycle Trail Westland Wilderness Trail, so keep an eye out for New Zealand Cycle Trail direction signs that will lead you back into town.

Glacier Tracks   ★ ★ ★ ☆

Two new cycling tracks at Fox and Franz Josef Glaciers provide fantastic alternatives to driving from the towns to the glacier car parks. They are both easy, and scenic.

Grade 1   **Time** 1–2 hours   **Distance** Both 10 km return

If you have to choose between the two glacier tracks, the Fox is better, because the track starts closer to town and finishes closer to the glacier.

From Fox township, ride south on the main road, and turn left just beyond the edge of town, weaving through a bike chicane, into the forest. The last kilometre to the car park is on the glacier road. The glacier is a further 1 km way, on a walking only track.

From Franz Josef township, ride south on the highway, across the main bridge, and up the valley on a signposted cycle track. After almost 5 km, you will reach a small bike rack beside an obese car park. Park and walk from here to the glacier, 2 km away on a walking track. Ride back the same way.

The glaciers themselves aren't that amazing, unless you do a guided walk up onto them. But the bike tracks are pretty cool.

Fox Glacier Track – a fine flowy piece of track work.

Jonathan Kennett

North Canterbury

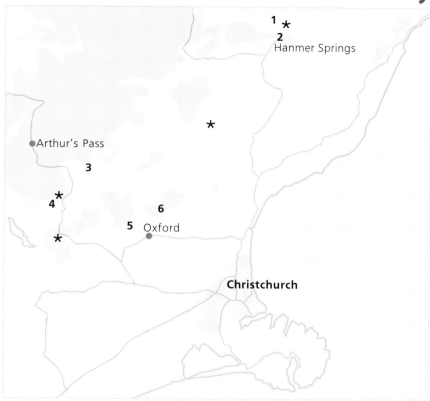

1 **St James Cycle Trail**
2 **Hanmer Tracks**
3 **Poulter Valley**
4 **Craigieburn Forest**
5 **Wharfedale Track**
6 **Blowhard Track**
★ Plus four other rides

NORTH CANTERBURY HIGHLIGHTS

Hanmer has a pot-pourri of tasty tracks (nicely rounded off with a marinate in the hot pools). Craigieburn Forest and Wharfedale Track offer fantastic mountain biking through beautiful beech forest for both intermediate and expert level riders.

1 St James Cycle Trail ★ ★ ★ ★

ADVANCED

Hanmer Springs, 130 km north of Christchurch

In November 2010, this became the first New Zealand Cycle Trail project to be completed and provides riders with the opportunity to experience the raw beauty of the retired St James Station.

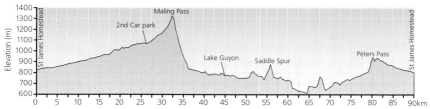

Grade 4   **Time** 1–2 days   **Distance** 64 km point to point or 90-km loop

Track Conditions 25% gravel road, 25% 4WD track, 50% single track

Maps NZTopo50 BT24 Ada Flat.

How to get there From Hanmer Springs, ride or drive out of town on Jacks Pass Road and turn right onto Clarence Valley Road to start the climb proper up to the pass. After descending into the Clarence Valley, turn left at Tophouse Road. When you are 13 km from Hanmer you will see the old St James Homestead on your left, comprising a few buildings, a car park and toilets. This is the official 'end' of the St James Cycle Trail. To do a loop trip, start your ride from here.

Route description

From St James Homestead, continue up Tophouse Road for another 26 km to the Maling Pass car park (on your left, just before Lake Tennyson). This is the official start of the St James Cycle Trail.

From the car park, an easy-gradient 4WD track leads up to Maling Pass, an hour away. At 1308 m, this is the highest point on the trail. On the other side awaits a 30-minute downhill into the Waiau Valley.

Saddle Spur swing bridge.   Jonathan Kennett

Once in the valley, the 4WD track soon morphs into a cycle trail, leading through grassland valleys and matagouri scrub to a signposted track intersection. Approximately 15 minutes ride to your left lies the picturesque Lake Guyon, where a fairly basic 4-bunk DOC hut awaits those who wish to stay overnight.

From Lake Guyon, head back to the main track and continue following the blue marker poles to Pool Hut, 2–3 hours away. The track becomes a lot rougher now, and after crossing the Waiau River on a massive swing bridge you may have to walk some of the way to the top of Saddle Spur. Some people get lost here, as the marker poles are scarce. Keep your eyes peeled and remember, you should generally be heading down valley. From the spur, it is mostly downhill or flat to Pool Hut, 5 km away.

If you don't stay at Lake Guyon Hut, then you'll probably stay at Pool Hut (another small 4-bunk hut, with mattresses, but no cookers). Pool Hut is not insect proof. You may prefer to sleep in an insect proof tent.

About 5 minutes south of Pool Hut, you will cross another large swing bridge. The trail is often loose and rocky from here to Scotties Camp Hut with a few walking sections. The exception is the final downhill from Charlies Saddle to the hut, which is great fun. Just a few hundred metres before the hut, you must wade across Edwards Stream. If this is in flood, do not attempt to cross it. Allow at least 1 hour to ride from Pool Hut to Scotties Camp hut.

From Scotties Camp up to Peters Pass Junction involves lots of easy 4WD track, several rough stream crossings, and a long steep hill that some people will have to walk. Give yourself at least 3 hours for this section.

At Peters Pass Junction there are two ways back to St James Homestead. The best option is to turn right here and continue following the blue marker poles on a direct route to the homestead. Otherwise just go straight ahead to Tophouse Road. Both options take around 1 hour.

From St James Homestead, it is mostly downhill back to Hanmer Springs, only 13 km away.

Notes DOC have built a flash new hut 7 km from the St James Cycle Trail, up the Henry River. They plan to build a track to it from Saddle Spur in 2012.

Fowlers Pass can be used to make a 'shorter' loop, but it's grade 5 (see Other Rides for more details). This area is usually closed by deep snow in winter.

2 Hanmer Tracks

EASY ADVANCED

Hanmer Springs, 130 km north of Christchurch

The hot springs and cool single track make this holiday town a brilliant weekend destination.

Grades 2–4   **Time** 1–2 hours   **Distance** 10–15 km

Track conditions 5% sealed road, 30% gravel road, 65% single track

Maps A map is essential for finding the single track treasures of Hanmer. Pick one up from the information centre or the Trust Camp (100% of the map price goes back into the trails).

Route description

Thanks to the efforts of the Hanmer MTB Club, there are a range of tracks in the forest from Chatterton River across to Dog Stream, and now many of them have been signposted.

Here's a good ride for starters: cycle 1 km out of town on Jollies Pass Road and turn left at Pawson Road. After another 300 metres, hang a right onto Dog Stream Track. This single track winds in and out of the forest, across Jolliffe

Simon and Rick high above Hanmer.

Road and down beside Menzies Road before turning left onto Jolliffe Saddle Track. It isn't far to the saddle, is mostly ridable and the downhill is a hoot.

At the bottom, turn right onto Jolliffe Road, head downhill for 100 metres and pick up Timberlands Trail. Turn left at Pawson Road to get back to the start of the loop.

If you're keen for more, cross Jollies Pass Road and ride back into town via a variety of tracks. The real gold, however, is shown on the Hanmer MTB Club map.

Notes This ride includes brilliant sections of single track that DOC encourage bikers to use. Their intention is to avoid conflict with other park users, so please cooperate by steering clear of walking tracks in the area.

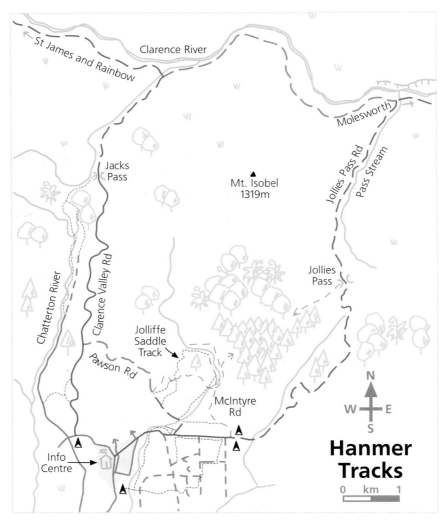

The pine forest owners ask bikers to observe the following:

- No smoking.
- Track closures due to fire risk.
- No camping or fires.
- Respect other track users.

Families with little 'uns in tow might enjoy the flat tracks in the forest just east of town.

3 Poulter Valley ★ ★ ☆ ☆

INTERMEDIATE

24 km east of Arthur's Pass

Here's the first track in a national park to be opened up to mountain bikes after the DOC policy was amended to allow for such extravagances. It's all on 4WD track and riverbed.

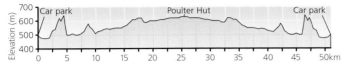

Grade 3   **Time** 5–8 hours   **Distance** 52 km return

Track conditions 98% 4WD track, 2% unridable riverbed

Maps Refer to NZTopo50 BV21 Cass or DOC's Poulter Valley Mountain Biking pamphlet.

How to get there From Highway 73, 24 km east of Arthur's Pass village, turn onto Mt White Road, then 1.5 km later, turn up Andrews Valley. The Poulter Valley parking area is 21 km from the highway, on a dusty gravel road, just before you reach the Poulter River.

Route description

The first hour of riding involves a tough climb and descent, but things get easier from the park boundary to Casey Hut (20 km from the car park). This is a good spot for an overnighter.

Beyond Casey Hut, riders can follow a rough 4WD track up the braided Poulter riverbed for a couple of kilometres. This section can be tricky to follow, and some walking is necessary, including crossing two rivers. Keep an eye out for the cairns marking the route. You'll find it a fair bit easier on the return journey with gravity on your side.

The Trust/Poulter Hut at the top end of the ride is tucked into the edge of the forest on the left.

Retrace your tyre tracks from the hut. Once back on the river terrace, you'll come to a fork in the 4WD track – head for the small cairn in the distance and then continue connecting the markers back to the permanent 4WD track and over the big climb to the car park.

Notes The Poulter is a sizeable river – best avoided during or soon after heavy rain.

⹂gieburn Forest ★ ★ ★ ★

∍st of Christchurch

‾∍ech forest, views to die for and mountain single track combine to make this our favourite ride in Canterbury.

Grades 3–4

Time 2–4 hours

Distance 16 km

Track conditions 5% sealed, 50% gravel road, 45% single track

Maps Refer to NZTopo50 BW21 Springfield.

How to get there Drive northwest from Christchurch towards Arthur's Pass on Highway 73 for about 100 km. Turn left at the 'Craigieburn Recreation Area' sign and park at the shelter/picnic area 100 metres from the highway.

Route description

Ride back out to the highway, turn left and ride up the road for 1 km before turning left again onto the Craigieburn ski field road. The scenic 7-km climb up to the ski field buildings takes about an hour and is well graded.

At the bottom of the rope tow, turn left and ride down and across a shingly slope. This is the start of The Edge, a hairy grade-4 track that requires some walking and includes a few sketchy drop-offs. After 4 km, you'll reach a fork in the track – veer right and climb up to Lyndon Saddle, 15 minutes away. From there, the short walk up to Lyndon Hill (also known as Helicopter Hill) rewards with some massive views.

Back at the saddle, turn west to enjoy The Luge, a grade-3 single track that weaves through beech forest for 3 km. Some of the bridges on the way down are narrow and slippery. Turn left when you hit the gravel road at the bottom and coast down to the picnic area 2 km away.

Notes Take it easy on these tracks, they are popular with walkers and cyclists. The ski field roads are used regularly by 4WD vehicles. Be prepared for snow in winter.

Dracophyllum Track ★ ★ ☆ ☆

This is an interesting there-and-back ride, best done in dry conditions.

Grade 3 **Time** 2–3 hours **Distance** 14 km return

Track conditions 40% gravel road, 60% single track

Follow the directions given above to the Craigieburn Recreation Area. From the shelter near the highway, follow the narrow gravel road up into the forest.

Summer in the beech beats summer at the beach – yeah!   Andy Cotgreave

After 10–20 minutes, you'll reach an intersection with a 'Dracophyllum Flats' sign on the other side. From here, a single track leads through forest and across a river to a climb up to the river flats. Although it's not marked on the map, there is a minor track, marked with poles, leading across the flats and through more forest to an ice skating rink (next to another ski field access road).

After a rest at the ice skating rink, head back the same way.

5 Wharfedale Track   ★ ★ ★ ★   *Possibly the worst mtb trail in the world!!*

INTERMEDIATE   ADVANCED

Oxford Forest, 70 km northwest of Christchurch

Who'd have guessed it; they knew how to build fine mountain bike tracks 130 years ago. Jolly good show!

Grades 3–4+   **Time** 3–8 hours   **Distance** 30 km from the car park to the hut and back; 75-km full loop

Track conditions 100% single track

Maps Take NZTopo50 BW22 Oxford to avoid getting lost.

Other users Walkers, some stock at either end of the track

How to get there From Oxford, drive southwest (towards Arthur's Pass) for just over 3 km and turn right, onto Woodstock Road, at the 'View Hill' signpost. Drive down the

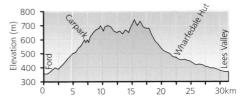

road for 10 km before turning right onto Ingrams Road at the 'Wharfedale Track' sign, and cruising down to the ford 1 km away. If it has been raining, you will have to park here. Otherwise, continue on up to the car park a further 6 km away.

Route description

This track was formed as a stock route and potential road to Lees Valley in 1879. It generally has a cruisy gradient, and beneath a layer of beech-tree leaf litter lies a smooth, responsive riding surface. There are also plenty of fords, roots and rocks to keep you challenged.

From the car park, follow the marked Wharfedale Track through lovely beech forest to a saddle about 2 hours away. Many people just ride this far and then turn back for a mostly downhill run, because that provides a good grade-3 ride that's about 3 hours long.

For a longer, more challenging ride, continue down to the far end of the track, beyond Wharfedale Hut, and then return the way you came (total riding time about 5 hours). This second section is much rougher and some walking is involved.

The ultimate Wharfedale ride requires continuing down valley and out to Oxford via Ashley Gorge. After following the 4WD track for about 30 minutes on from Wharfedale Hut, you should veer right (do not climb to your left) at an obvious Y-intersection. When you reach the gravel road, turn right again. Oxford is then 26 km away via the scenic and hilly Lees Valley Road.

Notes Watch out for the water channels – they get bigger and bigger as you go along, and the last two are real bike gobblers.

The track from the Coopers Creek car park, at the end of Mountain Road, (5 km northeast of View Hill) is also popular with local riders but is very steep in places. Refer to DOC's pamphlet, "Canterbury Foothills Forests – Oxford Forest", for more info. As with most tracks, the Wharfedale is a grade harder when wet.

6 Blowhard Track ★ ★ ☆ ☆

70 km northwest of Christchurch

This ride is a damn fine test for fit, technically skilled riders. The uphill is tough and requires a fair bit of bike carrying, but the view and downhill are fantastic.

Grade 4+

Time 4–5 hours

Distance 20 km return

Track conditions 10% 4WD track, 90% single track

Maps Refer to NZTopo50 BW22 Oxford and BW23 Cust.

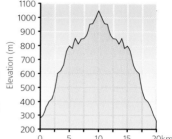

How to get there From Oxford, drive north on High Street, which becomes Ashley Gorge Road (then later Birch Road), for 16 km. Then turn left onto Maori Reserve Road and drive 4 km to the road end. (It's quicker to drive via Rangiora if you live in Christchurch's northern suburbs.)

Route description

The Blowhard Track is signposted at the end of the road. Ride past the sign and up a steep 4WD track into the bush. It takes over an hour to bike and hike up to the first summit, which just peeks out above the forest. The very top of Mt Richardson is a further hour away, with some downhill respite along the ridge but mostly more hard work. On the way up, turn right when you reach a 'Bypass Track' sign. A little later, it's easy to lose the track. Keep your eyes peeled for a small cairn. Turn left when you see it to keep following the orange triangles.

The top is well signposted and at 1047 m provides a stunning vista.

The ride back down takes about an hour. All the bits you couldn't quite ride on the way up are primo in the opposite direction – very challenging and deserving of respect.

Notes This track is exposed in places, slick when wet and definitely best ridden after a week of dry weather. If you get fine weather at the top, you'll want to spend some time there; if not, you'll wish you were home patching old tubes. Don't forget to take a parka, plenty of water and your beefiest fat tyres. The Mt Richardson Track is out of bounds for bikers.

Four Other Rides

Fowlers Pass, St James   ★ ★ ★ ☆

This old stock route provides fantastic technical challenges for expert riders; very old-school in nature.

Grade 5   **Time** 1 day   **Distance** Approx 48-km loop

All of this ride is shown on NZTopo50 BT24 Ada Flat. Start by riding the St James Cycle Trail to Lake Guyon Hut (2–3 hours from Maling Pass car park; see above).

From Lake Guyon Hut, head up the valley to Stanley Vale Hut, almost 5 km away. Now turn east and follow Fowler Pass Track up into the hills. Keep a keen eye on the map as there are two right turns that you shouldn't miss. This track gets quite rough, and up to half an hour of walking is required. The last zigzag section up to Fowlers Pass is very steep.

From Fowlers Pass, the old stock route provides 4 km of fantastic riding back down to Tophouse Road. At the bottom is Fowlers Hut – a good place to regroup.

From Fowlers Hut, either ride 10 km back up to Maling Pass car park or 25 km mostly downhill to Hanmer Springs.

Lake Sumner   ★ ★ ☆ ☆

Great scenery, no big climbs and lots of good camping areas.

Grade 1+   **Time** 3–6 hours   **Distance** 36 km return

From Amberley, drive 25 km north to Waikari and head northwest past Hawarden to Horsley Down. Then follow Lake Sumner Road for another 43 km before parking at the end of the gravel road beside Lake Taylor.

Skirt around the southwest edge of Lake Taylor on a 4WD track before heading north to do the same again round Loch Katrine. Carry on west past the end of Lake Sumner to the remains of No.2 Hut (2 km before Hurunui Hut). Admire the view over lunch and return the same way.

Alternatively, if you want to do an overnighter, carry along on a vague 4WD track 2 km up the valley to Hurunui Hut. Dump your gear here and head for the hot springs. They are 30 minutes riding plus 15 minutes walking further up the valley and are marked with a small red 'X' on the map.

Notes Take insect repellent. Refer to NZTopo50 BU22 Lake Sumner.

Castle Hill   ★ ★ ☆ ☆

Here's some sweet new single track to explore the beautiful countryside just out the back of Castle Hill village.

Heading up the Hogs Back, Castle Hill.

Simon Kennett

Grade 3   **Time** 1–2 hours   **Distance** Approx 14-km loop

Maps Check out www.castlehill.net.nz/castlehill/mtb/hogsback_mtb.htm for the latest information and map.

Head to Castle Hill village on Highway 73, almost 100 km northwest of Christchurch. Head through the village and along Castle Hill Drive to the trail-head car park (signposted 'Craigieburn Forest Park').

Ride away from the car park and almost immediately veer right up the single track, into the beech forest. It's signposted 'Track to Start of Lower and Upper Old Beech Forest Logging Tracks'. Climb up and over the Hogs Back Track into the valley beyond. Then pedal up to the Cheeseman ski field road, turn right and head back to Highway 73. Castle Hill is just a couple of kilometres back along the highway.

This track was given an official opening in October 2011. It is likely to be closed in winter to prevent track damage during the frost-heave season – this will be notified on the website above. In summer, this area can suffer chilly alpine weather or be hotter than hell.

If this ride leaves you wanting more, check out Craigieburn Forest (see above) just up the road.

Trig M   ★ ☆ ☆ ☆

This ride isn't much to speak of, but we've included it for anyone who's ever been intrigued by the DOC MTB markers visible from Highway 73 near Porters Pass ... like we were!

Grade 3+   **Time** 1–2 hours   **Distance** Approx 12-km loop

Before your ride, buy the "Korowai/Torlesse Tussocklands Park" brochure from DOC for a dollar. This loop starts/finishes near the bottom of the Porters Pass climb (east side) and does a huge climb up to Trig M at 1251 m. Expect a serious slog and some gob-smacking views. Some of this ride follows an easement through farmland, which is closed for lambing from 1 October to 20 November each year.

Dave Mitchell

Winter riding over Maling Pass, St James Cycle Trail.

Christchurch

1 **McLeans Forest**
2 **Bottle Lake Forest Park**
3 **Port Hills Crater Rim**
4 **Crocodile and Kennedys Bush**
5 **Flying Nun to Evans Pass**
6 **Godley Head Track**
7 **Victoria Park**
8 **Living Springs**
9 **Little River Rail Trail**
10 **Mt Fitzgerald**
★ Plus four other rides

CHRISTCHURCH HIGHLIGHTS

Despite the massive upheaval caused by the 2010/11 earthquakes, Christchurch's impressive cycling heritage continues, with council-supported tracks at Bottle Lake, McLeans Forest and the Port Hills. The Little River Rail Trail is the ultimate family-friendly cruise, and Mt Fitzgerald is a back-country classic. Many of the tracks on the Port Hills were damaged by the earthquakes, and at the time of writing, half of these were still closed for repairs.

1 McLeans Forest ★ ★ ★ ☆

BEGINNER

24 km northwest of Christchurch

A flat pine forested area on the southern banks of the Waimakariri River provides similar easy riding to Bottle Lake. Good for riders of all abilities.

Grade 1+
Time 1–1.5 hours
Distance Up to 12 km

Track conditions 100% smooth single track

How to get there Take Highway 73 out of Christchurch. Almost 14 km from the CBD, veer right onto Old West Coast Road. After another 4 km, turn right onto Chattertons Road and 5–6 km after that, turn left at the McLeans Forest entrance.

Route description

From the car park, ride 100 metres past the information centre to follow the MTB track signs into the forest and around a flat, fun 10-km loop. There are two extra loops that you can add on: the River Loop and the Coringa Loop. The River Loop is a bit boring, but the Coringa Loop is the best (and newest) bit of track at McLeans. It starts from a unique overbridge – you can't miss it!

The area also caters for walkers, so take care not to stray onto the walking track. If you have a copy of the McLeans Forest Map, produced by Environment Canterbury, you could use the forestry roads to shorten your ride.

Notes There are toilets, bike hire and a mapboard at the car park. The car park is locked at night. This area may be closed from time to time due to flooding or logging.

Gliding through McLeans Forest.   Jonathan Kennett

2 Bottle Lake Forest Park ★ ★ ★ ☆

BEGINNER   EASY

Christchurch

The tracks at Bottle Lake have been so well developed that the forest is now one of the most popular riding destinations in New Zealand. It's especially good for families and night riding.

Grades 1–2

Time 1–2 hours

Distance 9–15 km return

Track conditions Mostly gravelled single track

Other users Runners, walkers, dogs, horses

How to get there Head north out of town on Marshland Road. Turn right onto Prestons Road, left onto Alpine View Lane and left again onto Waitikiri Drive. After 700 metres, turn right into the car park.

Route description

Pick up one of the maps at the information centre by the car park and plan a loop trip around any two of the three main tracks shown. It will take up to an hour to do one loop. The far track along the coast is fairly straight and sandy. The rest are twisty, firm and fun.

Because this is a production forest, short sections of track are continually being logged out and replaced with new track, so don't presume you'll always have the whole area sussed.

There is also a skills area beside the car park.

Notes In case of emergency or for up-to-date information, contact the park ranger on phone 026 252 5093, or (03) 383 3795 after hours. The park is owned by the Christchurch City Council (CCC). This is a great wet weather riding area. In 2011, part of the park was being used as a dumping area for materials from the city centre earthquake recovery programme, but the main track is still open to the public.

Synchronised cycling at Bottle Lake Forest.   Simon Kennett

3 Port Hills Crater Rim ★ ★ ★

Christchurch

The Port Hills had one of the most impressive track netwo
country with over 40 km of tracks. Much of it is flowing si
with stunning views, traversing the crater rim of a huge extinct volcano.

Many of the Port Hills tracks were closed in 2011 due to rock falls
from the earthquakes. For the latest on track status, check out:
www.ccc.govt.nz/cityleisure/gettingaround/cycling/trackstatus.aspx Hopefully
much of the ride described below will be open again soon.

Amazing view, perfect
single track, ends at
the beach!

Grade 4   **Time** 4–8 hours   **Distance** 40 km

Route description

Start at Halswell Quarry and ride up the Crocodile Track and Kennedys Bush
Track (see below). Then cruise along to the Flying Nun, which leads to the
Sign of the Kiwi Tearooms. From there, you will be alternating between the
Summit Road and single tracks that run parallel with the Summit Road. The
main single tracks all start at obvious roadside signs and are, in order, Thomsons
Track, The Bowenvale Traverse Track, Mt Vernon Track, Witch Hill Track, Castle
Rock Track, John Britten Track, and the longest, the Greenwood Track.

From Evans Pass, take the Godley Head Track, followed by the Anaconda
Track, down to Taylors Mistake, with a final road hill to Sumner.

Notes This is one of the best day's mountain biking in the country. A word of
warning – we've had big crashes on these tracks (it's easy to go too fast).

4 Crocodile and Kennedys Bush ★ ★

EASY

Halswell, Christchurch

This is one of the best ways to ride up onto the Port Hills. A satisfying
plug uphill has you honing your turning skills on a series of tight corners.

Grade 2   **Time** 1 hour up, 20 minutes down   **Distance** 7 km

Track conditions A fairly even mix of 4WD track and single track

Maps Check out our Port Hills West map overleaf.

Other users Walkers, runners, farm stock

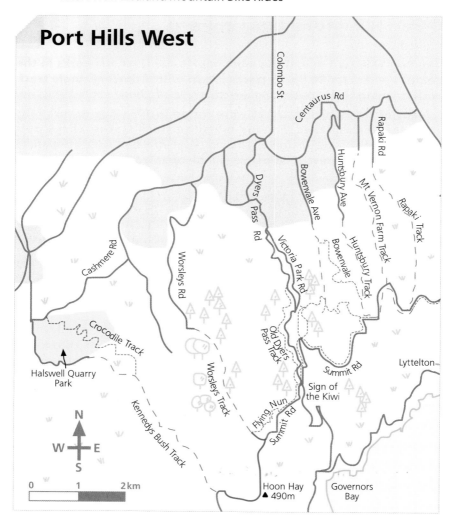

Route description

Start by heading up the Crocodile Track. It begins at Halswell Quarry Park on Cashmere Road and is well signposted. After crossing a valley near the bottom, this track is a steady grind up a series of switchbacks. When you get to the top of the Kennedys Bush 4WD track, cross over and keep following single track up hill for a further 1 km until you arrive at a gate after a short downhill section, at which point follow the 4WD track to the Summit Road, where you can turn left to head for Flying Nun.

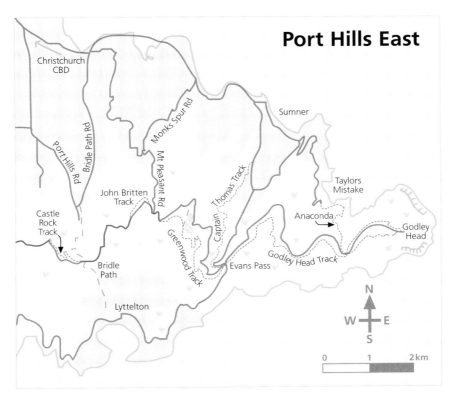

Port Hills East

Christchurch CBD

Monks Spur Rd

Sumner

Bridle Path Rd

Port Hills Rd

Mt Pleasant Rd

John Britten Track

Thomas Track

Taylors Mistake

Castle Rock Track

Captain

Anaconda

Godley Head

Greenwood Track

Godley Head Track

Bridle Path

Evans Pass

Lyttelton

N
W — E
S

0   1   2 km

Notes Both tracks are closed during lambing; August–September. The Crocodile Track was built by Dan van Asch over his farmland. It's the ideal place to start a traverse of the Port Hills.

5 Flying Nun to Evans Pass ★ ★ ★

INTERMEDIATE

Port Hills, Christchurch

This makes for an excellent round trip when linked in with Kennedys Bush Track (see above). Much of it was closed by quake damage in 2011, but we hope it will be reopened soon.

Grade 3   **Time** 20 minutes downhill   **Distance** 6 km

Track conditions Mostly purpose-built single track, stitched together with sections of sealed road and 4WD track.

Other users Walkers, runners and horses also use some of these tracks, which are two-way – take care on the descents. Flying Nun is also known as 'Marleys Hill Track'.

Route description

After chugging up Crocodile/Kennedys Bush tracks (see above), cycle left along the Summit Road. Just after crossing a cattle stop, turn left up a sealed road that leads to the top of Worsleys Track, 300 metres away.

Next, either head through the rusty iron gate and down Worsleys Track to Hoon Hay or carry along the Crater Rim on Flying Nun. The Flying Nun single track is 50 metres east of the gate and sidles down to the Sign of the Kiwi tearooms.

Dyers Pass to Evans Pass single tracks

From the Sign of the Kiwi, ride up the road for 100 metres before turning left onto Thomsons Track. This traverses around to the Bowenvale Traverse Track. Continuing along the Summit Road towards Evans Pass, there are several other signposted single tracks that you can take to get off the road. Three short ones are Castle Rock Track (1.5 km), John Britten Track (1 km) and finally Greenwood Track (3 km) on

Martin Langley on the Greenwood Track.

Jonathan Kennett

the other side of the road. This last track takes you right to Evans Pass. On the other side of the pass is the more difficult Godley Head Track.

Remember to check on the CCC website that all these tracks have been reopened since the earthquakes.

Notes Alternatively, if you're feeling like a challenge, try riding up Worsleys Track (see our map). The last 100 metres , aptly named The Body Bag, are extreme – give it heaps! At the top, go through an old gate and, after 50 metres, you'll see the track which connects to Flying Nun heading off on your left.

6 Godley Head Track

Sumner, Christchurch

The sweet single track and expansive views make this a great ride on a typically fine Christchurch day. Check out the CCC website to see if it is still closed due to earthquake damage.

Grade 4   **Time** 2–3 hours   **Distance** 12-km loop

Track conditions Mostly single track

How to get there Since the earthquakes, both Evans Pass Road and Captain Thomas Track have been closed. The best way to get to the track is to ride from the Greenwood Track (which starts 300 metres east of the top of Mt Pleasant Road). Alternatively you could ride from Dyers Pass (beside the Sign of the Kiwi tearooms). See the write-ups above.

Route description

From Evans Pass, ride east along the Summit Road for 100 metres and then turn hard right to ride up a steep track and over a MTB stile. This is the Scarborough Reserve Track, and it's sweet, although the first few minutes are very challenging! It spits you out at Breeze Col.

From Breeze Col, continue climbing one of the two tracks on the other side of the Col – we recommend the left one. The steep one on the right is for wannabe pro racers – we had a go at the bottom half and then decided to remain amateurs.

Once back at the road, take a look at the view from the car park (or just beyond).

Head back to Breeze Col on the relatively easy track that runs on the northern side of, and parallel to, the Summit Road. Once back at Breeze Col, check out DOC's roadside map for more info. You can either head back to Evans Pass on the track you've already ridden or turn right and descend to Taylors Mistake. Heading for Taylors Mistake gives you the chance to ride the fantastic Anaconda – fast, flowy and fun. It's the best option, so here are the directions: from Breeze

Returning from Godley Head.   Jonathan Kennett

Col follow the shared use track signposted 'Taylors Mistake Beach' for 2 minutes, then turn onto the signposted 'Anaconda MTB' track. Near the bottom, just before meeting a walking track, turn left onto the 'Mountain Bike Track' and sidle down to Taylors Mistake. It's easy to follow your nose from there over to Sumner following the road.

Notes Don't forget your camera!

7 Victoria Park ★ ★ ★ ☆

Cashmere, Christchurch

Victoria Park, on the side of the Port Hills, is riddled with several downhill tracks and lots of jumps.

Grades 2–5   **Time** 1.5–2 hours   **Distance** 8 km

Track conditions A wide range of purpose-built single track

Maps CCC has produced a map showing these tracks, available online at: www.ccc.govt.nz/cityleisure/gettingaround/cycling/findaride/mountainbiking/

How to get there From Cashmere, head up Dyers Pass Road to the Sign of the Kiwi tearooms or ride up Crocodile/Kennedys (see above).

Route description

From the Sign of the Kiwi tearooms, head north on the Summit Road and after 150 metres pop left onto the shared use Thomsons Track. Follow this for a few hundred metres, and you'll reach a clearing just below a car park. This is the top of the Victoria Park Tracks.

Follow the most obvious track down towards the city for 50 metres and you'll cross a fence (via a see-saw or a cattle stop). This is the top of 'Brake Free', a really cool grade-3 track for learning what flow and jumps are all about. It's only a few hundred metres long, but people just ride it over and over and over.

From there, you can bomb down through Victoria Park and explore the downhill tracks and jumps area, or head back up towards the Summit Road and follow Bowenvale Traverse Track round to the top of the Huntsbury/Bowenvale Track – an easier way back down to town.

8 Living Springs

15 km south of Christchurch

INTERMEDIATE ADVANCED

Living Springs is a private initiative involving the Christchurch Singletrack Club building several intermediate tracks over a mixture of farmland and forestry.

Grades 3–4 **Time** 2 hours **Distance** Up to 11 km

Track conditions Mostly purpose-built single track

How to get there From Christchurch, drive south over Dyers Pass, turn right at Governors Bay Road and after 3 km, park at the Living Springs Farm Park. The mountain bike tracks start near the car park entrance.

Route description

Track updates can be found at www.singletrack.org.nz

At the time of writing, there was a 6-km circuit of well built and maintained grades 3 and 4 tracks to explore, including The Pines, Mississippi, and Zanes, and the club were busy building a further 4–5 km loop on the upper slopes of the farm park.

Notes The best way to get to know this area is to attend a dig day and cap it off with a ride. Big thanks to Craig and Rebekah Tregurtha for opening up the area.

9 Little River Rail Trail   ★ ★ ★ ☆

Christchurch to Little River

This ride is mighty popular for the simple reason that it's so easy for anyone to ride. The trail is wide, flat, smooth and scenic. There is no traffic to contend with but plenty of interesting history and wildlife to enjoy.

Grade 1   **Time** 1–4 hours   **Distance** 45 km when completed

Track conditions 100% wide, flat, smooth path, paved and gravel

Maps Check out www.littleriverrailtrail.co.nz for maps and updates

Route description

The best part is 20 km long and runs from Little River down beside Lake Forsyth and then north, past Lake Ellesmere to Motukarara. There are lots of interpretation panels explaining the history and wildlife of the area along the way. Anyone, no matter what their fitness or age, will enjoy this ride.

The second part that is open runs from Shands Road in Hornby to Prebbleton, just southwest of Christchurch, and on out to Lincoln. It's on a sealed cycle path and is easy to ride, but the scenic values are not as high as the Little River to Motukarara section.

By 2012 it is expected that the link between Lincoln and Motukarara will be complete, with the trail connecting to cycle networks in Christchurch once the cycle route along the new southern motorway extention is finished.

Notes The track is exposed to the sun and wind. Of the planned 45 km of rail trail, 35 km had been completed by the middle of 2011.

10 Mt Fitzgerald   ★ ★ ☆ ☆

Also known as Double Fenceline

51 km southeast of Christchurch

While only 34 km long, this is a tough 'three-pie' ride with plenty of steep technical track and some challenging navigation. It provides a rewarding journey over Banks Peninsula high country.

Grade 3+
Time 4–8 hours
Distance 34 km

Track conditions 35% sealed road, 20% gravel road, 35% 4WD track, 10% semi-ridable single track

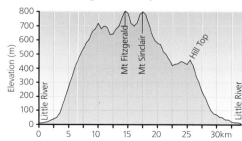

Maps Refer to NewTopo Banks Peninsula.

Landowners Although this track follows a paper road, it is closed during lambing, August–October.

Route description

From Little River, follow Western Valley Road towards Port Levy climbing steeply for 1–2 hours to the saddle. Take the 4WD track east, following a paper road (often between a double fence line) along an undulating ridge to Mt Fitzgerald (826 m). As you approach Mt Fitzgerald, cross a metal stile. Turn left, cross another fence and keep going for 200 metres, then turn right down a 4WD track, which sidles around the Mt Fitzgerald summit and avoids an unridable bit of walking track.

After a short descent, carry on up towards Mt Sinclair (841 m), from where the track drops towards Pettigrews Road. Soon after a small green hut comes into view, you'll reach a pair of gates. Hop over the left-hand gate. Don't climb the track to the TV transmitter – take the grassy 4WD track to the left for 1 km, and you'll link up with Pettigrews Road.

Once at the road, turn right, then after 500 metres, turn right again to get onto the Summit Road, which is sealed. From Hill Top, take Harmans '4WD Vehicles Only' Track and Puaha Road back to Little River where you can buy your well earned pies.

Notes While much of this route has orange markers along it, they are spaced too far apart to be seen and followed in thick cloud. The downhill from Mt Sinclair passes through one of the last remaining patches of totara forest on the peninsula. This is also a well-used walkway.

The farmer at the Pettigrews end has insurance to cover the possibility of his bulls goring a mountain biker. If this worries you, don't wear red.

Four Other Rides

Kaiapoi Island ★ ☆ ☆ ☆

A few easy tracks run parallel to the Waimakariri River, along stopbanks and through exotic forest. Fine riding for families and beginners in dry weather (quite slippery in wet weather).

Grade 1+ **Time** 1–2 hours **Distance** Up to 20 km

Drive 10 km north of Christchurch city on Highway 1. Just after crossing the Waimakariri River bridge take the Tram Road exit. Turn right at Tram Road, right at Main North Road and right at Wrights Road to enter the park. There are pamphlets

Road closed - Extreme rock fall danger!

with maps at the information centre beside the car parking area (where there is also a loo). The tracks are signposted, so you shouldn't have trouble finding your way.

From the information centre, cross the gravel road to ride alongside the road on a single track, which leads to the main track. Look out for the mountain bike signpost. This easy track weaves through forest. At the end, you can return the same way or pop up onto the stopbank road and ride back on that for a change and a bit of a view.

There is also a cycle track running from the information centre down river. It can be used for a short there-and-back riverside ride, or you can follow it all the way to Kaiapoi township.

The tracks are a mixture of gravel roads, purpose-built single track and shared cycle/walkways.

Rapaki Track   ★ ☆ ☆ ☆

This is the easiest track from Opawa in Christchurch up onto the Port Hills. It was closed by the 2010/11 earthquakes, but was just about to be opened as this book went to print in late 2011.

Grade 2- **Time** 20–40 mins   **Distance** 3.5 km

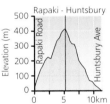

From the end of Rapaki Road, in Opawa, a smooth 4WD track climbs gradually 260 m to the Summit Road. Either backtrack or make this a loop trip by cycling around to one of the other Port Hill tracks (eg. Huntsbury or Mt Vernon Farm Track).

This track is well trod by walkers, runners and horses – take it easy on the way down.

Haven MTB Park   ★ ★ ☆ ☆

Banks Peninsula

This is a small, privately owned mountain bike park with several neat tracks under construction.

Grades 3–4 **Time** 1–2 hours   **Distance** 10 km

In 2011, several tracks had been built, adding up to 10 km of flowing single track. There were also plans to build a skills area, and plant loads more trees. To ride here, you must be a club member; check out www.havenmtb.org.nz to find out more and join up. Membership is cheap, and you get a free map.

Dave Mitchell

As with any developing mountain bike park, the etiquette is 'dig before you ride'. A big thanks to landowners Shailer Hart and Lisa Carter for expanding the mountain biking possibilities in Christchurch.

Mt Herbert   ★ ☆ ☆ ☆

At 920 m, this is the highest point on Banks Peninsula, making it irresistible for peak baggers.

Grade 4-   **Time** 4–6 hours   **Distance** 43-km loop

Maps Before heading out, pack the NewTopo Banks Peninsula map, as well as an extra layer of warm clothing.

From Diamond Harbour, head southeast through Purau. Take the Purau–Port Levy Road over Purau Saddle (passing the bottom of the Monument Track on your right) and almost all the way down to Port Levy. At the bottom of the hill, turn right and climb up Western Valley Road to Port Levy Saddle.

From the saddle, follow the marked track west across farmland. After about half an hour, you'll reach the signposted 'Monument Track' turn-off. The track from here to Mt Herbert requires considerable bike pushing on the way up and good technical riding skills on the way back down. There is a trig and two large aerials at the top.

From the summit, backtrack to the 'Monument Track' signpost and head down past the imposing cliffs, called 'The Monument', to Purau Saddle.

The tracks are closed during lambing (August–September).

South Canterbury

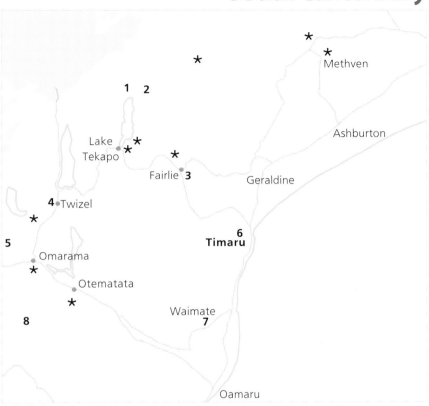

1 **Lake Tekapo Loop**
2 **Macaulay Valley**
3 **Fairlie Walkway**
4 **Twizel Area Tracks**
5 **Ahuriri Valley**
6 **Centennial Park**
7 **White Horse Trail**
8 **Omarama Saddle to St Bathans**
★ Plus nine other rides

Twizel is the main centre for track development through high-country land in South Canterbury, although Lake Tekapo has recently started to play catch-up. The region offers many rides up huge valleys into the Southern Alps.

1 Lake Tekapo Loop ★ ★ ☆ ☆

INTERMEDIATE

Lake Tekapo

Gravel roads and bumpy 4WD tracks circumnavigate Lake Tekapo, with spectacular mountain scenery and an optional side trip to Godley Glacier.

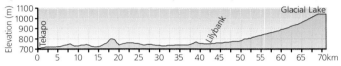

Grade 3 **Time** 1–3 days **Distance** 140 km return

Track conditions 50% gravel road, 50% 4WD track

Maps Take NZTopo250 22 Timaru and NZTopo50 BX17 Mount Sibbald.

Landowners If you plan to cross the Godley, phone Godley Peaks Station on (03) 680 6919 before your ride for permission to go through the station and to check the condition of the river crossing.

Route description

Ride east from Lake Tekapo village and take the first turn on the left. This gravel road heads along Lake Tekapo and up the Macaulay River. Cross the Macaulay River to Lilybank Station and go straight to the Godley River Valley.

Follow a rough 4WD track past a few 'Public Access' signs and on up the huge Godley River flats. Cycle over Lucifer Flat. Then shoot up to Godley Glacier Lake about 6 km north. Godley Hut is 600 metres from the lake. It's a basic tramping hut, with mattresses but not much else.

You can either head back the same way or, during times of low river flow, carefully cross the Godley River and ride down the other side of the lake (the river is fed by glacial melt and rises with temperature as well as rainfall). On your way back, it's worth visiting Lake Alexandrina (signposted from the road). It's a lot warmer for swimming in than the glacial ones in this district.

Notes Lake Tekapo village has shops, backpackers and a camping ground. This ride is raced once a year (see www.mtbpursuits.com).

Descending the Richmond Trail to Lake Tekapo.

2 Macaulay Valley ★ ★ ☆ ☆

EASY

39 km north of Lake Tekapo township

This beautiful valley, to the east of Godley River Valley, sees regular 4WD vehicle use, making it a fairly well-worn route into the foothills of the Southern Alps.

Grade 2+ **Time** 3–6 hours **Distance** 40 km return

Track conditions 95% 4WD track, 5% river

Maps Take NZTopo250 22 Timaru and NZTopo50 BX17 Mount Sibbald.

How to get there Leave Lake Tekapo as per the Godley Glacier ride (see above). There is a 'courtesy car park' by a shed 38.5 km from Lake Tekapo, just before the first Macaulay River ford.

Route description

From the car park, cross the Macaulay River, hang a right and then follow orange markers up to the flash Macaulay Hut, 20 km away.

After about an hour's cycling, the track becomes difficult to find as it negotiates its way up the middle of the braided river valley – keep your eye on the orange markers not the transient 4WD tracks. Return the same way.

Notes Macaulay Hut is free to stay at (although donations are welcome). Don't forget your camera – there are some mighty fine mountains at the top end of this ride.

3 Fairlie Walkway ★ ★ ☆ ☆

BEGINNER

Fairlie

Despite being surrounded by the worst weed infestations we've ever seen, this is a surprisingly fun track.

Grade 1+ **Time** 1–2 hours **Distance** 13 km return

Track conditions 100% single track

Maps Pop into the Twizel information centre for the latest maps and pamphlets.

Route description

Start on the Opihi river bank between the Top 10 Holiday Park and the main bridge out of town on Highway 79. Head downstream, following the Fairlie Walkway east and then the Opihi River Track to Opihi Gorge Road. Return the way you came.

This is an excellent introduction to single-track riding, but beginners should take care on the footbridges; if wet, consider walking across.

4 Twizel Area Tracks

There are several mountain bike opportunities close to Twizel. We describe our two favourites below.

Twizel River Trail ★★ ★ ★

Twizel

This little gem is an excellent beginner-grade single track, and during autumn, the turning leaves are a bonus.

Grade 1+   **Time** 1–2.5 hours   **Distance** 16–25 km

Route description

From the Twizel DOC centre, head out to the highway, cross the road and turn left, riding towards Lake Tekapo for about 100 metres to the trail-head sign beside the road. Head through the gate, onto the gravel road for 300 metres and then follow the orange poles beside the Twizel River. In places, you need to veer away from the river bank where erosion has formed new cliff edges.

The track branches away from the river and climbs up onto a barren, flat landscape. Turn back here if all you enjoy is single track. Otherwise, carry on, and after hopping over a fence, the track turns right (south) to a gravel road. Turn right again and follow this road back towards the highway.

When you are only 100 metres from the highway, you will reach a T-intersection. Turn right again and ride up to a substation, from where a signposted cycle path runs beside the highway back to Twizel.

Note The Twizel Bakery Cafe had the best hot chips we've eaten in years!

Ginny Wood spins along the Twizel River Trail.   Jonathan Kennett

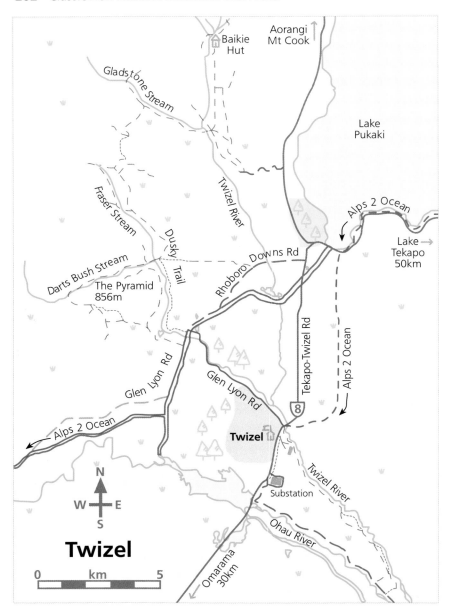

Dusky Trail ★ ★ ★ ☆

INTERMEDIATE

6 km northwest of Twizel

This ride is sandwiched between Gladstone Stream and the Darts Bush Stream Loop and contains some sweet flowing single track.

Grade 3   **Time** 2–5 hours   **Distance** 22–38 km

Route description

Ride from town or start from the 'Dusky Trail' sign on Glen Lyon Road – a couple of hundred metres before the Darts Bush car park. Follow the markers up Fraser Stream and into the foothills. This ride offers an interesting mix of single track and farm track passing through open tussock country.

You'll reach a picnic table at the ride's high point after 11 km. Either turn back here (the sheep track is excellent at 30 km/hr) or carry on to Gladstone Stream, which ends with a road ride back to Twizel or your parked car.

Note This ride includes a few stream crossings and is best avoided during or immediately after heavy rain.

5 Ahuriri Valley ★ ★ ★ ☆

EASY

39 km west of Omarama

Here's another simple valley ride with stunning scenery. As with so many South Island valleys, this one is huge.

Grade 2-   **Time** 2–6 hours   **Distance** 30–58 km return

Track conditions Gravel roads and 4WD tracks

Maps NZTopo50 BZ14 Mount Barth

How to get there From Omarama, drive 15 km west on Highway 8, then veer right onto Birchwood Road. It is a further 24 km to the DOC intentions booth and Ahuriri Conservation Park boundary – a good place to park.

Route description

The next 10-odd kilometres provide a good warm-up on a gravelly 4WD track that leads to the Ahuriri Base Hut. Then it's 5 km on a more natural 4WD track to the Canyon Creek camping area, another 3.5 km to Shamrock Hut and another 6 km to Hagens Hut. If you're feeling keen, carry on to Top Hut, 4.5 km up the valley.

Watch out for the devilishly slippery fords. Once you've had enough, turn around and ride back the way you came in.

6 Centennial Park ★ ★ ★ ☆

EASY

Church Street, Timaru

All up, Centennial Park has almost 20 km of ridable track now, making this area sweet for an hour or two's dabbling.

Grade 2+   **Time** 30–60 minutes   **Distance** Up to 20 km

Route decription

From the centre of Timaru, ride west down Church Street into Centennial Park. There are mapboards a short distance in from the main entrances.

The park comprises several dirt tracks scattered among the exotic trees and grass fields; they include a couple of mountain bike tracks built by the local club. Also, the walking tracks have recently been opened up to mountain bikers – enjoy, but remember to give way to pedestrians.

Centennial Park to the coast

If the tracks at Centennial Park aren't long enough for you, head back past the jumps area (near the Church Street entrance) and follow the three walkways listed below out to the coast.

Otipua Creek Walkway, 1 km: From the BMX track near the entrance to Centennial Park, ride a newish track down beside the creek to Coonoor Road. Cross this road and head right for 100 metres to the next track.

Saltwater Creek Walkway to King Street, 3 km: This track leads from Coonoor Road downstream to King Street. It is flat and easy. Cross the road at the end to continue.

Saltwater Creek to the coast, 2.5 km: The first half of this walkway follows the creek, then crosses it, and the railway line, to reach the coast. It then follows the coast south to the Caledonian Grounds and South Street, by the picnic grounds at Patati Point. This is 1 km from central Timaru.

7 White Horse Trail ★ ★ ☆ ☆

ADVANCED

West of Waimate

This sweet track has been built by local mountain bikers and is worth checking out, if only to break up a drive north or south. Why the name White Horse? You'll find out once you're there.

Grade 4
Time 1–2 hours
Distance 10 km return from Waimate

Track conditions 40% sealed road, 20% 4WD track, 40% single track

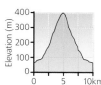

How to get there From Waimate, head northwest on Mill Road, then take a left onto Point Bush Road.

Route description
Follow the signs for the Waimate Walkway. The walkway starts at the car park beside Te Kiteroa homestay, 2 km out of town.

At the main gate, cross the stile and ride straight ahead, following the red and white markers to a second stile. These markers direct you to the track entrance on your left. Follow the track as it flicks back and forth up the hill. Just before the top, the trail meets up with the walkway, so be prepared for walkers from here on.

The lookout point (elevation 400 m) gives you a panoramic vista over Waimate to the Pacific Ocean. You can also spot the Waimate velodrome. Return the same way for an excellent downhill.

Notes Drop in to the Waimate information centre for an update on this and other tracks in the area. The nearby Noondale Forest has been sold, and that ride is now closed.

8 Omarama Saddle to St Bathans
Oteake Conservation Park

This is great back-country ride on old farm tracks, with the option of doing a loop trip if need be. The hills are long and the scenery stark in a beautiful sort of way.

Grade 4   **Time** 3–4 hours   **Distance** 31 km

Track conditions 100% 4WD track

Maps Take NZTopo50 CA15 Omarama, and CB15 Idaburn.

How to get there Head southwest from Omarama for 1 km before turning left onto Broken Hut Road. Go past Twin Peaks, and 17 km from Omarama, veer left at the 'Access to Oteake Conservation Park' sign. Almost 2 km further on, you'll reach a parking area with a DOC information sign.

Route description
Head through the gate behind the sign and follow orange marker poles on the West Manuherikia Track. After 4 km, veer left and settle into an hour-long, 8-km, climb to Omarama Saddle.

At Omarama Saddle the track forks. Drop straight over the other side to go to St Bathans, or head left over Saddle Ridge to do a loop back to Omarama (Note: Saddle Ridge is not all ridable).

If you are going straight to St Bathans, then a fast downhill soon gets you to Top Hut (8 bunks). Another half hour down and you will reach Boundary Hut (8 bunks). These DOC huts are mostly used by 4WDers. They are in good condition.

From Boundary Hut, there are several stream crossings, and after 7 km, you will see a signposted track off to the right. It looked unridable to us, so we continued straight ahead to a gravel road with a DOC signboard, turned right and nipped up to the homestead campsite among the trees 1.5 km away. This is 31 km from the Broken Hut Road car park. The historic Vulcan Hotel at St Bathans is 15 km away, down the gravelly Hawkdun Runs Road, then right up Loop Road.

Warming up on the West Manuherikia Track en route to Omarama Saddle.

Nine Other Rides

Mt Hutt   ★ ☆ ☆ ☆

Several downhill tracks have been built below the ski field at Mt Hutt, and you don't need a DH rig to ride the easier ones.

Grades 4–6   **Time** 1–2 hours   **Distance** Up to 10 km

From Mt Hutt township (110 km west of Christchurch) drive south for 6 km then turn right onto McLennans Bush Road and follow the signs towards the ski field. Drive up the hill for 2 km and then park at the toll-gate building.

There are up to 10 tracks in this area; most include jumps and structures for downhilling, but all the really gnarly stuff can be avoided. The best tracks are higher up. From the toll gate, ride up the ski field road for at least 2 km. Then you'll see a DOC MTB sign on your left. This grade 3+ track heads back towards the toll gate. You can also ride another 1.5 km up the road and start higher up.

On the way down, turn left to ride FUZZ, one of the easier tracks at grade 4. These tracks become horrendously muddy after a bit of rain. Drop in to Big Als Snow Sports in Methven for an update on track conditions.

Methven Walkway   ★ ☆ ☆ ☆

If you're stuck in Methven, waiting for some snow, try this short jaunt.

Grade 1+   **Time** 30–60 minutes   **Distance** 8 km

Pick up a pamphlet on the walkway (50 cents) at the information centre in town, then ride northeast out of Methven on Barkers Road for 1 km. At Holmes Road, ride into the forest and enjoy the first few hundred metres of purpose-built mountain bike track. It weaves tightly through the trees and has some cool dips and jumps.

When you reach the canal, either backtrack or turn left onto the 4WD track beside the canal and carry on to the second road, turn left there and follow Pudding Hill Road back towards town.

The Beast of Otematata   ★ ★ ☆ ☆

Looking for a bit of a blast near Otematata? Try this scenic and hilly ride across a private farm in the Waitaki Valley.

Grade 4   **Time** 2–3 hours   **Distance** 28 km

This ride is over farm tracks, and has the stunning scenery typical of this area. It costs $10 for a map and access to ride this private track. You must book first. Check out www.otematataventures.co.nz for full details or phone (03) 438 7800.

Hakatere Conservation Park ★ ★ ☆ ☆

This park covers 60,000 hectares of the stunning Ashburton Lakes area, 70 km west of Methven, and can be traversed on a variety of 4WD tracks.

Grades 1–3   **Time** 1 hour–1 day   **Distance** 3–45+ km

Take NZTopo50 BX18 Lake Clearwater and BX19 Hakatere. DOC gives brief descriptions for some of the tracks in their "Mountain Biking in Canterbury" pamphlet, which can be downloaded from: www.doc.govt.nz/publications/

As there are some good camping areas and huts in this area, we recommend loading the car up with double rations and your extra-comfy sleeping bag and spending a couple of days exploring around Lakes Heron, Clearwater and Emma.

The austere scenery in Hakatere is the product of its harsh climate – if it's not blistering hot, it's likely to be freezing cold, and you can expect plenty of matagouri along the track edges.

North Opuha ★ ★ ☆ ☆

This is a traditional there-and-back high-country ride that will leave you wishing for more.

Grade 2+   **Time** Approx 2 hours   **Distance** 18 km return

Head north out of Fairlie township on Highway 79 and take the first left after crossing the Opihi River bridge, onto Clayton Road. After 25 km, turn onto Fox Peak ski field road. Park by the conservation area signs, 29 km from Fairlie.

Once on your bike, it's a 7-km, 4WD track ride up through high-country pasture to the North Opuha Conservation Area and then another 2 km to Spurs Hut (built in 1890). Just follow the orange markers, and don't turn left at the saddle.

The hut sleeps four and is a perfect spot for a break. From there, turn around to head back the same way.

Richmond Trail ★ ★ ☆ ☆

A nice introduction to the unique landscape of the Lake Tekapo and Two Thumb Range area.

Grade 4   **Time** 2–3 hours   **Distance** 27-km loop

This ride is one of many described in DOC's "Mountain biking in Mackenzie/ Waitaki" pamphlet (www.doc.govt.nz/publications/parks-and-recreation/activities/ mountain-biking/mountain-biking-in-mackenzie-waitaki/).

Head up the eastern side of Lake Tekapo on Lilybank Road to the Boundary Stream car park, 14.5 km away. Warm up on the road for the next 10 km, then head right up the Round Hill ski area access road. After a few kilometres, you'll pick up the Richmond Trail signposts. They'll soon direct you south, along the

Ditte van der Meulen enjoys a blue day at Lake Heron.

glacial terrace at the foot of the range, and then back down to Lilybank Road just 200 metres north of Boundary Stream.

Lake Tekapo Regional Park ★ ★

This is a great area for a quick blat or a gentle cruise with the family.

Grade 2 **Time** 1–2 hours **Distance** Up to 12 km

If you are staying at the Lake Tekapo Motorcamp, start by cruising east along the lakefront track around to the Tekapo River bridge. Cross the bridge and then head upstream on the Cowans Hill Track. Follow the markers and, after just over 2 km, you'll reach Highway 8 near the end of Lilybank Road. Lake Tekapo Regional Park is across the road – head over and pick up the tracks. They are a mix of single track and old road, mostly in forest, but there's also some lake shore action.

The entire park is only just over 1 km long by 1 km wide. In 2011, the tracks were less developed at the northern end. Once you're done exploring, you can head back the way you came, or follow the water's edge back to town via the Church of the Good Shepherd.

Alps 2 Ocean Cycle Trail ★ ★ ★

Travelling from the base of the Southern Alps to the east coast town of Oamaru, this is the longest New Zealand Cycle Trail in the country.

Grade 2–3 **Time** 1–6 hours **Distance** up to 310 km

The Alps 2 Ocean was still under construction as this book went to print (late 2011), but it was shaping up to be a beauty. If you don't have time for the full trip we recommend you sample the section from Lake Pukaki to Lake Ohau and then on to Omarama. That would be a fine weekend trip. For more information, check out *Classic New Zealand Cycle Trails* (published 2012).

Melina Ridge Track ★ ☆ ☆ ☆

This back-country epic near Omarama has scenery you'll remember for the rest of your life, which is good, because you won't dare go back for seconds! The main climb is an absolute monster.

Grade 5   **Time** 4–8 hours   **Distance** 35–50 km

Pack extra rations, warm clothes and NZTopo50 CA14 Lindis Pass map, then head west from Omarama, over Lindis Pass to the signposted entrance to Lindis Conservation Area. Follow the marked route to Melina Ridge (just below Mt Melina at 1925 m). Don't be suckered by the DOC sign into attempting a direct ascent of Mt Prospect (it's mostly unridable).

From the ridge, either return the way you came or descend a good 4WD track to the Avon Burn River and continue to the Birchwood car park (in the Ahuriri River Valley). Hang right to complete the loop back to Omarama.

Simon earns altitude the old-fashioned way up Mt Melina.   Simon Kennett

Otago

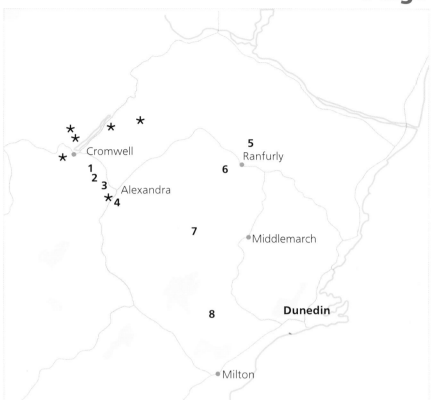

1 **Cairnmuir Mountains**
2 **Omeo Gully Loop**
3 **Alexandra Anniversary Track**
4 **Lake Roxburgh Walkway**
5 **Naseby Forest**
6 **Otago Central Rail Trail**
7 **Dunstan Trail**
8 **Government Track**
★ Plus six other rides

OTAGO HIGHLIGHTS

The Otago Central Rail Trail has been a huge success for this region. It combines safe riding with social overnight stops. Naseby Forest has excellent single track options for intermediate and experienced riders, and Alexandra has several short rides to choose from or the massive climbs into the Old Man Range to push your boundaries.

1 Cairnmuir Mountains ★ ★ ☆ ☆

Clyde

Reckon you're fit? Looking for a space so large and open that it makes you feel tiny? Here's the hill for you.

DOC has marked out the Cairnmuir Hill Track, from Clyde to Bannockburn, with yellow marker posts. The route (which is mostly 4WD track) traverses the Cairnmuir Mountains. The track climbs to an impressive 1100 m.

Grade 4- **Time** 2.5–4 hours **Distance** Approx 30 km

Track conditions 18% sealed road, 18% gravel road, 57% 4WD track, 4% single track, 3% unridable

Maps There is some faint walking track involved, so have NZTopo50 CC13 Alexandra with you to be sure of your navigation. In cloudy conditions, a compass would be handy, too.

Route description

From Clyde, cross the old Clyde Bridge and head south for a few hundred metres before turning up Lookout Road (also known as Hawksburn Road). This is steep and rutted, and you'll soon be so deep in oxygen debt that you could be forgiven for missing the turn onto the Cairnmuir Track. Keep your eyes peeled for a DOC sign on the right, 5 km from the bridge. Don't veer right until you see the DOC sign. From there, simply follow the markers.

Ten kilometres into the ride, you'll be heading up towards some large tors (rock stacks); head through the gate on your right just before reaching them. Another 15–20 minutes later, you'll come to a hut. If you have some single track riding skills, take the sweet water race detour to the right. You'll rejoin the main route 1 km later.

When you reach the end of the track at Cornish Point Road, turn left and cruise a few kilometres round to the Bannockburn Inlet picnic area – a nice spot to be picked up. Bannockburn is an easy 5 km spin from Cromwell.

   Notes Take plenty of water and warm clothing and be sure to leave all gates as you find them. Access is restricted during lambing (from mid-October to mid-November). If you've got a long summer's day on your hands and are feeling particularly staunch, consider riding back to Clyde over Hawksburn Road. Watch out for Spaniards on the walking track section!

2 Omeo Gully Loop ★ ★ ★

8 km from Alexandra

For those with good navigation and technical riding skills, this ride rewards a hard uphill slog with awesome views. There is an option to ride up to the incredible Obelisk on top of the Old Man Range, 1682 m.

Grade 3+

Time 3–7 hours

Distance 28 km

Track conditions 65% 4WD track, 30% gravel road, 5% no track

Maps Take NZTopo50 CC13 Alexandra and a compass or GPS. DOC's 'Prospect Hill Track' and 'Omeo Track' brochures also cover this area.

How to get there From Alexandra, head south over the main bridge, then west to Blackmans (8 km away via Earnscleugh and Blackman Roads).

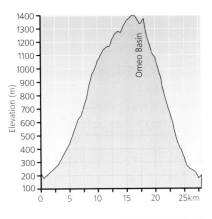

Route description

From the Blackmans intersection, ride up Fraser Dam Road for about half an hour. Just after the crest of a hill, you'll see a DOC sign stating 'Access to Kopuwai Conservation Area' on your left. That's your invitation to start some serious climbing. Follow the yellow marker posts and leave the gates as you find them.

   Keep heading up the Prospect Hill Track past some eerie rock formations and a couple of huts until you get to a locked gate at 1400 m. Now drop southeast into Omeo Basin and pop up to spot height 1377 on the other side. This is where the navigation starts to get tricky.

Where the 4WD track turns hard right, hop over the fence on your left. Now head northeast across tussocklands, directly away from the fence, aiming to keep the gully on your right and some major erosion on your left.

Due to the thick Spaniard grass, you can expect to walk much of the next kilometre. After about 40 minutes, you should reach a 4WD track. Continue heading generally northeast (with a few decent zigzags thrown in for good measure) along Omeo Gully Track and then Omeo Gully Road. This stretch is a real hoot, but be careful of running stock off their legs.

At the bottom of the gully, turn right and cruise 1 km back to Blackmans and then on to Alexandra.

Notes If you are super keen, ride another 5 km up to the impressive Obelisk (1682 m).

Many of the tracks in this area follow access easements across private land – please stick to the marked route.

Also, head elsewhere during winter (when snow covers the tops) and during lambing: mid-October to mid-November.

3 Alexandra Anniversary Track ★ ★ ★ ☆

Alexandra

This ride from Alexandra to Clyde is an excellent introduction to single track. Pick a fine autumn day, and you'll be rewarded with some stunning scenery.

Grade 2   **Time** 1–2 hours   **Distance** 12 km

Track conditions 100% single track

Route description

From Alexandra, cross the big iron bridge heading south, turn left and immediately duck under the bridge onto a single track beside the river. This is a short cut to the car park at the start of the Anniversary Track, which is 1 km from the shops in town.

From the car park, you can't get lost. Follow the main track up river to a car park and road bridge beside Clyde. The track follows the Clutha River and is a lot of fun, in a cruisy sort of way.

Cross the river to enter Clyde, sniff out a cafe to grab a bite to eat, then return via the Otago Central Rail Trail (on the northeast side of the highway), although, heading back the way you came is more fun.

4 Lake Roxburgh Walkway ★ ★ ☆ ☆

INTERMEDIATE

Also known as Mt Rock

Alexandra

This rocky single track is ideal for riders looking to test their skills. Nice scenery, too.

Grade 3   **Time** 1.5–3 hours   **Distance** Approx 15 km return

Track conditions 15% gravel road, 85% single track

Route description

From Alexandra, cross the Manuherikia River on Shaky Bridge before turning right and cycling to the end of Graveyard Gully Road. From the graveyard, where there is a 'Lake Roxburgh Walkway' sign, follow a fun single track beside the Clutha River up to the historic stone huts at Butchers Point. In years gone by, one of these huts was the local hotel!

Riding becomes very difficult beyond Butchers Point, so it's best to turn around and head back the same way. Some riders choose to turn back earlier.

Notes Avoid this narrow track when it's likely to be chocka with walkers, and always give way.

5 Naseby Forest ★ ★ ★ ☆

EASY   EXPERT

12 km north of Ranfurly

If you're looking for great single track and reliable sunshine close to Dunedin, look no further – Naseby is the place to be.

Grades 2–5
Time 1–8 hours
Distance Up to 50 km

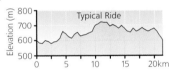

Landowners Naseby is a production forest, and logging is ongoing. Ask for an update at the forest headquarters in Naseby. The forest is occasionally closed because of fire risk. Walkers and forestry trucks always have right of way.

Accommodation Most mountain bikers stay at the Naseby motor camp because it's right on the edge of the forest and it has well-priced cabins. There are also two hotels.

How to get there From Palmerston, take Highway 85 (the Pigroot) for 65 km towards Ranfurly. The historic little town of Naseby is a further 12 km north.

Route description

Most of this exotic forest lies northwest of Naseby village and is festooned with forestry roads and 4WD tracks with numerous single tracks branching off

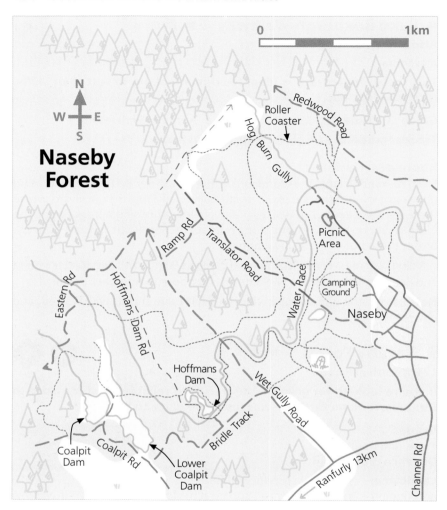

them. The Skatebowl, Ejector Seat and Roller Coaster are some of the features that local riders rave about.

According to our dodgy Internet poll, this is the most popular riding destination in Otago. Many of the tracks are cruisy and scenic; others simply 'flow' amazingly well. You'll feel like riding some bits over and over again until you're knackered.

Start by heading to the top of Hog Burn gully, then explore.

Zigzagging through Naseby Forest.

Zane Smith

6 Otago Central Rail Trail   ★ ★ ★ ★

BEGINNER

Alexandra to Middlemarch

The disused railway from Alexandra to Middlemarch has been upgraded over the years and is now a world-class cycling trail. Out-there scenery, zero traffic and unique Otago hospitality make this one of New Zealand's most popular cycling holidays.

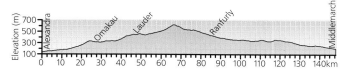

Grade 1   **Time** 2–3 days   **Distance** 148 km

Track conditons 100% gravel, some rough, but becoming smoother with time

Maps Pick up the free "Otago Central Rail Trail" pamphlet, which includes a good map, from any local information centre. Alternatively, go to www.otagocentralrailtrail.co.nz for an encyclopedia worth of information.

Bookings If you want someone to organise your trip along the rail trail, contact Trail Journeys (www.trailjourneys.co.nz) in Clyde. They organise bikes, accommodation, meals and transport. Altitude Adventures in Alexandra offer a similar service (www.altitudeadventures.co.nz).

How to get there Start from either Alexandra or Middlemarch. From the centre of Alexandra, simply ride north on Tarbert Street for 800 metres before turning left onto Little Valley Road, which is part of the Otago Rail Trail.

From Dunedin you can start in style by catching an historic train to the trail. For details about the train, from Dunedin to Pukerangi (or Middlemarch on Sundays), phone Taieri Gorge Railway on (03) 477 4449.

Route description

The rail trail officially starts/ends at Clyde, and follows a straight, flat 8 km to Alexandra. We recommend you either skip this boring section, or take the Alexandra Anniversary Track (see details above) instead. It is much more scenic and fun, but a grade harder.

From Alexandra, the ride starts with a gentle climb up the huge Manuherikia Valley. On your right is the Raggedy Range, which the trail soon climbs over.

The section from Lauder Station to Ranfurly involves riding over the highest point of the trail (620 m), through gorges and tunnels and over old viaducts.

The section from Ranfurly to Daisybank includes a 96-metre-long steel truss bridge across the Taieri River, and from Daisybank, at the 109 km mark, there

All aboard for New Zealand's most popular multi-day ride.

Jonathan Kennett

are three more bridges en route to Hyde. There are good camping sites at various places where the trail passes close to Taieri River.

The trail has a slight downhill slope most of the way from Hyde to Middlemarch – the end of the line, so to speak. From here, the most fitting end to your trip is to catch the train to Dunedin (see details above). Most days, it leaves from Pukerangi (25 km from Middlemarch). For very fit riders, the most appealing option from here is to cycle back to Alexandra via the Dunstan Trail (140 km; see below). Alternatively, Dunedin is 75 km away via Highway 87.

Notes There are plenty of accommodation options at every town and village along the trail. See www.otagocentralrailtrail.co.nz for over 100 options!

7 Dunstan Trail

Dunedin to Alexandra

This trip is a collection of quiet gravel roads, 4WD tracks and old wagon trails pioneered as a bike route by gnarly cycle tourers in the 1970s.

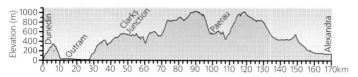

Grade 3+   **Time** 2–4 days   **Distance** 170 km

Track conditions 35% sealed road, 45% gravel road, 20% 4WD track

Maps To follow the Dunstan Trail proper, it is essential to take NZTopo250 26 Alexandra and NZTopo50 CD15 Paerau. The existing road diverts from the trail twice.

Route description

To leave Dunedin by the shortest possible route, cycle straight up Stuart Street from the Octagon and veer right onto Taieri Road, which turns into Three Mile Hill Road. Soon after crossing Silver Stream, turn right onto Milners Road. Carry straight on and you'll reach Highway 87 a few kilometres north of Mosgiel. It's mostly uphill cycling, northwest on Highway 87, to Clarks Junction 49 km from Dunedin.

Alternatively, a fun way to start is to catch the train to Middlemarch or Pukerangi (see Otago Rail Trail).

The Old Dunstan Road turns off to the left here, and you head into an isolated and barren Central Otago landscape. From Clarks Junction, it is 48 km of up and down (but mostly up) to the abandoned Paerau township (called 'Styx' by the locals) where there is an esplanade reserve by the Taieri River. The jail here has a fireplace that may be useful if it's raining or snowing. If you go any further than the river, you'll be on private land.

It's a hard 71-km day from Paerau to Alexandra with a lot of uphill and heaps of downhill. Cycle north out of Paerau on the Styx-Patearoa Road for 1.5 km. A fence heads off to the left 150 metres after a hay shed. The next 800-metre section of the old trail you're looking for has been ploughed up, but if you cycle along the northern side of the fence up towards the hills, you'll soon pick up two historic cartwheel ruts in the grass. They're marked on the map as a 4WD track and lead to a derelict house on Linnburn Runs Road, 7 km away. In this stretch, you'll need a compass to avoid drifting onto new, misleading 4WD tracks.

From the house, head north for 300 metres before turning west onto another 4WD track, which is also part of the original Dunstan Trail. After 3 km, this track meets up with the Old Dunstan Road. Route finding from here on is relatively easy. From Poolburn, it's 50 km mostly downhill to Alexandra.

Notes The historic Dunstan Trail was the route originally used by goldminers in the 1860s to travel from Dunedin to the goldfields in Central Otago. This area experiences extremes of weather any time of year, so go well prepared. In wet conditions, parts of the trail are unridable because of sticky mud.

During a northwesterly wind, it's easier to do this trip in reverse, from Alexandra to Dunedin.

If it's wide open spaces free from man-made structures that you're after, get in quick. The area is earmarked for large-scale windfarm development.

8 Government Track ★ ★ ★

40 km west of Dunedin

INTERMEDIATE

Government Track is a classic, pre-mountain biking single track through beautiful native forest.

Grade 3

Time 3–5 hours

Distance 23 km

Track conditions 45% gravel road, 10% pylon track, 45% single track

Maps Take NZTopo50 CE15 Waitahuna.

How to get there From Dunedin, drive towards the township of Waipori Falls, west of Taieri Plains.

Route description

Start from the picnic area, which is marked on the map beside Waipori Falls Road, 2 km after entering the bush. Cycle back down the road for 1 km before turning left onto Government Track. This old coach road sidles its way up to a wide pylon track on top of the ridge. Most of the track runs through beech forest, but about 30 minutes into the climb, you'll reach a patch of farmland where navigation is tricky. Dip down to the left very briefly at the arrowed 'Track' sign and then just keep climbing gradually through the paddock. A stile awaits on the other side of the paddock. We found the climb to be about 90% ridable.

From the gravel road at the top (by the 'Government Track' sign), you have two options. Either turn right and continue on to Lake Mahinerangi via the forestry roads, then cross the dam and go back along Waipori Falls Road, or go left for a short cut to Waipori Falls township (as per the altitude graph). The latter route turns into a steep single track, which is unridable for a minute near the bottom. A permit is required to head through the exotic forest to the lake. Visit Wenita Forest Products Ltd in Harstonge Avenue, Mosgiel, phone (03) 489 3234 or go to their website: www.wenita.co.nz

Notes Expect to encounter windfalls if you're heading in after a big blow; these are normally cleared in early autumn. Government Track can be covered by snow in winter. Walkers also use this track, so be wary.

Six Other Rides

Packspur Gully   ★ ★ ☆ ☆

The Packspur is the east side of the Cardrona-Cromwell Pack Track, which traverses the gigantic and impressive Pisa Range.

Grade 4   **Time** 3.5–7 hours   **Distance** Approx 21 km return

Most of this ride is shown on NZTopo50 CB12 Cardrona. Take it along with DOC's 'Wanaka Outdoor Pursuits' brochure.

Head north from Cromwell on Highway 6 for 3.7 km before turning left up Lowburn Valley Road. Two kilometres later, turn right up Swann Road. Another 2 km on, you'll come to a sign and stile at Lowburn Station. Follow the markers across the yards and over a small bridge, then enjoy your last easy breaths. For the next 1.5–3 hours you'll be grinding your granny gear up the Packspur Gully Track.

Eventually the gradient mellows and you'll need to turn left onto the Cardrona-Cromwell Pack Track. There's even a little bit of descending as you pass a large shed and then a 9-bunk hut. But the difficulty of the riding ramps up another notch as the track narrows and speargrass closes in. We just went on for another 2 km and then turned around and enjoyed the ride home

If you have extra rations and a hankering for a hike 'n' bike, you can carry on to Meg Hut and Tuohys Saddle. Then return to Cromwell via Roaring Meg or head on over to the Cardrona Valley (see Southern Lakes: Pisa Range). Good luck!

Extra water, tyre sealant and sunblock will doubtless come in handy in this region.

Devils Creek Track ★ ☆ ☆ ☆

Old farm tracks in the Bendigo Conservation Area make for an excellent test of lungs and brakes.

Grade 4   **Time** 2.5–5 hours   **Distance** Approx 21 km return

Refer to NZTopo50 CB13 Tarras for this ride.

Head 7 km northeast of Cromwell bridge on Highway 8 (beside Lake Dunstan) until you see the DOC sign, 'Devils Creek Track' (there's a lakeside picnic area across the road).

From the sign, a ridiculously steep 4WD track climbs up to Mt Oho and on to Mt Kinaki (1309 m). Some bike pushing will be necessary on the way up, but the views and ride back down make it all worthwhile. Never mind the blurry vision as you approach the tops – that's a perfectly normal reaction to near vertical grades at this altitude.

You can also access the Bendigo Conservation Area from near the top of Thomsons Gorge Road by riding over Mt Moka (see Rise 'n' Shine below). From there, the riding all the way to Mt Apiti is much easier.

Dave Mitchell's retro body armour.

Tour de France racers think 12% is a steep grade – the first kilometre of this ride averages 20%!

Rise 'n' Shine, Thomsons Saddle   ★ ★ ☆ ☆

Here's a great ride for anyone wanting to check out the Dunstan Mountains without the challenge of tricky navigation or the hassle of contacting landowners.

Grade 2   **Time** 2–4 hours   **Distance** 50 km

Head out of Cromwell across Lake Dunstan and drive northeast on Highway 8 for 13 km to The Stables shop, Crippletown (1 km north of a lakeside picnic area).

From Crippletown, jump on your bike and follow the gravelly Bendigo Road east to Thomsons Gorge Road. Keep heading generally southeast, over Thomsons Saddle (980 m), through Thomsons Gorge and on to Highway 85 at Omakau. Like most of Central Otago, this trip offers expansive views but is exposed to the elements.

From Omakau, you can follow the Otago Central Rail Trail (see above) down to Alexandra, 28 km away – no hills or cars to contend with.

Dunstan Lakeside Track   ★ ★ ☆ ☆

A good Cromwell-based introduction to mountain biking.

Grade 1+   **Time** 30–60 minutes   **Distance** 10–20 km

From the Old Cromwell historic district, follow a mix of road and dirt tracks north around the lakefront to Lowburn. Then head up Lowburn Valley for 500 metres to cross the valley without using the main highway bridge. Once back at the lakeside, continue on up to Brittany Cove and Pisa Moorings. This is the end of the track. Give yourself time to check out the sites and the fresh fruit. If you run out of time, return to Cromwell via Highway 6.

If that ride left you wanting more, try the south lakeside track, which heads southwest from Old Cromwell to the Bannockburn bridge and beyond towards Kawarau Gorge.

The "Walk Cromwell" brochure (available from the Cromwell information centre) is loaded with useful maps.

Carricktown Loop   ★ ★ ☆ ☆

This excellent day trip from Cromwell is loaded with history and awesome scenery.

Grade 3+   **Time** 3–6 hours   **Distance** 31 km

Before getting packed for this trip, call Don Clarke of Carrick Station, on (03) 445 0977, for permission to ride from Duffers Saddle down to Carricktown. Then, with NZTopo50 CC12 Bannockburn in hand, cycle out of town west, past Bannockburn and all the way to the top of Nevis Road. Turn right and ride north, into the midday sun, on an undulating 4WD track. After 5 km, turn right again and enjoy the downhill past Carricktown on to Quartzville Road and Schoolhouse Road, which takes you back to Bannockburn.

Remains of stone buildings are all that are left of Carricktown, but the Young Australian waterwheel a short distance away is worth a look-see (to your right).

Sarah Drake on the Carricktown Loop.   Simon Kennett

Roxburgh Gorge Trail ★ ★ ☆ ☆

Grade 1   **Time** 1–2 hours   **Distance** Up to 33 km

This trail between Alexandra and Roxburgh Dam started construction in late 2011. It is one of the New Zealand Cycle Trail projects and should be an excellent beginners' day trip.

This easy graveled cycle path will start from just south of the large Highway 8 bridge on the edge of Alexandra. Follow signs down to the track and then along the western side of the Clutha River. You will soon enter the impressive Roxburgh Gorge. Turn around and head back when you feel like it. The first 10 km should be complete sometime in 2012. It is unclear when the trail will be finished all the way through to the dam.

Exploring near St Bathans.

Mike Wilson and Freeload Ltd

Dunedin

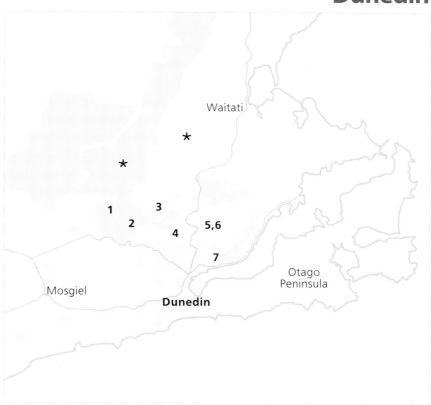

1 **Racemans Track**
2 **Whare Flat**
3 **Swampy Summit**
4 **Wakari Creek Tracks**
5 **Forrester Park Track**
6 **Bethunes Gully**
7 **Signal Hill**
★ Plus two other rides

DUNEDIN HIGHLIGHTS

In Dunedin, in summer and autumn, you can get out there with your bike and thrash yourself on some of the best purpose-built single track in the country. However, in wet winter conditions, you will have to be choosy as many tracks get churned up.

1 Racemans Track ★ ★ ☆ ☆

ADVANCED

15 km northwest of Dunedin

A well-graded, technical track through native forest. Best ridden when dry.

Grade 4   **Time** 2–3 hours   **Distance** 13 km return

Track conditions 40% gravel road, 60% single track

Maps You can pick up a pamphlet on this area from the Dunedin information centre at the Octagon.

How to get there Drive west out of Dunedin on Stuart Street, then Taieri Road and then Three Mile Hill Road. When you are 10 km from the Octagon, turn right onto Silverstream Valley Road and go for another 5 km. Stop at an obvious parking area that is 200 metres past the Scout Camp.

Route description

From the car park, pass the gate and continue up the gravel road, across a ford and look out for the signposted Racemans Track on your right. There is a little bit of walking to get up to the actual tail-race, but then the riding improves. There are still a few short walking sections, but after about 1 hour, you will reach the top weir.

After a rest, head back from the weir the way you came until you reach the signposted intersection where you can turn right down to the Powder Creek Track. This provides a 15-minute diversion from Racemans Track. Then you will cross a ford and be back at the gravel road you cycled in on, only 5 minutes from the car park.

Notes The tracks around here can be very boggy and slippery after rain, and tree falls are common after storms.

The uncompromising Racemans Track.

Jonathan Kennett

2 Whare Flat ★ ★ ★

6 km from central Dunedin

People who enjoy technical challenges will want to spend all day on the freaky tracks at Whare Flat.

Grades 4–5   **Time** 1–3 hours   **Distance** 12 km

Track conditions 30% forestry road, 70% single track

Maps For a map and updates on tracks at Whare Flat, take a look at www.mountainbikingotago.co.nz

How to get there To ride or to drive there, that is the question. Ride southwards from town via the Switchback Track (see below), or drive out on Stuart Street, Taieri Road and then Three Mile Hill Road. One kilometre past Halfway Bush, you'll reach Flagstaff Whare Flat Road on your right, next to a reservoir. Climb halfway up Flagstaff Whare Flat Road towards the 'Bull Pen' car park, before stopping at Laings Road on your left.

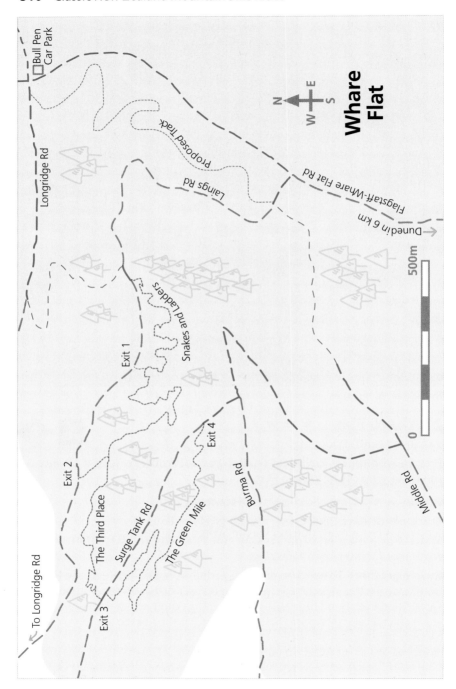

Bull Pen
Car Park

Longridge Rd

Proposed Track

Laings Rd

Flagstaff–Whare Flat Rd

Dunedin 6 km

Whare
Flat

N
W E S

500m
0

Snakes and Ladders

Exit 1

Exit 2

Exit 4

Burma Rd

Middle Rd

The Third Place

Surge Tank Rd

The Green Mile

Exit 3

To Longridge Rd

Route description
Head up Laings Road for almost a kilometre and you'll find a sweet single track called Snakes and Ladders only 40 metres away on your left.

Snakes and Ladders leads on to The Third Place, which leads to The Green Mile. All three together are 5 km long and are smattered with dozens of interesting obstacles (some are grade 5 and not all have bypasses so treat them with respect). The track is grade 4 if you don't ride any of the obstacles.

There are big rock drops, see-saws, log rides, and of course, ladders. No snakes yet, but the track is still under construction. If you like a technical challenge, you will love this track. None of the built obstacles are over 1 m high.

The Green Mile leads to Surge Tank Road. Follow it to the right to Burma Road, then take the next two left-hand turns. You will climb back up to Laings Road, only 100 metres from where you started.

Notes The tracks must be dry to be fully ridable. Local mountain bikers plan to build a single track link from the Bull Pen to Laings Road in 2012/13. We've tentatively marked it on our map.

3 Swampy Summit
8 km northwest of Dunedin

This is an old classic for Dunedin mountain bikers that has been overtaken by the new single track popping up all round the place.

Grade 3
Time 2–4 hours
Distance 16-km loop
Track conditions 50% gravel road, 25% 4WD track, 25% grassy single track

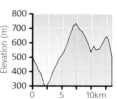

How to get there From the Octagon in town, head south up Stuart Street, Taieri Road, and over Three Mile Hill Road, and after 5.5 km, turn right onto Flagstaff Whare Flat Road and drive 2.5 km up to the 'Bull Pen' car park. Alternatively, ride out via the Switchback Track (see below).

Route description
From the Bull Pen, continue straight ahead on the gravel road, and enjoy a fast 5-minute downhill. Turn right at Rollinsons Road and then settle in for a steady half-hour climb to Swampy Summit.

Turn right at the ridge and pass the Doppler radar, which looks like a UFO. Go right at the next two intersections and watch out for the nasty rut on the way down. Then you'll be riding along the ridge, past the turn-off to the Switchback Track, which is now the best way from Swampy Summit back to Dunedin.

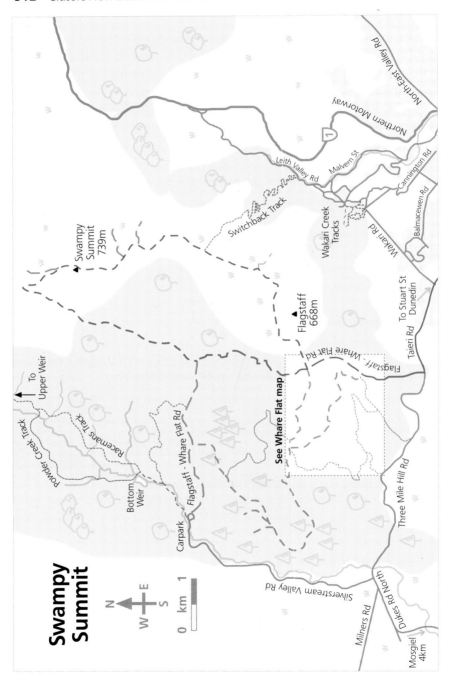

If you wish to return to the Bull Pen, take the next two right-hand turns (but don't turn right down a really steep track near the end).

Notes The Pineapple Skyline Walkway also starts from the Bull Pen, but be warned: this is the sole domain of pavement plodders and the haunt of old ladies (with thermos flasks and woollen mittens) who lie in wait for law-breaking mountain bikers, with the intent of shoving their ivory-handled walking sticks through the offending spokes and then trampling the hapless rider under slippered feet – this high-conflict walkway is best avoided.

Mid-summer's morning bliss, Swampy Summit.

Jonathan Kennett

Switchback Track ★ ★ ★

This single track is by far the best way to ride between Dunedin and Swampy Summit. Use it to create a loop to Swampy Summit or Whare Flat and back.

Grade 3 **Time** 1–2 hours **Distance** 9 km

Route description

From the north end of Malvern Street, Dunedin, head up Leith Valley Road roughly 1 km and stop at a small bridge across Nicols Creek. The track starts 10 metres past the bridge on your left. The first couple of kilometres have been gravelled and ride brilliantly. From there on, the track narrows a bit and can be muddy in winter.

Boardwalk masterpiece on the Switchback Track.

After climbing several kilometres from Leith Valley Road, the mountain bike track stops and meets up with an old farm track – forge ahead to reach Swampy Summit ridge. At the ridge, turn right to go to the summit or left to go to Whare Flat.

To do it the other way round, ride from the Bull Pen at Whare Flat up the 4WD track towards Swampy Summit for 3 km, then look out for a minor track on your right (it's at the top of the second crest along the ridge).

Notes Be prepared for a wintery climate at the top any time of year.

4 Wakari Creek Tracks ★ ★ ★
3 km north of central Dunedin

Once completed, this pair of single tracks will be the best 'easy' grade ride in Dunedin.

Grade 2 **Time** 30 minutes–1 hour **Distance** 6 km

How to get there Head over to Wakari Road, about 3 km from the north end of George Street.

Route description
In 2010, a sweet 3-km loop through redwood forest was built. In 2011, a second 3-km loop was being added. The tracks are being gravelled, have a mellow gradient and are sheltered – an excellent spot for a spin at any time of year.

If you rode across, there's a track entrance just north of the corner of Wakari and Burma. If you drove, there's a car park and mapboard near the northeast end of the Wakari Road straight. From either spot, simply get your bearings by following your nose around the lower loop in a clockwise direction.

Notes Please steer clear of the Ross Creek Walking Track.

5 Forrester Park Track ★ ★
Normanby, Dunedin

This is a great beginner's ride or warm-up for Bethunes Gully (just across the road).

Grade 2
Time 15–20 minutes
Distance 2.5 km

Track conditions 100% single track

How to get there Head out to North East Valley and cruise up Norwood Street. About 100 metres past the last house, turn right at Forrester Park (signposted).

Route description

Forrester Park Track skirts around the back of the playing field, then the back of the Dog Club building, before entering the pine forest and squiggling through this small block of trees. After 5 minutes, you'll pop out, back near the top and can ride across the BMX track towards Bethunes Gully (see below).

This is an ideal ride for young kids just getting started.

6 Bethunes Gully ★ ★ ★ ☆ Tues Feb 4, 2014 🚵 INTERMEDIATE

Normanby, Dunedin

This forest area has some awesome single track built for XC racing.

Grade 3   **Time** 1 hour   **Distance** 5 km

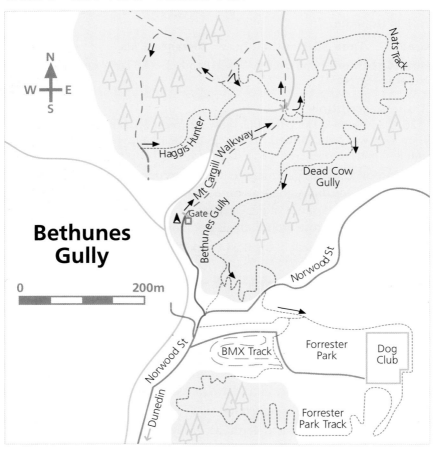

Bethunes Gully at race pace.   Celia Lie

Track conditions Mostly purpose built single track with a little bit of wide walking track thrown in the mix

How to get there Start with a warm-up on Forrester Park Track (see above for directions).

Route description
After Forrester Park Track, cross Norwood Street and ride up to the Bethunes Gully picnic area. Check out the signboards, and the map on the facing page. Now ride up the gravelly Mt Cargill Walkway for almost 1 km before turning left at some recently felled pines (it should be signposted). Follow this forestry track for 300 metres, then turn left again onto some purpose-built single track called the Haggis Hunter. Och Aye!

This brings you back to the walkway, but not for long. After re-crossing the main stream at the bottom, look out for the start of Nats Track on your left. This climbs up to a clearing, then rewards you with a fun descent through pines. It will spit you back out onto Norwood Street.

Notes Respect the 'walking-only' status of the upper Mt Cargill Walkway.

7 Signal Hill ★ ★ ☆ ☆

North Dunedin

This scrub and pine forested hillside bears some of the oldest and newest MTB single track in Otago.

Grades 2–5
Time 1–2 hours
Distance 5–10 km

Track conditions 100% single track

Maps For the latest information and a map of Signal Hill see 'Rides and Tracks' at: www.mountainbikingotago.co.nz

How to get there A new track from the back of Logan Park High School, on Butts Road, climbs at an easy gradient up to all other tracks on Signal Hill. You access the track from the driveway to the left of the school grounds.

Signal Hill revitalised.   Hamish Seaton

Route description

With map in hand, ride to the top of Signal Hill and then tackle whatever route takes your fancy. We started with the Zig Zag, the Contour and the Haggis Basher – all good tracks but quite short. The older XC tracks are on the top half of the hill and can be ridden within 2 hours.

Once you're done with the XC tracks, start heading downhill to Logan Park. Aim to emerge at the playgrounds behind Logan Park High School. Watch out for killer jumps on the way down to the park. The safest retreat is via the new track you climbed up on.

Notes This area was getting a major overhaul in 2011, with several kilometres of new track being built.

Two Other Rides

Pulpit Rock ★ ★ ☆ ☆

This old-school enduro ride leads you into the depths of the remote Dunedin outback.

Grade 3+ **Time** 5–8 hours **Distance** 48 km return

First up, get yourself an access permit from Wenita Forestry. Pop into their office on Hartstonge Avenue in Mosgiel (turn off Gordon Road at the New World) or try their website: www.wenita.co.nz

Warm clothes and NZTopo50 CE17 Dunedin are also essential.

Ride from North Taieri (15 km west of Dunedin) and head up Taioma Road. From the top, stay on the main gravel road for the next 10 km and, at the bottom of the second long downhill, you'll reach a four-way intersection, next to Big Stream. Hop over a gate to your right and cycle up beside Big Stream. After 4 km, turn right onto a steep, somewhat marginal 4WD track heading up into pine forest. Zigzag up this rutted track to a gravel road on a ridge, then turn left.

Sunday morning at Pulpit Rock. Hallelujah!

Adrian Robinson

You can see Pulpit Rock in the distance, about 6 km away as the cyclist pedals. If the weather is fine, it's worth climbing the last 50 metres to the rock – leave your bike near the gate below the top and walk up a little track on your left.

Once back with your bike, continue north from Pulpit Rock. After 1 km, you'll pass a turn-off on your right, which leads to Mt Silverpeak (777 m), the highest spot in the Silverpeaks. Head west along the ridge, passing several turn-offs, for almost 7 km, until you reach a sharp left turn signposted 'Boggy Burn'. This drops you back down to Big Stream. Watch out for the spiked gate at the bottom. From there, head back out the way you came in.

Parts of this pine forest were closed for logging in 2010. Wenita will let you know when access is open when you apply for your permit. The first 12 km of this trip can be driven, but beyond that, it's a bit rough for 2WD cars.

Green Hill   ★ ☆ ☆ ☆

This is an old-school ride for those who love the outdoors. The track must be dry to be fully ridable.

Grade 4   **Time** 2 hours   **Distance** 10+ km

Take NZTopo50 CE17 Dunedin with you. The best way to start this ride is via Swampy Summit. Then continue north on the Swampy Ridge Track for another 4 km. Alternatively, drive over to Blueskin Bay and head up Double Hill Road and Semple Road for about 7 km.

If riding via Swampy Summit, when you reach the ridge, turn left at the signposted 'Swampy Ridge Track' and ride north for 4 km. Then, turn left again at the 'Green Hill' sign.

The next 4 km is reasonably technical single track. Stop at the old Green Hut clearing for a breather before heading back the same way.

If driving, park at the roadside clearing opposite the 'Green Hill' signpost along Semple Road. The first part of this track is badly rutted by motorbikes. You will have to walk some of it.

On the way down, you can come out via the signposted 'Mountain Track' road, which is more ridable, and then ride along the road (which becomes Semple Road) for just over 1 km to get back to your car.

Notes Green Hill is only 1 km from Pulpit Rock, but the track between the two is an unridable slog.

This is a remote area, go well prepared for bad weather and mechanicals.

Southern Lakes

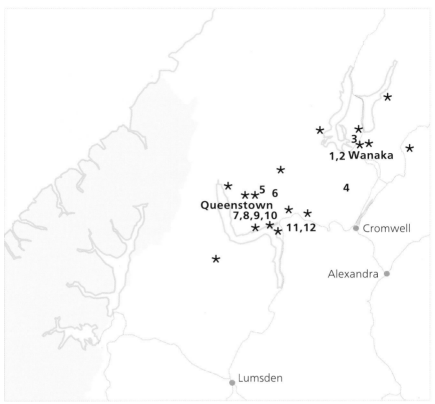

1. **Wanaka Lakeside Tracks**
2. **Plantation Trails**
3. **Dean's Bank Track**
4. **Pisa Range**
5. **Skippers Canyon**
6. **Macetown**
7. **Moke Circuit**
8. **Seven Mile MTB Area**
9. **Queenstown Bike Park**
10. **Fernhill**
11. **Kelvin Peninsula Track to Jacks Point**
12. **Ben Cruachan**
★ Plus sixteen other rides

Racer's Edge-Great bike shop in Wanaka

SOUTHERN LAKES HIGHLIGHTS

Nowhere in New Zealand are you more spoilt for choice than Queenstown and Wanaka. There are loads of stunning old walking tracks, purpose-built single tracks, challenging free-riding trails and several gnarly all-day missions in the mountains. Queenstown even has a gondola to take you and your bike up a mountain side.

1 Wanaka Lakeside Tracks ★ ★ ★ ★
Wanaka

Here are two great rides to do from downtown Wanaka. Load up on coffee and buns before hitting the trails. It's worth picking up DOC's "Wanaka Walks and Trails" brochure on the way out of town.

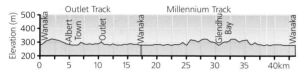

Wanaka Outlet Track

BEGINNER

Grade 1+   **Time** 1–2 hours   **Distance** 18-km loop

Track conditions A mixture of 4WD track, gravel road and single track

How to get there Ride from Wanaka to Albert Town via Highways 84 and then 6. Just before the Albert Town bridge over the Clutha River, hang a left and drop to a track along the river's edge.

Route description
From beside the bridge, follow the track and marked route beside the river, back towards Wanaka. You'll pass Beacon Point and Penrith Beach (a great swimming spot), from where another signposted single track leads to Bremner Bay.

At the end of the track, follow the road, either straight ahead or to the right, back to Wanaka township. If you head right, through the pines, you'll connect up with a third section of single track.

Notes If you want to avoid the road riding, simply ride the single track there and back. Expect to see walkers and runners along the way.

Cruising the Wanaka lake front.

Jonathan Kennett

Millennium Track to Glendhu Bay

EASY   INTERMEDIATE

Grades 2–3+   **Time** 1–2 hours   **Distance** 26 km return
Track conditions Almost 100% single track

Route description

This track follows the lake front from Wanaka township to Glendhu Bay. From the Wanaka shops, ride west around the lake front for a few hundred metres, and you'll pass a 'Waterfall Creek 20 min' sign. From there, it's easy single track most of the way to Waterfall Creek Reserve 3 km away. Sweet!

From the signboard at the reserve car park, the Millennium Track continues around the lake to Glendhu Bay. This section includes a few steep, loose bits and the potential for a killer fall, so you may want to walk in places.

Notes This is a popular walking track, so take it easy and ride elsewhere during busy holiday times. If you like this track and would like to support the development of more like it, check out the Upper Clutha Trails Trust at www.uctt.org.nz

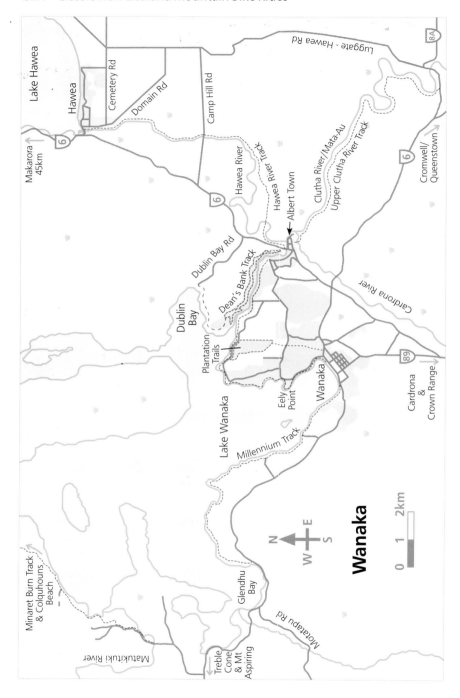

2 Plantation Trails ★★★

INTERMEDIATE

EXTREME

Also known as Sticky Forest *Really fun tracks!*

Wanaka *Helps to ride them with the locals. Lots of tight corners, jump + berms.*

A maze of fantastic trails has been built on the edge of Wanaka – but before you jump on your bike, visit one of the bike shops in town or the information centre to get a map of the tracks. Without it, you're lost.

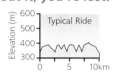

Grades 3–6

Time 1–4 hours

Distance 10–30 km exploring

Track conditions 15% 4WD track, 85% single track

How to get there From the Wanaka information centre, ride north, past the Lismore Bike Park (a jumper's heaven) along a short bit of Kings Drive and onto the Scurr Heights Track. Follow it all the way to the bottom of Hoe Down track, near the southern end of the forest.

Route description

We recommend the following intro for intermediate riders: ride up Hoe Down (track number 1), along Easy Street (3), through the Double Gate, down Venus (10), then up Cranking Fine (33) and down 4G (9). Now you're at The Hub, which offers a smorgasbord of track beginnings and ends. We headed up Scooby (7) a couple of times to ride Dizzy Turns (54) and then Venus again.

A guaranteed fun way to finish is to Hoe Down (1) back to the nearest cafe, via Scurr Heights Track. Yeehaa!

Notes In 2011, the status of these trails was still up in the air, as the long-term use of the land was being reviewed.

The less developed tracks in Hikuwai Reserve to the east of the Plantation are on DOC land. These can be accessed from the Outlet Track (see Wanaka Lakeside Tracks above), adjacent to the Clutha River, or from the Plantation Trails via the narrow and smooth Sidle Track (number 32).

Bilantis rock drop, Sticky Forest.

Simon Kennett

3 Dean's Bank Track ★★★★

EASY

Albert Town, Wanaka   *Unreal- rode this 4 times!*

Wanaka is fast becoming a mecca for MTB family holidays, with the smooth-flowing, purpose-built track at Dean's Bank being a star attraction.

Grade 2+   **Time** 1–2 hours   **Distance** 11.5 km

Track conditions 100% single track

How to get there From Wanaka, head to Albert Town via Highways 84 and then 6 or ride via the Outlet Track (see Wanaka Lakeside Tracks above). Cross the Clutha River bridge and then immediately turn left into the Albert Town camping site entrance. The Dean's Bank trail head is to your right, about a hundred metres away.

Route description

Check out the mapboard before hopping over the stile and heading up the bank. Most of the climbing is tackled in an impressive series of switchbacks. Just keep following the markers to complete a loop of this sweet single-track network (in a clockwise direction).

There are a couple of obvious bailout options should you find yourself running out of time, energy or light.

Notes Water and toilets are available at the camp ground. Much of this ride heads through areas thick with wild rose – a fresh puncture kit might come in handy. This area can also be accessed from Dublin Bay, via the old Dublin Bay Track.

Jenny Taylor mellows out on Dean's Bank.   Sarah Drake

4 Pisa Range

Between Lake Wanaka and Queenstown

The Pisa Range is a massive yet benign-looking set of hills. It provides the highest altitude cycling in New Zealand but is subject to polar weather conditions for half the year.

How to get there A couple of pamphlets promote mountain biking on several access roads and tracks up to the Pisa Range. The tracks are nearly all too steep to ride up (eg, the Roaring Meg access leads to an unridable poled route). The best access up is via the snow farm road or off the Crown Range Road (described below).

Tuohys Gully ★ ★ ★

Cardrona, 24 km south of Wanaka

Grade 4
Time 3–5 hours
Distance 27 km
Track conditions 40% gravel road, 60% farm track
Maps NZTopo50 CB12 Cardrona is essential.
How to get there From Wanaka, head 20 km south on the Cardrona Valley Road (Highway 89). Soon after passing a

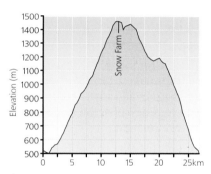

'Cardrona Alpine Resort' sign, turn left at the 'Waiorau Snow Farm' sign, then right at the 'Roaring Meg Pack Track' car park sign.

Route description

From the car park, backtrack to the snow farm entrance and follow the main snow farm road up the hill for 12 km. There are marker posts every kilometre.

At the 12-km marker post, you should turn right and ride past the building closest to you (this is the edge of the snow farm). Ride along a straight flat for 100 metres, then follow a 4WD track to the bottom of a ski tow in the gully on your right. Climb out of the small gully and across to the high point 1460 marked on the topomap. Veer right again towards some transmitters, hop over a gate and then turn left just before the transmitters. There has been development around here, so you'll need the map to confirm you're heading in the right direction.

Now follow the main farm track all the way to Tuohys Saddle, which is signposted. The ride from here on is very cool indeed.

From Tuohys Saddle, you can nip over to Meg Hut (DOC), 2 km away, or turn right and follow a fast and furious track down the gully to the car park you started from. Red waratahs mark the way. About 500 metres before the car park, you have to veer right, off the farm track and across a flattish paddock to a stile. It's marked but easy to miss if you're blazing.

Notes This track is impassable in winter due to snow, but you can hire skis up at the snow farm instead. Throw plenty of warm clothes and extra food into your pack at any time of year.

If you are feeling fit and don't mind some road riding, start by riding 17 km up the Crown Range Road to the Crown Range Saddle and then head to Tuohys Gully via Mt Hocken, Mt Allen, and Quartz Knoll (1593 m) – a fine test of the old ticker!

Pisa Range Snow Farm ★★☆☆

INTERMEDIATE

Grade 3 **Time** 1–4 hours **Distance** 55 km

Maps The snow farm lodge has an up-to-date map of the trails.

From December to April, you can drive up to the snow farm lodge (13 km up from the valley floor) and explore 55 km of ski trails by bike. They are cross-country ski trails, so the riding is easy, and the scenery is fantastic. If the weather is perfect, ride up to Mt Pisa. At 1963 m, it is the highest fully ridable mountain in New Zealand.

You must check in at the lodge office before starting your ride. There is a fee of $10 per adult for 'Area usage' and 'Trail fees' – it's less for families and children.

Notes The lodge hires out bikes as well as offering meals and accommodation. For more information, check out www.snowfarmnz.com or phone (03) 443 7542.

Cardrona-Cromwell Pack Track ★★☆☆

ADVANCED

Grade 4+ **Time** 1 day **Distance** Approx 36 km from snow farm

Maps Definitely take NZTopo50 CB12 Cardrona.

Here's a great wilderness trip in the Pisa Conservation Area. From the very top of Mt Pisa, follow a 4WD track south along the main range for about 12 km to connect up with the Cardrona-Cromwell Pack Track. This rough track heads west to Meg Hut (DOC) and involves some walking through speargrass as well as some stretches of technical riding.

From Meg Hut, a 2-km 4WD track leads up to the saddle above Tuohys Gully. Take the steep track down to the car park in Cardrona Valley (at the bottom of the snow farm road).

Nicky gets some authentic altitude training on top of the Pisa Range. Tim Dennis

Alternatively, descend east from the tops via the Packspur Gully track (see Otago, Other Rides).

Notes This is big country. For further information about the 22,000 ha Pisa Conservation Area, contact the DOC office in Wanaka. Take lots of water and warm clothing. If you are at all unsure of the weather, also carry a compass or GPS, extra food and a survival blanket.

5 Skippers Canyon ★ ★ ☆ ☆

EASY   ADVANCED

Queenstown

As the name suggests, this is dramatic, steep and rocky terrain. The area's long history of mining and farming has left a network of old 4WD tracks waiting to be explored.

Grades 2–4

Time 2 hours–3 days

Distance 10+ km

Maps NZTopo50 CB11 Arrowtown is essential for trips beyond Skippers Bridge.

How to get there Ride north from Queenstown on Gorge Road. After 12 km, turn left up the Coronet Peak ski-field road. After another 4 km, turn left again onto Skippers Road.

Route description

From Skippers Saddle, either continue down Skippers Road or dive down the Skippers Pack Track.

Skippers Pack Track

This superb, pre-mountain biking single track starts at Skippers Saddle and rejoins Skippers Road after 5 km. The round trip down the track and back up the road to the saddle takes about 1 hour. The track is grade 3 in dry conditions. See our Mt Dewar map later in this chapter.

Skippers Ghost Town

Track conditions Mostly rough gravel road and 4WD track, some single track

Almost 16 km down from Skippers Saddle, on one of the narrowest and scariest public roads in New Zealand, you can turn left and drop 1 km down to Skippers Bridge and then climb 500 metres to a picnic/camping area near Mount Aurum Station. There are several excellent interpretation boards and a water supply here.

A couple of great walking trips start from the Mount Aurum camping area. Try heading up to Dynamo Flat or the Phoenix Battery. Both routes were much-travelled goldminers' trails back in the old days and are steeped in fascinating history.

Notes There are scary drops off the side of the single lane road down to the Shotover River hundreds of metres below. To do a guided trip in Skippers Canyon, check out www.vertigo.co.nz

Zoot Track

If you are riding back to town from Skippers Saddle, check out the 1-km Zoot Track, south of the saddle. It's a short cut down to the sealed Skippers Road. Be prepared for lots of ruts and jumps – best take it real easy your first time down.

6 Macetown ★ ★ ★ ☆

Arrowtown

Macetown is a great ride for a group with riders of all abilities. The track is generally easy, and it is an interesting destination to aim for.

Grade 2+
Time 2–4 hours return
Distance 30 km
Track conditions 95% 4WD track, 5% water

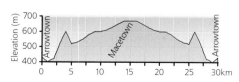

Martin Langley, Macetown bound.

Jonathan Kennett

Maps DOC's 'Arrowtown Walks and Trails' pamphlet and NZTopo50 CB11 Arrowtown show the route.

Other users 4WD vehicles, motorbikes, equestrians, walkers

Route description

From the west end of the Arrowtown shops, you'll see a 'Macetown' sign 100 metres away. From this sign, a slightly confusing jumble of tracks heads up into the valley. Follow the main 4WD track northeast (to your right).

En route, you'll cross the Arrow River over a dozen times. Often there are short sections of single track, which bypass a couple of fords. If you find yourself on one that involves clambering up a large bank, turn back – you're heading up the side valley to Soho.

There are small yellow pegs along the way marking points of interest – for the self-guide brochure describing these points contact the Lakes District Museum in Arrowtown or DOC in Queenstown.

At peg '3', make sure you turn right.

At the 'Macetown Historic Reserve' sign, you should follow the main 4WD track as it crosses the river and then heads left, up the obvious side valley to Macetown.

At the Macetown Historic Reserve, there are interpretation boards and loads of great picnic spots. You can continue a further 2 km up valley to check out the Anderson Battery if you're interested in that sort of thing. Return the same way.

Notes Best done on a stinking hot day. With so many deep fords to cross, taking some oil is a smart idea.

7 Moke Circuit ★ ★ ★ ☆

Queenstown

INTERMEDIATE

Moke Circuit provides a quiet yet challenging journey by bicycle through the rustic Ben Lomond Station.

Grade 3+

Time 3–6 hours

Distance 33 km

Track conditions 40% sealed road, 40% 4WD track, 20% single track

Landowners You'll be passing through Ben Lomond Station, but no longer need to call for access permission.

Route description

Head southwest out of Queenstown and cycle around the lake front for 7 km. Turn right at the 'Moke Lake' signpost and climb the road to Moke Lake. The gravel road leads past the lake to a fence with an 'Arthurs Point' sign on it. Climb over the stile and continue for a few minutes before hopping over a fence beside two gates and riding up valley on a well-formed gravel road.

After a few kilometres of sidling around the hill high above Moke Creek, you'll pass a small car parking area and drop steeply down to the valley floor only to climb straight up again after crossing a side stream.

After passing 'Seffertown', the track eventually becomes narrow and technical, and a little bit of bike carrying is necessary. Most intersections are signposted, and before long, you'll start descending to Arthurs Point. The last few kilometres of single track (known as the Moonlight Track) are used for horse trekking. When you reach a cluster of houses, follow McChesney Road down to Arthurs Point.

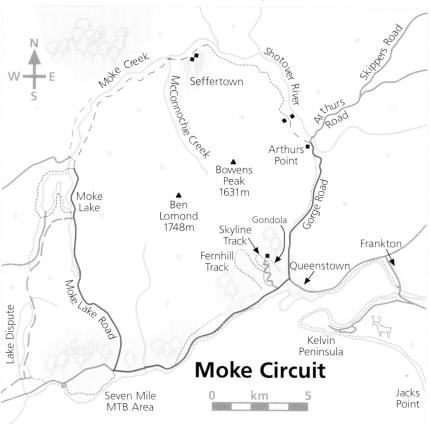

Moke Circuit

David Drake

Simon coasting past Moke Lake.

Queenstown is 5 km to your right, down Gorge Road (much of which has a shared path running alongside it).

Notes If you are a fit expert rider, try this loop in an anticlockwise direction. You can add in the Lake Dispute Track and then the Lakefront Tracks at the end as the icing on the cake. This turns it into an excellent 41-km, grade-4 loop with 1200 m of climbing.

For a shorter trip, ride up and around Moke Lake and back via Lake Dispute (see Other Rides below).

8 Seven Mile MTB Area
EASY   EXPERT

Queenstown

There are 11 MTB tracks jam-packed into this DOC recreation reserve. The tracks are managed by the Queenstown MTB Club. Get hold of a copy of their MTB trail guide from a bike shop in town.

Grades 2–5
Time 20 minutes–2 hours
Distance 1–12 km
Track condtions 100% single track

How to get there From Queenstown, drive/ride out of town on the road to Glenorchy for 8 km before turning left down to the Wilsons Bay parking area. The tracks are signposted from there.

Alternatively, only ride out of town for about 6 km before heading left onto the rough Seven Mile Point Track, which is two-way and dual use.

Route description

Make your way up to The Hub, where there's a large map and groovy wooden structures to test your skills on – a great place to meet other riders. From The Hub, we recommend checking out Cool Runnings, Kirks Terrace, Kachoong, and Grin & Holler (with a detour through Fruit Loop).

After that, you'll either be finding your bearings or totally confused. Regardless; we guarantee you'll be wanting more. These are some of the best flowing tracks anywhere!

Notes If, like us, you are not a big jumper, take it easy on your first run down these tracks. If the largest jumps in this area leave you wanting more, check out the Wynyard Freestyle Terrain Park, Fernhill, Queenstown.

Expect to meet walkers on the original DOC Seven Mile Point Track.

Richard Goldsworthy testing his latest hand-built bike on Hammy's Track.   Jonathan Kennett

9 Queenstown Bike Park ★ ★ ★ ★

Queenstown

This is the riding area with all the buzz in Queenstown now. The trip up in the gondola takes 6 minutes, and the ride down through Ben Lomond Forest takes 10–20 minutes. There is a range of half a dozen tracks to choose from. The tracks are closed over winter.

Grades 3–6

Time 1–4 hours

Distance 5–50 km

Track conditions 100% single track

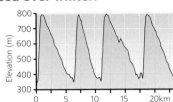

Timing The gondola carries bikes from 10 am to dusk daily, mid-September through to the end of April, except for busy holidays such as Christmas and Easter. Check out www.queenstownbikepark.co.nz for more information.

Route description

From downtown Queenstown, ride up Brecon Street to the bottom of the gondola. There you will be offered one trip up for $30, or 5 hours of trips for $45. Trust us – take the $45 deal; these tracks are great fun, and you'll want to ride them more than once.

You can still ride up the Skyline/Gondola Access Road (off Lomond Crescent). It takes around 40 minutes and is an excellent cardiovascular workout.

At the top of the gondola, there is a small bike repair and hire shop called Vertigo. There they also sell Queenstown trail maps and run guided trips (phone them on (03) 442 8378). To get to the tracks, ride to the left of Vertigo, then veer right and aim for Hammy's Track 100 metres up the road.

Hammy's Track

This is the most popular track in the park, and the easiest. It took us 20 minutes down the first time and 15 minutes the second time, on hardtails. It is a damn good grade 3 track, if you avoid all the jumps and wooden obstacles (and they are easy to avoid), but if you take every gnarly line possible, it's grade 5. Lots of grade 3 riders are pushing their luck and breaking bones.

Vertigo and more

This is an old classic that has recently been given a beautiful makeover with big berms and jumps. It's good to try after you've dialed Hammy's. It's grade 4, with some harder grade 5 options.

After Vertigo, there are a number of grade 5 tracks to try. The easiest is Turd Sandwich (marked as Single Track Sandwich), and the hardest is Grundy (it's a grade 6). All these options lead to a track called Original, which leads to the

Flying through Ben Lomond Forest.

...dred metres of Hammy's, which takes you right back to the bottom
...ola.

...al runs down these purpose-built tracks, you may start craving for
...natural single track – not a problem! Fernhill branches off Hammy's
about a quarter of the way down (see Fernhill below).

Notes These tracks are exciting, but don't get too carried away. More riders
are being carried out of Ben Lomond Forest than any other area in the country.
Just take it easy, and you'll still be riding at the end of your holiday.

10 Fernhill ★ ★ ★ ★

Queenstown

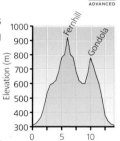
ADVANCED

**This is a fantastic natural track, highly rated by locals
and visitors alike for its great views and interesting
technical riding.**

Grade 4+
Time 1–2 hours
Distance 5–10 km

Track conditions 100% single track

Route description

There are two ways to start this ride: take the gondola or ride up the road. If
you take the gondola (see above for details), then ride down Hammy's Track
for a few hundred metres, watching out for Fernhill branching off on your right
at a switchback.

Alternatively, cruise round to the bottom of the Skyline/Gondola Access Road,
on Lomond Crescent. It's a 5-minute ride to the track, and there's a 'Ben Lomond
Walkway' sign at the bottom.

From the sign, climb the main gravel road for 1.5 km to the Halfway Hub
(centre of the gondola downhill tracks). A stone's throw up from the clearing
is the Fernhill Track. Climb through beech forest and onto tussock country for
an awesome view, then head back the same way.

On the way back down, merge with the crowds and take Hammy's Track
back to Queenstown.

Notes This track has been built by local mountain bikers and DOC. It is steep
in places and therefore prone to damage by skidding tyres. If you haven't
got the skills to avoid skidding, then stick to gravel roads. The Skyline/Gondola
Access Road is a private road with a locked gate at the bottom.

11 Kelvin Peninsula Track to Jacks Point ★ ★ ★ ☆

Frankton

This ride comprises brilliant single track, with awesome lakeside vistas.

Grade 2 **Time** Approx 1.5 hours **Distance** 15-km loop

Maps A map of the Jacks Point Tracks is available at:
www.jackspoint.com/downloads/JP-Trail-Map-Summer-2010.pdf

Route description

From the southern end of the Kawarau River Bridge just out of Frankton, head southeast for a minute before climbing up Peninsula Road. Two minutes later, drop down Willow Place to the water's edge, veer left and shortly you'll be following single track close to the lake's edge. After about 20 minutes, you'll pass a playground and golf course; carry on to the very end of the peninsula.

After riding around the peninsula, head left up the first road you reach, and you'll soon see the playground again, only 300 metres away. Cruise back to Frankton by the main road or the track. Alternatively, carry on around the lake to Jacks Point.

Jacks Point (also known as Lakeside Trail) ★ ★ ★ ☆

If the Kelvin Peninsula Track (see above) left you champing at the bit, then you'll enjoy this technical and scenic single track.

Grade 3- **Time** Approx 1.5 hours **Distance** 12 km return

From the peninsula golf course, continue southeast around the lake. The first kilometre is tight and technical – many riders avoid this by starting from the reserve at the end of Jardine Park Road (where there's a short track and jumps in the pine forest). From there on, the track is a much higher standard, although there are still some steep sections to test expert riders.

Wherever you start, the impressive rock outcrops of Jacks Point are your goal. After soaking in the view from the outcrops, head back the way you came or, if you are full of beans, head around Jacks Point Loop (adjacent to the new golf course). This loop has some very, very steep bits.

12 Ben Cruachan ★ ★ ★ ☆ Not good!

Gibbston, 30 km east of Queenstown

Pick a fine day, and this ride will take your breath away; it's one of the most sustained climbs, and descents, in the country.

Grades 4–5 **Time** 4–7 hours **Distance** 40 km return

Maps Take NZTopo50 CC11 Queenstown and CC12 Bannockburn.

Route description

From Gibbston, 30 km east of Queenstown, follow Coal Pit Road for 7 km, climbing 700 vertical metres to Coal Pit Saddle. From the saddle, an easy water-race track heads southwest around the hills for 4.5 km. A steep 2-km-long track then climbs up to a 4WD track on the main ridge. You can follow this track over Mt Salmond and all the way to Ben Cruachan (1895 m). Turn around when you feel like it to enjoy the massive downhill.

Remarkables–Ben Cruachan

EXPERT

Grade 5   **Time** 6–10 hours   **Distance** 44 km

Alternatively, if you're feeling wired, ride up to the Remarkables ski field from Queenstown and hoof it across rough terrain to Ben Cruachan. This takes up to an hour of tramping over steep rocky slopes, so you will have fully earned the 1500 m downhill to Gibbston.

The key to this route is riding to the top of the eastern ski tow and then picking a good line up rocky slopes to carry your bike up to the prominent ridge. Aim for a spot about 500 metres south of high point 2057. From there, it is 50% ridable over to Ben Cruachan, which sets you up for the massive downhill. The scenery will blow your mind.

Notes If you're feeling lazy, give Vertigo a call on 0800 VERTIGO. They can transport you to Coal Pit Saddle or Ben Cruachan and from Gibbston back to Queenstown. Extra food and clothes and gallons of water are essential.

Sixteen Other Rides

Isthmus Peak   ★ ★ ☆ ☆

The ultimate example of a long, barely ridable climb rewarded by a remarkable vista and warp-speed descent.

Grade 4-   Time 2–4 hours   Distance 16 km

This ride is mentioned in DOC's 'Wanaka Outdoor Pursuits' pamphlet: www.activedownunder.com/images/wanaka-outdoor-pursuits-brochure.pdf

Drive north from Wanaka and set your odo at the Albert Town bridge. Continue north on Highway 6 and at 26.8 km, park up just north of Stewart Creek. Hop on your bike and head back over Stewart Creek before following the marker poles up, down, up, up and away … A couple of hundred metres are unridable, but the rest is do-able, just. When you get up to the ridge between Lakes Wanaka and Hawera, turn right and tackle the last stretch up to Isthmus Peak at 1386 m.

Don't forget an extra warm layer, emergency rations and your camera. The ride is closed from 20 November to 20 December for fawning.

Descent from Isthmus Peak.

Simon Kennett

Lake Hawea Circuit ★ ★ ★

Public access to the full circuit has been restricted to one day a year, during the Contact Epic mountain bike race, held in April each year.

Grade 2 **Time** 1 day **Distance** 95–125 km

There are two courses, the 95-km Classic and the 125-km Epic – both are worthy of those familiar superlatives, and all entrants will feel a great sense of accomplishment at the end of the day. The 125-km Epic is a full lap of the lake, starting and finishing in Hawea. The 95-km Classic starts at Kirks Bush, cutting out the first quarter of the Epic. The scenery is fantastic around Lake Hawea, so rather than race through, you may prefer to cruise with some mates at the back of the field. It's still a long way though.

For more information, and an entry form, go to www.contactepic.co.nz

Minaret Burn Track ★ ★ ☆ ☆

Another little beauty courtesy of the high-country Tenure Review process; this ride provides breathtaking views across Lake Wanaka.

Grade 3+ **Time** 3–6 hours **Distance** Approx 34 km return

Refer to DOC's "Minaret Burn Track" pamphlet, then head west out of Wanaka. Four kilometres past Glendhu Bay, turn right onto West Wanaka Road, and after another 5 km look out for the DOC car park at Homestead Bay.

Follow the DOC markers over a rambling mix of single track and farm track. You'll reach the Rumbling Burn Stream after 10 km – if you're not bursting with energy, this is a good spot to check out the beach and then turn back.

From Rumbling Burn, the track climbs to a high terrace and traverses it before dropping down to Minaret Burn. We went just far enough to get a view up the valley, then headed back the way we came.

Minaret Burn Track.   Simon Kennett

Hawea River Track ★ ★ ★ ☆

An easy gravel path follows the Hawea River most of the way from Albert Town to Hawea township.

Grade 2+ **Time** 1–2 hours **Distance** 10.7 km one way

Ride or drive from Wanaka out to Albert Town. Cross the highway bridge and take the first right to the signposted Hawea River Track. From there follow the gravel track all the way to Domain Road, on the outskirts of Hawea township, at the southern end of Lake Hawea. There is a café in town less than a kilometre away.

If you have a trailer or tag-along bike, be aware that there is a big swing bridge near the start of the track with a sizeable set of steps forming the main hurdle in this ride.

Upper Clutha River Track ★ ★ ★

A scenic ride above the Clutha River with the odd steep hill to raise your heart rate, but otherwise an easy, smooth track.

Grade 2+   **Time** 1–2 hours   **Distance** 14 km one way

From Wanaka, head 5 km northeast to Albert Town. Then turn right down Kingston Street, and a few hundred metres later, right again into Kinnibeg Street. Follow the 'Upper Clutha River Track' signs to a car parking area down a narrow gravel road. You can ride from Wanaka to here around the lake front tracks.

From the car parking area, check out the signs, and then ride up to a bridge and, on the other side, turn left and climb up the gravel track. It is easy to follow for 14 km to Shortcut Road (Highway 8A). In mid-2011, the track ended here.

There are plans to extend the Upper Clutha River Track all the way to Cromwell. Check out www.uctt.org.nz for trail building progress and to make a donation.

Fantastic views from the Upper Clutha River Track.   Jonathan Kennett

Lindis Loop ★ ★

This road and farm-track loop offers fantastic views, a historic site and one awesome descent through iconic high country.

Grade 2+   **Time** 4–8 hours   **Distance** 53 km

Check out the DOC pamphlet "Lindis Valley Tracks" before driving north from Tarras (33 km east of Wanaka) on Highway 8 for 17.6 km and parking on the left at the start of Old Faithful Road.

Ride up Old Faithful Road to the derelict Lindis Pass Hotel (a good camping spot). Then carry on to the Lindis River ford.

After crossing the ford and joining the highway again, head south for 1 km before turning left onto Goodger Road. Follow this road past the Tim Burn and Pleasant Valley car parks on to the base of McPhies Ridge. By now, the route follows DOC markers along faint grass 4WD tracks.

Climb up onto McPhies Ridge, past the high point of 836 m, along the tops and finally down a fast, silky smooth descent to Lindis River. Cross the river bridge, climb a few hundred metres up to the highway and turn right. Eight fast kilometres on the road will lead you back to where you started.

Notes This area is closed from June to 5 December due to wicked winter weather and then lambing. Be prepared for cold weather any time of the year. The neighbouring Lindis Peak and Chain Hills tracks are extremely steep.

Whakaari ★★★☆

Grade 3+ **Time** 2.5–6 hours **Distance** 14–20 km
Here's a new conservation area 43 km northwest of Queenstown that is loaded with interesting historic mining sites and old access tracks.

Check out DOC's wee booklet on this area for a small map and brief history tour; available from the DOC office above Outside Sports in Queenstown. The Jean and Bonnie Jean huts are uninhabitable.

Just 2 km east of Glenorchy, you will find the main entrance to the Whakaari Conservation Area (altitude 390 m).

Head past the display panels and up, up, up to top out nicely with the Bonnie Jean Hut (940 m). The first and last kilometres are very steep, but much of the rest is good satisfying riding. You'll want to walk the last few hundred metres from the stream to the hut. Check out the displays before returning the way you came.

If you are feeling in the zone and ready for some hike 'n' bike, try the loop up to Heather Jock Hut at 1300 m (via Bonnie Jean Hut) and back via Jean Hut.

Motatapu Valley ★★☆☆

The ride from Glendhu Bay to Arrowtown via Motatapu Valley passes through three private properties and is not generally open to the public. There is an exception …

Grade 3 **Time** 3–6 hours **Distance** 50 km
Once a year, in mid-March, the Motatapu Icebreaker mountain bike event passes through this area. The entry fee in 2012 is $140. For more information on this

opportunity, contact Iconic Adventures, phone (03) 441 1025, email info@iconicadventures.co.nz, or visit www.iconicadventures.co.nz/motatapu-home/

Lake Dispute ★★☆☆

Although the track is fairly tame, this is a fun wee ride if you enjoy exploring new areas.

Grade 3+   **Time** Approx 1.5 hours   **Distance** 13 km

Head southwest out of Queenstown and cycle around the lake front for 7 km. Turn right at the 'Moke Lake' signpost and climb the road to Moke Lake – a fairly stiff climb. Immediately before the lake, leave the road at the DOC signpost, following a single track with many boardwalks to your left. Continue following the DOC signs and markers to Lake Dispute. Some of the riding is slow going through lumpy grassland, but you'll pick up an easier gravel road shortly before the lake. Then, not far past the lake, the DOC signs will direct you off to a steep single track descent back to the main road. Turn left to head back to town.

Mt Dewar ★★☆☆

A classic back-country trip with a little bit of everything – ups, downs, arounds, great views, interesting navigation.

Grade 3+   **Time** 2–4 hours   **Distance** 19 km

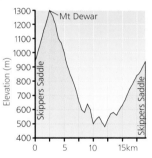

Take NZTopo50 CB11 Arrowtown on this ride. From Queenstown, drive north towards Coronet Peak. After 12 km, turn left at the 'Skippers Road' sign, drive for another 600 metres and park at the saddle.

A DOC mapboard at the saddle shows the route you are about to take. Start by tackling the half-hour climb up to Mt Dewar (1310 m). From the top, you can just about see Sydney (on a fine day).

Now follow a steep 4WD track down to the huts beside the Shotover River. Watch out for the bike-bucking water bars.

From the huts (one old and one new), a rough track takes you past a slip face to Butchers Point. The track then veers away from the Shotover and joins up with Skippers Road just a few hundred metres from the bottom of the Skippers Pack Track (too steep to ride up). From there, the well-graded but rough Skippers Road leads back up to Skippers Saddle. It's only a 300 m climb; should take about half an hour.

Notes This ride is on retired high-country leasehold land now administered by DOC. Don't forget your jacket; things can get nippy on the exposed tops.

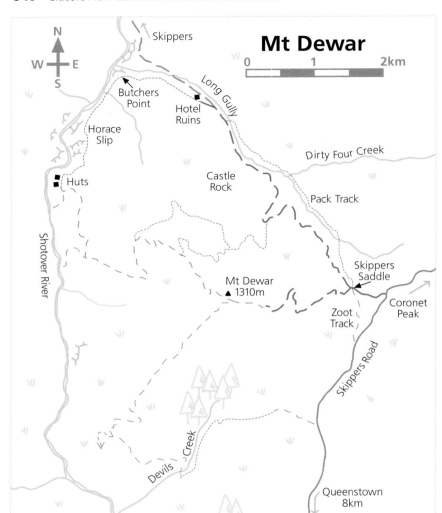

Mt Dewar to Devils Creek ★ ★ ☆ ☆

Grade 3+ **Time** 3 hours **Distance** 20-km loop from Arthurs Point

From the top of Mt Dewar, you can also ride southwest to an intersection at grid reference 576 125, then drop down to Devils Creek. The climb out of the creek is only slightly hellish and won't take an eternity. From a small saddle, an old farm track leads back down to Skippers Road, a few kilometres north of Arthurs Point, which is just north of Queenstown.

Queenstown Lakefront Tracks   ★ ★ ☆ ☆

Grade 3+   **Time** 30 mins–1.5 hours   **Distance** Up to 17 km one way

From Queenstown, a series of single tracks leads southwest around Lake Wakatipu, providing an envigorating way to, or from, the Seven Mile MTB Area and Moke Lake.

Sunshine Track: (Grade 3+, Distance 2 km) The first single track heading along the lakeside west of Queenstown is Sunshine Track. It's very steep and technical in places but worth the effort.

Start from the Fernhill roundabout, a few hundred metres southwest of central Queenstown. Simply follow the single track heading away from town. Expect walkers around any corner.

Seven Mile Point Track: (Grade 4, Distance 3.5 km) From the end of Sunshine Track, you can spin round the lakefront road for a couple of kilometres to Seven Mile Point Track or climb up Fernhill Road and Arawata Terrace for 500 metres to do the Arawata Track. Expect a little bit of walking.

Arawata Track: (Grade 3, Distance 2 km**)** Arawata Track starts from the end of the drive below 45 Arawata Terrace and leads you down to the Glenorchy Road about 4 km from Queenstown. It is all ridable.

About 6 km from Queenstown, turn left off Glenorchy Road at the 'Seven Mile Scenic Reserve' sign. Follow the main track through the Seven Mile MTB Area, around to Wilson Bay.

Twelve Mile Delta Track: (Grade 3, Distance 6.5 km) From Wilson Bay, you can cycle along Glenorchy Road for 2 km to the start of Twelve Mile Delta Track, which is signposted. Start by heading down a gravel road for 600 metres, veer right and follow the main 4WD track for 300 metres. This then becomes a single track.

There are two historic stone kilns worth checking out along the way. After 5 km, you'll reach a fork in the track; turn left to extend the ride by 5 minutes or right for a short cut.

Then drop down to Bobs Cove and take three consecutive right-hand turns to return to Glenorchy Road. You're now 13 km west of Queenstown.

Bobs Cove Track: (Grade 4+, Distance 1.5 km) This short track is not 100% ridable but goes through some splendid native forest. In fact, it's also a nature trail, with some trees labelled for your edification. You might want to ditch the bike part of the way along the track and join the leaf peepers.

These tracks are very popular with walkers – expect loads of tourists, particularly at the Queenstown end. In 2011, maintenance on some of these tracks was a bit lacking.

Frankton Walkway   ★ ★ ☆ ☆

This track follows the edge of Frankton Arm between the Botanic Gardens in Queenstown and the Kawarau River Bridge at Frankton. It's used a lot by local walkers and bikers, so take it easy.

Grade 1+   **Time** 45 minutes   **Distance** 9 km

From the Kawarau River Bridge at Frankton, hop up to the turbine and follow a short track down to the lake edge 100 metres away. Turn right and follow the gravel road for a few hundred metres before veering left onto a gravelled track. From here, the walkway is a mixture of single track, 4WD track, gravel and sealed road. Just after passing the wooden boat club, cycle up Park Street to cruise into the centre of Queenstown.

This track is also an excellent way to get to Lake Hayes (see below).

Lake Hayes   ★ ★ ☆ ☆

Lake Hayes offers a quick, easy, single-track spin around a beautiful lake – ideal for a family outing.

Grade 2-   **Time** 40–60 minutes   **Distance** 9 km

From Queenstown, head northeast on Highway 6. A couple of kilometres past the Shotover River bridge, turn into the signposted car park on the left. Ride down to the lake and complete a lap in either direction. Apart from a couple of stiff wee climbs, this ride makes for an easy, good time for the whole family.

Best ridden in autumn when the leaves are turning. Avoid this ride in weekends and public holidays when it will be swarming with tourists and dog walkers. This ride can also be accessed from Arrowtown via Lake Hayes Road.

Gibbston River Trail   ★ ★ ☆ ☆

This is a nicely graveled path that offers stunning scenery with just a few short steep hills to keep you honest.

Grade 3   **Time** 40–60 minutes   **Distance** 7 km one way

From Queenstown, you can cycle off-road trails to the historic Kawarau River bridge (where they do the bungy jumping) or just drive there. 100 metres from the bridge, on the edge of the big car park, you will find a 'Gibbston River Trail' sign. From there, navigation is easy. At the far end, turn around and ride back the same way. This is well worth checking out, but be aware of other users around any corner. Sight lines are generally good, but there are a few massive drops off the side of the track.

Notes We did the so-called 'dangerous' Wentworth Bridge Loop and thought it was fine for any expert rider.

Jonathan Kennett

Southern Lakes single track - virtually impossible to beat on a fine autumn day.

Mavora Lakes   ★ ★ ☆ ☆

Mavora Lakes are a great destination for fat-tyred cycle tourers. The roads and 4WD tracks between Queenstown and Te Anau are quiet and the scenery stunning.

Grade 2   **Time** 2 days   **Distance** Up to 160 km return

Refer to NZTopo50 CC09 North Mavora Lake.

From Queenstown, catch the steamboat *Earnslaw* across Lake Wakatipu to Walter Peak (phone 0800 656 501 to book in advance). One adult plus bike cost $34 one way in 2011. Over summer, the *Earnslaw* is scheduled to leave Queenstown at 10 am, 12 noon, 2 pm, 4 pm, 6 pm and 8 pm. If you just want to do a day trip, then check out www.aroundthemountains.co.nz and book an independent trip (it's quite good value).

From the jetty at Walter Peak, cycle west 12 km around to Mt Nicholas Station, then head south on the quiet Von Road for almost 40 km. Turn right at Mavora Lakes Road and within 8 km, you'll reach the official road end at the second lake.

From the road end, follow the 4WD track beside North Mavora Lake for about an hour to Carey's Hut. 4WD vehicles have thrashed the track in places, so you'll have to nip out to the lake edge from time to time to avoid some boggy sections. Carey's Hut (DOC, 6 bunks) is a good place to shelter from either rain or sandflies.

If you're keen to explore further, you can ride for another hour up to Boundary Hut (DOC, 6 bunks; no fireplace) or 2 hours up to Forks Hut (DOC, 4 bunks).

From the huts, turn around and backtrack to Mavora Lakes. You can then either head back to Lake Wakatipu and Queenstown, or ride south to Te Anau 65 km away.

This ride is particularly popular with Southland-based riders and the lakes are a great place to go camping ($5 per tent site). In winter, take your skis instead!

Southland

1 **Percy Pass**
2 **Mt Bee**
3 **Dog Box Hut**
4 **Waikaia Bush Road**
5 **Bald Hill**
6 **Sandy Point**
★ Plus three other rides

SOUTHLAND HIGHLIGHTS

For a short ride close to Invercargill, the tracks at Sandy Point are great fun. For hard-core adventurers, the magnificent Percy Pass is a must. For something in between, the Eyre Conservation Park has a few intermediate rides with fine scenery.

1 Percy Pass ★ ★ ★ ★

EXPERT

Manapouri, Fiordland

This is the stuff that epics are made of! Long miles, a difficult and remote bike-carry section, unpredictable and often wild weather. Even if everything goes according to plan, it's a hard ride but like all good adventures, very rewarding.

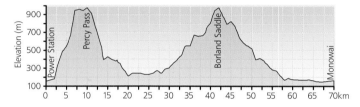

Grade 5   **Time** 8–12 hours   **Distance** 70 km

Track conditions 80% rough gravel road, 18% 4WD track, 2% unridable

Maps Take NZTopo50 CD07 Manapouri, CD06 Deep Cove and CE07 Lake Monowai.

How to get there Catch the tour boat across Lake Manapouri to the hydro power station at West Arm. A one-way ticket costs $38 (plus $7 for a bike). Phone Real Journeys on 0800 65 65 01 to pre-book.

Route description

From the wharf, ride past the right-hand turn-off to the power station. After a few minutes, take the left-hand turn across the Spey River and towards the power station hostel. Turn left just before the hostel garages and hop over a gate. From here, recalibrate your pain-meter as you climb, climb, climb for an hour or two until you reach a wide hanging valley. Cross this valley and climb just a wee bit more to the top of Percy Pass, next to a telecommunications hut.

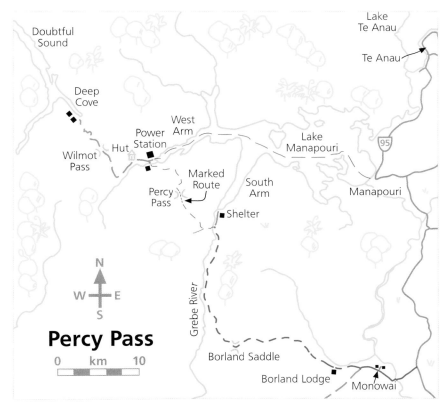

From here, the power transmission line, which is your guide for most of this ride, dives down to another hanging valley almost 300 m below. There is a basic route heading left, then down, marked with a handful of waratahs and cairns. You must carry your bike across steep scree slopes and through thick native bush for around an hour before reaching the pylon track that leads to Monowai.

The marked route wisely stays just above the bushline for as long as possible before diving down to the far pylon. That way it avoids any crazy bush-bashing. Travel light or you'll be making two trips down this tricky route.

Next comes a rocky descent with numerous switchbacks down to a river. Cross the river and take the left fork, past pylon 30. Continue to a T-intersection beside Grebe River. If you're looking for a campsite, turn left at the bridge and ride a few kilometres to the South Arm of Lake Manapouri, where there are toilets, a shelter and flat land for camping.

Otherwise, turn right to carry on to Monowai. A gravel road follows the bush-clad valley floor for almost 15 km before climbing steeply up to Borland Saddle, way off in the distance. From here, it's a long gentle descent to Monowai, 27 km away.

From Monowai to Manapouri, it's an extra 42 km of quiet sealed road through rolling farmland.

Notes Manapouri township has the only shop anywhere near this route – stock up well. Insects in this area are so fierce that power station workers receive a special 'sandfly allowance'!

There is a DOC hut near West Arm (Lake Manapouri) and backpacker accommodation at the far end of the ride at both Monowai Lodge and Borland Lodge.

The hydro power station is worth a visit – it's New Zealand's largest, built 200 m underground into solid rock.

2 Mt Bee ★ ★ ☆ ☆

ADVANCED

21 km north of Lumsden

A huge climb up onto the tops is rewarded by fantastic views, improved fitness and a long descent back the same way.

Grade 4

Time 2–5 hours

Distance 18–32 km

Track conditions 100% 4WD track

Maps Refer to NZTopo50 CD10 Eyre Peak.

How to get there Head north from Lumsden for 13 km on Highway 6, then turn left at Five Rivers. Cruise towards Te Anau for 3 km before turning right onto Irthing Road. Park by the DOC sign at the end of Irthing Road, almost 5 km away.

Route description

At the end of Irthing Road, hop over a gate and follow a farm track north across the paddocks for 2 km. The track then veers left and enters a Rayonier Forestry pine forest (recently logged).

The track you're after then starts climbing seriously – whenever it forks, take the high road. The Mt Bee huts are just over 9 km (and 600 vertical metres) from the road end.

Dave Mitchell

Busy as a bee approaching the mountain top.

From the huts, the track deteriorates as it climbs another 300 m up the spine of Mount Bee. The views are fantastic, but watch out for the razor-sharp rocks around here. As the topomap shows, the track finishes just short of spot height 1203. The downhill back to Irthing Road is a blast.

Notes Mt Bee huts have eight bunks and four mattresses. DOC has no plans to maintain this track. There is an official camping area beside Mulholland Road, 2 km north of the start of the ride.

3 Dog Box Hut ★ ★ ☆ ☆

INTERMEDIATE

120 km north of Invercargill

This ride follows the Eyre Creek Valley into the Eyre mountains, through an interesting mix of farmland and native forest.

Grade 3 **Time** 2.5–5 hours **Distance** 30 km return

Maps There are some handy maps in DOC's "Eyre Mountains/Taka Ra Haka Conservation Park" pamphlet. Alternatively, refer to NZTopo50 CD10 Eyre Peak.

How to get there From Highway 6, 1.5 km west of Athol, turn up Eyre Creek Road. About 5 km from the highway, there is a DOC sign at the Eyre Creek Station boundary. There are frequent farm gates for the next 5 km (if you're driving by yourself, it would be easier to cycle this stretch). After another 5.5 km, the gravel ends at the Glen Eyre Station boundary.

Route description
Follow orange marker poles along the public access easement to the park boundary and continue up the 4WD track to the 'three-star' Shepherd Creek Hut.

The next 5 km to the historic Dog Box Hut offer difficult riding in places, but you won't want to slow down for long – the sandflies are as ferocious as a swarm of hungry flying piranha.

Dog Box Hut is perched above the track on the right, just past Dog Box Creek. Return from here the way you came.

Notes Mataura River, just to the north, provides an alternative ride, but both the track and the scenery are better on the Dog Box Hut ride.

4 Waikaia Bush Road

80 km north of Gore

Although it starts out on a scenic gravel road suitable for the whole family, don't be fooled; this ride eventually ends up tackling an extreme 4WD track on the Old Man Range.

Grade 3   **Time** 2–4 hours   **Distance** 24–40 km

Track conditions 34% gravel road, 66% 4WD track

Maps See NZTopo50 CD12 Piano Flat.

How to get there From Gore, head northwest on Highway 94 to Riversdale, then north, past Waikaia, to the Piano Flat camping area.

Route description
Park at the DOC Piano Flat camping area and ride northeast on a quiet dirt road through pristine native forest with a few chunky hills for 12 km. A few hundred metres after emerging from the bush, you'll reach a group of large signs (the derelict Christies Hut is half a kilometre away).

From the signs, give yourself a serious workout by heading east, straight up towards a high point on the Old Man Range (1366 m). The first couple of kilometres are super steep and rutted, but the views just get better and better the higher you climb, and the gradient mellows out a bit after halfway.

Head back the same way for some great downhills, but beware of 'Mystery Corner', which, according to MTB folklore, takes out half the riders who race their way back to Piano Flat. It is closely followed by the 'Death Drop'!

From the fork by the gates, you can also drop down to Canton Bridge, 1 km away, for a look at the upper Waikaia River. There is a locked gate at the bridge, and from there a 4WD track heads west over some massive hills to Blue Lake 20 km away. Get the OK from Glenary Station, phone (03) 202 7898, before heading past the bridge.

Notes The road above the bushline is closed from 10 May to 18 October due to extreme weather.

5 Bald Hill

40 km northwest of Invercargill

This ride climbs through Longwood Forest to the very top of Bald Hill. At 804 m, this is the highest point on the Longwood Range and one of the best lookout points in Southland, with views of Fiordland, the Southland plains and Stewart Island.

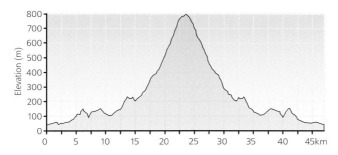

Grade 3   **Time** 3–6 hours   **Distance** 47 km

Track conditions 100% forestry road

Maps Take NZTopo50 CF08 Tuatapere and CF09 Nightcaps.

Landowners You will need to pick up a forest permit from Rayonier Forestry, 176 Spey Street, Invercargill – it's free.

How to get there From Invercargill, set your car's trip meter to zero to follow these directions. Drive out of Invercargill on North Road. At 5 km, turn left towards Riverton on Highway 99. At 25.9 km, turn right at Thornbury Road. At 35 km, turn left onto Omutu Road. At 40.1 km, turn right onto Ermdale Road. At 42.5 km, park at the first right turn, which is Harrington Road.

Route description

From your car, pedal up Harrington Road. At the first two intersections, just go straight ahead. After 6.4 km, you will reach a 3-way intersection where you should veer right (left goes to the Pourakino picnic area). Stay on Harrington

Road at the next intersection, then, 9 km into the ride you should veer left at Mill Road.

Stay on Mill Road and climb up to a large gravel pit. This is where the fast riders practise jumps while waiting for the rest of the group. It's a relatively sheltered spot.

From the gravel pit, it's another 20 minutes climbing to the Telecom buildings on top of the rounded Bald Hill. This is a scenic alpine zone with massive views. We would have spent hours up there, if a storm from Antarctica hadn't arrived at the same time.

The ride back takes an hour. Watch out for the treacherous ruts and occasional vehicles.

Notes It's very exposed above the gravel pit.

6 Sandy Point ★ ★ ★ ☆

10 km west of Invercargill

The Invercargill City Council has designated part of the Sandy Point Recreation Area for mountain bikers, and the local club has done a great job of building tracks there.

Grade 2
Time 1–2 hours
Distance 6+ km

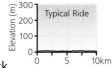

Track conditions 35% grassy 4WD track, 65% single track

Maps To check out a map of the area before your visit, click on 'Trails' at www.southlandmtbclub.co.nz

Route description

From Invercargill, head west on Stead Street and then Dunns Road towards Oreti Beach and ride for 7 km. Once you've crossed Oreti River, turn left onto Sandy Point Road. After another 3 km, you'll see a 'Mountain Bikes' sign on your right.

This is the start of several handmade single-track loops. There is a mapboard at the parking area, and the tracks are well marked.

We started with the Yellow Trail. It was a fun 6-km twisty track; about grade 2. The Red Trail explores more of the forest and is a better option if you really want a workout.

Note The area is sheltered from bad weather, so it's a good ride any time.

Blitzing through Sandy Point on a cyclo-cross bike.

Lionel Benjamin, Laben Photography

Three Other Rides

West Dome ★ ★ ☆ ☆

32 km northwest of Lumsden a forestry road, followed by a tramping track, leads to the remote and scenic Windley Bivouac.

Grade 3+   **Time** 4–8 hours   **Distance** 41 km return

Landowners Before your ride, you need to get a permit from Rayonier Forestry, 176 Spey Sreet, Invercargill.

After getting your land access permit, go and buy NZTopo50 CD09 South Mavora Lake and CD10 Eyre Peak.

From Mossburn, head northeast on the Mossburn Five Rivers Road for 6 km. Turn left onto Hillas Road and drive for 5.6 km to a fork in the road. There will be a bridge on your right and a 'West Dome Block' sign on your left. Park here.

Ride west on the forestry road and after 800 metres, at a second forestry sign, go straight ahead. Follow this hilly road, through a mixture of pines, scrub and tussock, as it arcs around the flanks of West Dome. There are great views along the way. Eventually the forestry road descends to Windley River.

When you reach the river, follow a 4WD track up valley for 2.5 km. This track is difficult to follow in places, so keep the map handy. The track ends 1 km before the biv. We left our bikes and made a beeline for the biv on foot. First we crossed a grassy dell and then followed a vague track that weaved through beech forest and led right to the small, well-hidden hut. It has two bunks and is situated in an idyllic spot facing the river.

Now that you have the route sussed, the return trip will be a breeze.

Hokonui MTB Track ★ ☆ ☆ ☆

The Gore MTB Club have been busy building a gnarly wee single track through native bush near Dolamore Park.

Grade 3–5   **Time** 30–60 minutes   **Distance** Approx 3 km

Maps There's a map in the trails section of www.southlandmtbclub.co.nz

Drop into the Gore information centre for a map, then head west out of town on Reaby Road. Just over 6 km from downtown Gore, turn right onto Pope Road at the 'Hokonui MTB' sign. There's a DOC sign and car park 700 metres up the road.

Another 500 metres further on, you'll cross a stile and enter the bush. When you come to a fork, veer right and try creating an anticlockwise loop. Some of this track is very steep and best avoided when wet.

Oreti Beach   ★ ★

The ideal beginners' ride. Oreti Beach is wide and the sand firm, during low tide.

Grade 1   **Time** 2–4 hours   **Distance** 35 km

Ride west from Invercargill on Stead Street and then Dunns Road. The route is signposted 'Oreti Beach 10 km' from Dee Street. Aim to be there 1 hour before low tide.

When you ride out onto the beach, head left down to Sandy Point, 10 km away and then leave the beach on a sandy 4WD track. You'll pass some houses and reach a gravel road. Continue north on the main road – it turns into Sandy Point Road and leads back to Dunns Road. You'll pass several picnic spots and the Sandy Point mountain biking area.

On the way back, try the signposted 'McShanes Track'. This 4WD track weaves through forest back to the main gravel road. It's named after an infamous bootlegger who collapsed drunk beside his fire one night and cooked one of his own legs!

Notes Clean the salt off your bike thoroughly after this ride. This is an enjoyable moonlight ride, but do it in reverse at night; the last street light on Dunns Road will guide you off the beach.

Index

Also from the Kennett Brothers

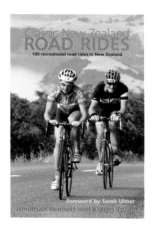

Classic New Zealand Road Rides

100 recreational road rides in New Zealand

By Jonathan Kennett and Kieran Turner

The best road rides New Zealand has to offer, complete with:

- Maps and altitude graphs
- European climb categories
- New Zealand's most popular cycling events
- Important safety information
- Comprehensive route guide details.

Kieran Turner is CEO of BikeNZ and competitive road cyclist. Jonathan Kennett is the author of several cycling books including Classic New Zealand Mountain Bike Rides.

Tararua Adventure Guide

Tramping, Rafting, Mountain Biking and Running in Tararua Forest Park

By Jonathan Kennett

Stunning rivers, lush forests and breathtaking alpine landscapes. Right there, on Wellington's doorstep.

- 16 short walks
- 15 classic weekend tramps
- 7 mountain bike rides and runs
- 7 rivers to kayak, tube or canyon.

This compact guide offers a range of adventures from easy day trips to inspirational epics.

Classic New Zealand Cycle Trails

Great rides and back country roads

Due out October 2012

All you need to know to enjoy a great cycling holiday in New Zealand.

Complete information on all the Great Rides from the government's New Zealand Cycle Trails project, plus

- Otago Central Rail Trail
- Taranaki's Forgotten World Highway
- and numerous other multi-day classics.

Includes information on how to get started, buying a bike, setting it up, and going on your first ride, plus sections on training, nutrition and safety.